# TELEVISION FOR RURAL DEVELOPMENT

# Television for Rural Development

BSS RAO

CONCEPT PUBLISHING COMPANY, NEW DELHI 110059

ISBN 81-7022-377-6

First Published 1992



*Published and Printed by*
Ashok Kumar Mittal
Concept Publishing Company
A/15-16, Commercial Block, Mohan Garden
NEW DELHI-110059

*Lasertypeset by*
Microtech Advance Printing Systems (Pvt.) Ltd.
H-13, Bali Nagar
NEW DELHI-110015

*DEDICATED*

*TO*

*ALL MY TEACHERS*

# PREFACE

IT IS generally recognized that among the mass media television is the most powerful instrument yet devised. Whether it is for influencing public opinion or for reshaping social life, its potential is considered to be immense and far-reaching. Likewise, its contribution to both formal and non-formal instruction is being increasingly appreciated. In our country, though this medium is still in its infancy, it is being nursed with high hopes to take up new challenges. The most formidable task assigned to it lies in the field of communication with the rural masses for national development. However, there have not been many attempts to understand its status as a means for accelerating the process of socio-economic change. This prompted me to undertake a qualitative study in five villages in Maharashtra.

The study has encouragingly revealed that TV holds a promising future, provided the delivery and feedback systems are carefully planned and organized.

It has been my endeavour to present the results of the study in a simple and readable form. While doing so, the requirements of media administrators and communicators concerned with the growth and management of television have been kept in mind.

Chapters 1 to 3 provide the background material and theoretical explanations of various concepts relating to development communication. Chapter 4 outlines the Methodology adopted for the study and Chapters 5 to 8 give the analyses of field data. The main conclusions of the study are reviewed and summarized in Chapter 10. The Appendix Tables contain a detailed analysis of data under different socio-economic variables.

From anthropology to television communication may not be a far cry, but definitely a long way to traverse. And, for this I owe my gratitude to my teacher, late Prof. A. Aiyappan, who has not only taught me anthropology but also largely shaped my outlook as a man.

Prof. R.K. Mutatkar, of the Department of Anthropology, University of Poona, was gracious enough to accept me as his student for this doctoral work. But for his unstinted support, guidance and help, it would not have been possible for me to complete the work in time. He extended his cooperation even to the extent of adjusting his timings to suit my official commitments. I have no words to adequately express my gratitude.

I am grateful to the Film and Television Institute of India, for encouraging me to work on this project. I could profitably avail myself of the excellent facilities available in the Institute for research, especially in the Prototype Unit, with which I have had long association.

My colleagues in various departments in the TV wing of the Institute were not only a source of inspiration but also of immense help in writing this thesis. I am grateful to all of them. My friend, Shri V. Rama Rao, was kind enough to critically examine the statistical presentation of the data and offer valuable comments. I am highly obliged to him.

Words are inadequate to acknowledge the affection, hospitality and cooperation that I was fortunate to get from the people in the five selected villages. I am greatly indebted to them.

I am duly grateful to M/s Concept Publishing Company which, appreciating the fact that this work documents the realities of rural communication and the role of television prior to the large-scale expansion of the TV network in the country, and also that the growth of the transmitters, the increase in the transmission hours and the acquisition of the new hardware have neither altered the rural scenario, nor the fundamental requirements of "accessibility" and "accountability" of the public service broadcasting services to the people at large, have accepted the dissertation for publication.

Last but not least, my sincere thanks to Dr. Binod C. Agrawal without whose motivation and guidance this book may not have seen its completion.

BSS RAO

# CONTENTS

*Preface* 7
*List of Tables* 10
*List of Appendices* 12
*List of Figures, Maps and Plates* 13

1. INTRODUCTION 15
2. COMMUNICATION FOR DEVELOPMENT 39
3. TELEVISION IN INDIA 61
4. METHODOLOGY AND STUDY DESIGN 95
5. THE AUDIENCE – A PROFILE 106
6. THE STATUS OF THE MEDIUM 125
7. MEETING THE INFORMATION NEEDS 151
8. THE PARAMETERS OF RESPONSE 186
9. TELEVISION FOR CULTURE CHANGE 213

*Appendices* 231
*Bibliography* 252
*Index* 260

# LIST OF TABLES

3.1 Distribution of TV sets in SITE clusters **80**
3.2 Telecast schedule of ETV/ITV programmes during SITE **83**
3.3 Content of SITE Instructional Programmes **85**
3.4 Expenditure on SITE **90**
4.1 Composition of the sample **105**
5.1 Growth of TV receiver licences in Maharashtra **111**
5.2 Demographic profile of the study area **114**
5.3 Statistical profile of the villages **123**
6.1 Pattern of exposure to newspapers **126**
6.2 Place of reading of newspapers **127**
6.3 Selection of newspapers **128**
6.4 Radio ownership in the villages **130**
6.5 Radio ownership by occupation and social status **130**
6.6 Frequency of radio listening **131**
6.7 Place of listening to radio in case of non-owners **132**
6.8 Pattern of exposure to radio programmes **133**
6.9 Frequency of exposure to films **135**
6.10 Reasons for lack of frequent exposure to films **136**
6.11 Contacts with urban area **138**
6.12 Contacts with block headquarters **139**
6.13 Contacts with Village Level Worker **141**
6.14 Frequency of TV viewing **145**
6.15 Regularity of TV viewing during SITE **145**
6.16 Reasons for occasional viewing of TV **147**
6.17 First generation media participants **148**
6.18 Frequency of TV viewing according to exposure to newspapers and radio **149**
7.1 Knowledge of current political scene **164**
7.2 Programme preferences on television **167**
7.3 Broad content of Marathi programmes of Bombay TV **168**
7.4 Extent of awareness of Rural TV programmes **171**

7.5 Primary source of information on occupation **173**
7.6 Can TV provide information on occupation? **175**
7.7 Why TV is installed in the village? **176**
7.8 Preferred channel for delivery of developmental messages **178**
7.9 Should television be extended to other villages? **180**
7.10 Specific utility of television **181**
7.11 The most preferred facility for village development **183**
8.1 Content analysis of the rural service of Bombay TV **187**
8.2 Growth of Community TV sets in Maharashtra **202**
8.3 Community viewing facilities in Pune region **203**

# LIST OF APPENDICES


1. Pattern of exposure to newspapers 233
2. Frequency of radio listening 234
3. Awareness of radio rural programmes 235
4. Frequency of exposure to films 236
5. Contacts with urban area 237
6. Contacts with Block headquarters 238
7. Contacts with Village Level Worker 239
8. Frequency of TV viewing 240
9. Knowledge of current political scene 241
10. Awareness of rural TV programmes 242
11. Primary source of information on occupation 243
12. Can TV provide information on occupation? 244
13. Why TV is installed in the village? 245
14. Preferred channel for delivery of development messages 246
15. Most preferred facility in the village 247
16. Telecast schedule of Bombay Doordarshan, (April-June, 1979) 248
17. Community TV in Maharashtra: Operational System (chart) 250
18. Variables of rural TV communication (chart) 251

# LIST OF FIGURES, MAPS AND PLATES

## FIGURES


6.1 Exposure to mass media 142
6.2 Frequency of TV viewing 144
7.1 Programme content of Bombay Doordarshan 169
7.2 Can TV provide information on occupation? 174
7.3 Why TV is installed in the village? 176
7.4 Preferred channel for delivery of developmental messages 179
7.5 Most desired facility for village development 184


## MAPS


1.1 Maharashtra : Television coverage 19
3.1 India : Doordarshan Kendras and Relay Centres 73
3.2 SITE clusters 79
4.1 Pune District : Communications 97
4.2 Location of selected villages 100
5.1 Maharashtra : Communications 109


## PLATES


6.1 Sharing of newspapers 129
6.2 Domestic radio listening 129
7.1 Publicity to entertainment TV programmes 166
7.2 Community TV viewing 166
7.3 Exchange of information through personal channels 172
7.4 Guidance from experienced farmers 172

# 1

# INTRODUCTION

IN THE traditional communication system, interaction is a personalized drama, forming part of the social process. The patterns of message delivery and reception are culturally defined. The interactive situation is informal but result oriented. There is very little scope for distortion or seepage in communication, as it is regulated according to the receiver's response. However, the communication is localized and highly restricted. There is no sharing on a wider plane, as there is no scope for multiplication.

Mass media are a gift of the technological revolution. They command the benefit of increased output, greater accessibility and wider reach. But, the communication through the mediated channels — print, radio, televisions or film — suffers from separation, lack of personal touch and absence of simultaneous feedback. So, the endeavour in mass communication is to overcome these constraints and establish satisfactory links for achieving effective message delivery and desired response.

In India, television has a mandate to provide support to the national goals of social justice, welfare and development. In view of these social objectives, the medium cannot afford to ignore the realities and pump out its output indiscriminately. It needs to ensure that whatever little communication support it provides does not go waste and is purposeful, convincing and effective.

### *Objectives*

The main aim of this study is to examine how best the potential of television could be exploited and utilized for developing the rural base in the country. Its specific objectives are:

1. To assess the status and role performance of television *vis-a-vis* other media in villages;
2. To identify the informational needs of the audience and to examine if television is responding to these requirements;
3. To analyse the critical parameters of response; and
4. To suggest the means for effective performance of TV as an instrument of culture-change and development.

In concrete terms these objectives are explained with two illustrations:

1. Bavaji Arjun Chimte is an illiterate tribal aged about 40 years, living in one of the hamlets of an interior village. He owns less than two acres of forest land but has no draught animals. The yield from the land being very meagre he and his wife work mostly as labourers in other's fields. None of his children go to school as they keep themselves busy in looking after the house and collecting minor forest produce.

   His exposure to outside world is limited, as there is no need for him to go out, except for the weekly market, which he or his wife visits once a month, to get provisions like salt, chillies, cooking oil and kerosene. He has travelled by bus only twice in his life and has not seen a train.

   He struggles for survival and his joys and sorrows are limited to his wife and children. Neither he nor his family members have ever seen the community TV located in the main village, a kilometre away, during the past two years of its existence. His first reaction was that he cannot go during night as the route is bad. Later, he added that the TV does not provide him any food nor does it concern his life.
2. Kondiba Nathu Hule is a middle-aged literate Maratha peasant from a village with adequate communication facilities. He possesses eight acres of land having irrigation facilities. He grows commercial crops and has achieved a status as a progressive farmer. Occasionally he listens to the farm programmes on the radio in the house, but mostly depends on his own initiative and experimentation. He seldom consults the Village Level Worker as he feels that his practical knowledge is wider than the arm-chair experience of the extension workers. Whenever he has a problem, he prefers to seek information and guidance from fellow farmers in the village or neighbourhood.

> Kondiba and his family members occasionally watch the entertainment programmes on the community TV. But, he is not aware of the farm telecasts. He is not against extension of TV to other villages, but does not see much necessity in view of the pressing problems like drinking water, irrigation facilities, land development, supply of agricultural inputs, etc. However, he admitted that he has resources to diversify his activities if some money spinning avenues could be shown to his children.

Why does Bavaji feel that television does not concern his life? Why does he keep aloof when it was provided free of cost? Why Kondiba feels that his fellow farmers are better sources to provide information on agriculture than radio, television and the Village Level Worker? Why does he miss the farm telecastes? How can TV prove its worth to persons like him. These are some of the pertinent questions for which answers are sought in this study.

### *Scope*

The study is confined to five selected villages in the Pune region of Maharashtra, where television transmission facilities are existing since 1973. Its scope is limited to the instructional programmes for the adult audience in villages. It excludes the pure entertainment and curriculum-based educational services.

### *Justification for the Study*

Anthropologists have studied the phenomenon of culture-change and explained the process primarily in terms of acculturation. But, the communication systems and channels, which are crucial to the process of diffusion of information and adoption of new innovations, have not been studied in depth.

Spicer's *Human Problems and Technological Change* (1952), Mead's *Cultural Patterns and Technological Change* (1953) and Foster's *Traditional Cultures and the Impact of Technological Change* (1962) are considered to be pioneering works in the anthropological analysis of cultural determinants of technological change and development. They have pointed out the need for understanding the responses to the forces of change in the context of specific cultures. Their explanation of the concept of "cultural relativity" and emphasis on the need for analysing cultures as "integrated wholes" prompted others to interpret the process of adoption or rejection of innovations from the angle of cultural compatibility. Foster particularly emphasized the need for recognizing the change-inhibiting forces (barriers) and the change-promoting factors (stimulants), and relating them to the programme of socio-cultural change.

One of the missing links in the anthropological studies in villages on culture-change in India, either by Srinivas (1976), Bailey (1963), Beals (1962), Epstein (1962), Aiyappan (1965), Sachchidananda (1968), Vidyarthi (1970), or others is the inadequate focus on the forces of change, particularly the media, Dube (1958) initiated anthropological studies on communication, change and development. Analysing the role of Village Level Worker (VLW) in the Community Development Project, he explained the human aspects of communication in stimulated change. Y.V.L. Rao (1963) also studied the flow of information through various channels of communication to explain the socio-economic changes in two villages. But, his analysis was limited to personal channels, print and radio. Ajit Kumar Danda and Dipali Danda (1971) have also explained briefly the role of VLW in the diffusion of innovations. But, they did not analyse the role of mass media in the change-process and development.

Other sociological studies by Prodipto Roy *et al.* (1969) and Kivlin *et al.* (1971) discuss the role of radio in the diffusion of agricultural and health innovations in the villages. But their basic objective is to measure the relative effectiveness of media in the diffusion process. Similarly studies by Mathur and Neurath (1959) and Mathur and Saksena (1963) have the limited objective of evaluating, in quantitative terms, the effects of pilot experiments on radio and television respectively.

Due to its late start and meagre coverage, television did not attract any serious anthropological studies. Research on the status and contribution of the medium in the dynamics of culture-change is extremely meagre. The Report on the holistic study of selected villages during the recent Satellite Instructional Television Experiment (SITE) by Binod Agrawal (1978) is the only major contribution in the field. The present study is an attempt to understand the potentialities and limitations of television as an instrument of culture-change, for accelerating the development process in the rural and tribal areas of the country.

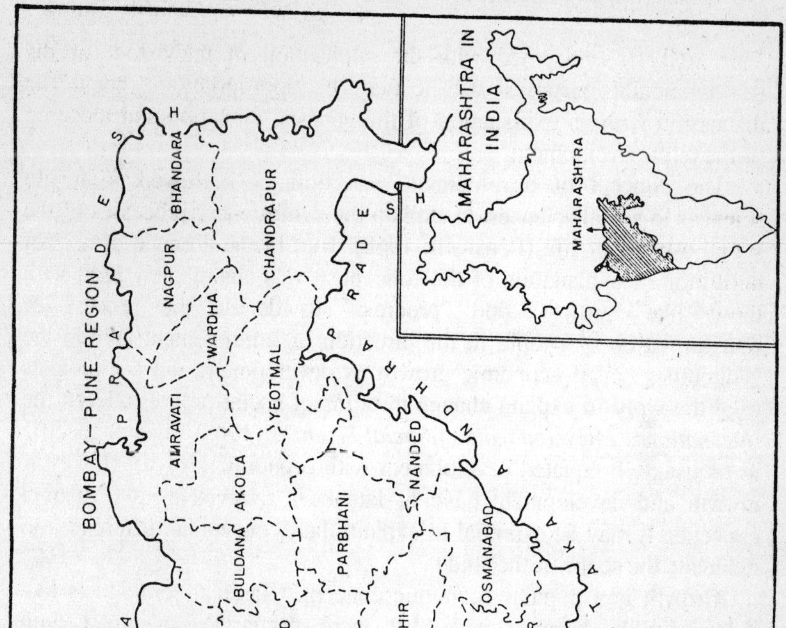


MAP 1.1: Maharashtra : Television Coverage

### *The Concept of Development*

This study is concerned with the application of television for the developmental purposes. So, it may be appropriate to begin the discussion with an explanation of the genesis, evolution and meaning of the term development.

The concept of development was initially borrowed from life sciences to social sciences, to explain the evolutionary processes of the social aspects of life (Ponsioen: 1968). But, in the absence of a clear definition or explanation of the concept, it was analogously used with terms like "growth" and "progress" to denote the process of transformation of people in the direction of improvement. While the economists called economic growth as development, the sociologists used the word to explain change in terms of social progress. Even the *International Encyclopaedia of Social Sciences* (1968) was not specific in its usage. It equated development with economic growth. However, growth and development have of late been evolved as two distinct concepts. It may be essential to explain their conceptual differences to delineate the scope of the study.

Growth is a popular economic concept. Classical economists like Adam Smith, Ricardo and Mill were primarily concerned with increased productivity and economic growth. Adam Smith, in his *Wealth of Nations*, analysed the role of capital formation and indicated the means by which the material output is increased and growth is achieved. But, from 1850 onwards Western economists concentrated more on allocative efficiency, distribution systems and stability, taking for granted the process of growth, in terms of increased output (Bhagvati & Richards: 1972). Marxian economic theory of capitalist evolution was based on such sociological hypotheses. Karl Marx believed that all social institutions are determined and conditioned by the modes of production. His arguments for economic equality by way of ownership of the means of production reflect the broad social philosophy of humanism and welfare that became very popular after the Industrial Revolution. However, the Marxist theories of economic liberalism were also primarily concerned with growth, in terms of production and distribution.

The growth theories of the classical economists were conceived in the context of industrialization of otherwise unindustrial societies. Therefore, the growth process was explained in terms of transition from pre-industrial economy to industrialized economy. Technological development and innovations were set as goals for achieving growth and prosperity.

The neo-classical Keynesian model envisaged growth, more or less, as an automatic process, once the institutional set-up in terms of competitive economy is built. Keynes General Theory of Employment, Interest and Money analysed growth in terms of national output, savings and investment. He argued that a big push in terms of aid can take the economy from stable low equilibrium to growth process and high-level stable equilibrium (Bhat: 1978).

Based on the monetary devices of the Keynesian system, the economists of the forties evolved the Capital-Output Ratio for the measurement of growth rate. The objective of the country's growth was conceived exclusively in terms of enlarging its total and per capita Gross National Product (GNP).

**Meaning of Development**

Development emerged as a distinct concept during World War II. Between the years 1940 to 1944, the Allied governments were keen in adopting higher productivity, greater welfare and democratic governments as goals for the colonial territories (Brookfield: 1975). With the formation of the United Nations Organization (UNO) in 1945, the disparity between the rich and poor countries became a matter of international concern. The preamble of the United Nations mentioned economic development of the underdevelopment, backward or less developed countries (LDCs) as one of its Charters.

Simultaneously, the nationalist movements in Asia and Africa gained momentum and opposition to the colonial rule and dominance increased. During the struggle for independence more concern was voiced for the welfare of the masses, not merely restricted to economic well-being and material progress. This found expression in the term "development". Around 1950, the philosophy of development became an integral part of word polity. It emerged as a subject of wide concern, not only of the economists but also of those who were interested in social transformation and political change.

Subsequently, the term "growth" was restricted to denote a process which is self-generating and is a gradual evolution. Ponsioen explained that while growth is conceived as something stimulated from within and as realization of the inherent potential, development is accepted as an engineered process primarily initiated by the government machinery. "Development as a policy concept designates not a spontaneous growth, but a process of induced change; induced by consciously framed policies of indigenous as well as assisting agencies" (Ponsioen: 1968). As referred to earlier, development was adopted as a broader concept than growth which was hitherto interpreted in more economic terms. Coyle (1963) explained that the development doctrine has social, economic and political overtones. "The underlying philosophy of development is that the poor will have to get a larger share of the national income and a better hope for the future."

This broader perspective for development is stimulated by the authors who did not consider material progress as the end in itself. "Development is not simply a matter of learning how to use radios, automobiles and how to manufacture them. It touches every aspect of national life: political, social, even religious" (Coyle: 1963). According to Demis Goulet "the concept of development is best expressed in the phrase - the human ascent, the ascent of all men in their quintessence of humanity, including the economic, biological, psychological, social, cultural, spiritual, transcendental dimensions" (Higgins: 1970).

One important and distinctive attribute of development is its application to low-income countries, in Asia and Africa. It is not applied to Western countries, Australia and even Latin America. They are said to have their economies expanding and growing. Development is restricted to countries close to subsistence level of economy.

Gunnar Myrdal's *Asian Drama* (1968) is an illuminating study of the poverty of nations in South Asia. It deals with the problems of underdevelopment, development and planning for development. Explaining the basic valuations of the countries in the region he states: "These valuations which for brevity we label the 'modernization ideals' were impressed on the nations of South Asia in the Great Awakening, following independence, though people there had been gradually conditioned to them by influences from the Western world during colonial times, and more recently by influences from the Soviet Union. They have become the 'official creed' almost the national religion and one of the powerful stands of the "new nationalism."

Myrdal specified these modernization ideals in the following aspects:

1. *Rationality:* Adoption of scientific reasoning and application of the modern technology for all economic and social relations.

2. *Development and Planning for Development*: Development is conceived as an improvement of the host of undesirable conditions in the social system that have perpetuated a state of underdevelopment.
3. *Rise of Productivity*: Higher per capita output.
4. *Rise in Levels of Living*: The main reason for desiring a rise in output per head is that it would raise levels of living.
5. *Social and Economic Equalization*: This is desired to promote equality in status, opportunities, wealth, incomes. Development is interpreted as creating conditions for raising levels of living for the masses.
6. *Improved Institutions and Aspirations*: Change in attitudes to permit mobility, enterprise, effective competition and greater equality.
7. *National Consolidation*: A national system of government, courts and administration that is effective, cohesive and united in purpose and action.
8. *National Independence*: The ideal is independent nationhood.
9. *Political Democracy*: Ambition to become a democratic nation status with universal adult suffrage and free elections, guaranteeing civil liberties.
10. *Democracy at Grassroots*: The ideal of local and sectional self-governments by democratic decentralization.
11. *Social Discipline versus Democratic Planning*: This implies that politics should be decided on by democratic political procedures and they should as far as possible be implemented with the cooperation and shared responsibility of local communities.

The outlook of the emerging poor nations was, thus, oriented towards the socio-political aspects of development than mere increase in per capita incomes or productivity. Economic planners emphasized the social objectives of development. Oommen explained that the basic objective in development is to make people more human, by lifting them out of dehumanising conditions of poverty, unemployment, ill-health, ignorance and the like. "Development is humanism. It takes place when the dignity of man is fully assured" (Oommen: 1973). Looking from the same broader perspective Rainer Schickele stated that in the drama of development the central protagonist is the worker, the peasant, the small craftsman, the clerk, the poor man working in the factory, field, workshop and office. The plot of drama deals with his frustrations and triumphs as he struggles to human dignity and citizenship, from poverty to wealth, under the guiding spirit of human ideology of democracy and equality of man (Schickele: 1973).

**Means of Development**

Development theories of the fifties were mostly based on the economic growth models. It was assumed that a backward country tends to remain stagnant due to its inability to set the process of development in motion by its own means. Hence, it was argued that it is possible to induce development by injecting the right amount of capital, domestic or foreign. But, the extra economic variables of development were not explained by these theories (Ricardo and Charles: 1964). The economic concept of development was confined to the policies aiming to build an economic system in developing countries that would be able to produce by itself enough commodities for improving the standards of living for all levels of population.

Industrialization was regarded as the golden remedy for underdevelopment for more than a generation. The general theory of economic development provided a rationalization for the hypotheses of the Western economists, who saw growth only in terms of industrialization. During the forties Rosenstein Rodan argued that industrialization was the way of achieving a more equal distribution of incomes between areas of world by raising incomes in underdeveloped areas at a higher rate than in developed areas. In the fifties Regner Nurkese advocated investment across wide fields and enlarging size and volume of markets under his Balanced Approach Theory. Till 1960 it was not fully realized that economic growth by itself is insufficient as a prescription for development.

*The First Development Decade*

The United Nations General Assembly adopted a resolution in 1961, envisaging a programme of development for the sixties, which became popular as the First Development Decade. The goal envisaged for development was "to attain for each country a substantial increase in the rate of growth, with each country setting its own target, taking as the objective a minimum annual rate of growth in aggregate national income of five per cent at the end of the decade". The resolution added that it was to be widened by an improvement in official and private financial flows from the developed to the less developed countries to equal one per cent of the former's GNP.

The Western development experts continued to see development purely as an economic process and paid very little attention to the social and political dimensions, except in the capacity as means for economic development. Development was accepted to be more than economic growth, but per capita income designed to measure economic growth rate continued to be adopted as the general indicator of development.

It was not until the mid-sixties that is was realized that acceleration of growth rate required not only an increased capital but also other human factors, especially skills. Analysing the social aspects of economic development in Latin American countries, Benjamin Higgins (1963) argued that economic analysis itself cannot afford an explanation of the dynamics of social change. These arguments created a new awareness about the complexity of development as a process of social change.

The stimulus for awareness can be seen in the models of economists like W.W. Rostow and Arthur Lewis, who stressed inter-linkages in the process of economic growth. Rostow analysed the five stages of growth, adopting the historical method (popular with the anthropologists), viz.: 1. The traditional, 2. the preconditions for take-off, 3. The take-off, 4. The period of drive, and 5. The period of high mass consumption. Passing from one stage to the other requires re-arrangements in society. According to him this "re-arrangement" consists mainly in the introduction of new institutions, educational systems, expanding markets, new forms of transport, and communications facilitated by new monetary institutions, new forms of production, effective government and administration (Rostow: 1960).

The hypothesis postulated by Arthur W. Lewis stresses that "the will to economize" is the key factor. But, the value system, the attitudes and the socio-cultural institutions which inter-act in the process were to be seen as parts of the whole. "All sectors are independent in such a way that advance in one sector or any one front will bring in others as well" (Lewis: 1959).

### *The Second Development Decade*

During the First Development Decade (1960-69) even countries with respectable rates of growth (more than five per cent of national income) like Kuwait and Venezuela did not enjoy development in the sense of welfare of the masses. The per capita incomes increased because of the oil boom. But, the number of undernourished and illiterates increased. Health targets could not be achieved. Higher rates of growth did not bring about social mobility or equality of opportunity (Higgins: 1963). It was slowly realized that no development is possible unless social and political infrastructure is assured.

The United Nations General Assembly adopted the resolution on the Second Development Decade in 1970 for the years 1970-79. Growth remained central, with a target of six per cent per annum in gross terms and 3.5 per cent in per capita terms. But, the aim was accompanied by a series of strategy resolutions concerning the need to reduce regional, sectoral and social disparities (Brookfield: 1975).

The U.N. Research Institute for Social Development identified a number of general economic and social indicators of development and set them as norms. These norms were defined in terms of birth rate, life expectancy, mortality rate, consumption of cereals and proteins per capita per day, school enrolment, reach of mass media like newspapers, radio, TV and cinema, telephone, agricultural production per worker, electricity consumption per capita, imports and exports per capita, etc.

Despite this elaboration, those who were concerned with the qualitative improvement of the masses were not convinced with the bias for growth, measured in terms of per capita incomes. Oommen argued "it never tells us anything about the quality of life of the people for who all growth is meant. It tells us very little about the social cost with which growth is achieved" (Oommen: 1973). The same viewpoint was expressed by Dube. "Development as an ideal lost much of its magical quality. It is no longer the panacea for the ills of the contemporary world. It is now evident that the notion has been poorly defined: economic development has often been confused with development as such. Economic growth measured in terms of GNP and per capita income is a false indicator of development as it has little bearing on the distributive aspect of fruits of development and does not significantly alter the quality of life of the ordinary people. It is common knowledge that the impressive rise in national income often accentuates deprivation and misery by consolidating inegalitarian structures" (Dube: 1978).

Development is seen today as an integral whole, as the elements of the culture are interdependent. Development is not seen in parts as it enjoins economic activity, social process, education and learning, exploitation of environment, political consciousness and participation. Secondly, needs are specific to culture, so development effort has to be specific to each society.

Explaining the aspirations of the South-East Asian countries the Indonesian economist, Soedjatmoko stated "when we speak of development, we speak of a movement, of goals, of values, of motivation. We are essentially concerned with developing a new sense of direction of society, and with deepest, often moral motivation for social action. When we speak of development, we are really speaking about modernization of the soul" (Soedjatmoko: 1969).

In the recent past, the basic needs model has emerged as a popular model of development. Soedjatmoko, who is associated with this model, explained "the Basic Needs Model requires an appropriate macro-policy framework for development. This should include the adoption of employment and equity as developmental goals. It also means a commitment to development from the bottom" (Ploman: 1979).

The Basic Needs Model emphasizes a direct attack on poverty by meeting the basic needs in the fields of food, nutrition, health, education and housing as well as through employment and income-generating activities among the lowest 40 per cent income groups. The Antyodaya concept advocated in India during 1977-79 for the development of the poorer sections was conceived on these lines.

Development strategy is currently advocated on the following lines:

1. The objective should be to satisfy the essential needs – material as well as non-material – of the people, starting with the most underprivileged groups, struggling for survival.
2. The process demands changes in the institutions, structures and functioning of the whole society. Hence, it cannot be compartmentalized into parts.
3. The focus of development being human beings, it must be carried out by and with people but not for them.

Development is a complex process. It envisages a national effort. As Adler has pointed out, "there is no short-cut to development – neither via industrialization nor via import substitution, nor via infrastructure investment nor via education. . . . The path to development is far longer and much more arduous than it appeared to be when a conscious drive towards development and development aid began in the fifties" (Adler: 1972).

## Rural Development in India

Having explained the evolution and broad meaning of the concept of development, it is proposed to review how the process of development was initiated through planning in India and what have been the priorities to achieve the developmental goals. The strategies for rural development in the overall context of national development have been briefly explained later.

The Constitution of India offers to all citizens, individually and collectively, some basic freedoms. These are guaranteed in the Constitution in the form of Fundamental Rights. Over and above these rights, it also lays down certain Directive Principles of State Policy. These are not justiciable, but are fundamental to the governance of the country; and it is the obligation of the State to evolve laws in accordance with these Directive Principles.

The Directive Principles in the Constitution enunciate that the State shall strive to promote the welfare of the people by securing and protecting as effectively as it may a social order in which justice, social, economic and political, shall inform all the institutions of the national life. They also make it clear that the State policy should be directed towards securing among others: (1) equal rights to an adequate means of livelihood; (2) distribution of material resources for the common good; and (3) an economic system that does not result in concentration of wealth. The Government is obliged to draw all the schemes for development within the framework of these constitutional commitments.

The Planning Commission was set up in March 1950, with the objective of preparing a blueprint for the development of the country. In formulating Plans and drawing the strategy for augmenting the resources in relation to the nation's requirements, it was directed to work within the ambit of the Directive Principles of State Policy, having regard to the Fundamental Rights and in furtherance of the declared objectives of the Government. These objectives were specified as: to promote a rapid rise in the standard of living of the people by efficient exploitation of the resources of the country, increasing production and offering opportunities to all for employment in the service of the community (Planning Commission: 1952).

*First Five Year Plan*

While drawing up the country's First Five Year Plan, the Planning Commission had made certain observations in respect of our developmental goals and the means for their achievement. Some of them form the premises of our developmental planning even today and it may not be out of context to discuss them here in detail: (Planning Commission: 1952).

1. "The problem of development of an economy is one of utilizing more effectively the potential resources available to the community, and it is this which involves economic planning. But, the economic condition of the country at any given time is a product of broader social environment, and economic planning has to be viewed as an integral part of a wider process aiming not merely at development of human facilities and the building of an institutional framework, adequate to the needs and aspirations of the people.
2. "The urge to economic and social change comes from the fact of poverty and of inequalities of income, wealth and opportunity. The elimination of poverty cannot be achieved by redistributing existing wealth, nor can a programme aiming only at raising production remove existing inequalities. . . . The problem is not one of merely re-channellizing economic activity within the existing socio-economic framework; that framework has itself to be remoulded.
3. "It is important to ensure that in the process of development, the forces of growth from within are not stifled by attempts abruptly to superimpose preconceived patterns of life and society.
4. "The rapid advances in science and technology over the last few decades have opened new possibilities in the direction of abolition of want and the restoration of man to a new sense of dignity but they also carry the potentialities of harm and danger.
5. "Development is an all-embracing process which cannot be compartmentalized. But, the accent of endeavour under the present conditions of India has to be on economic development."

The country was forced to import foodgrains on a large scale during 1951. Accordingly the Plan accorded the highest priority to agriculture earmarking about 45 per cent of the total public sector outlay for its development. It was indicated that without a substantial increase in the agricultural production, it would be difficult to sustain a higher tempo of industrial development. In quantitative terms the aim of the Plan was spelt out as to increase the rate of investment from five to seven per cent of the national income.

*Second Five Year Plan*

In 1954, Parliament adopted a resolution directing that the main objective of the country's economic policy should be to achieve a socialistic pattern of society. In pursuance of this national commitment the subsequent Plans were drawn up. The goals of the Second Five Year Plan were to rebuild rural India, to lay the foundations of industrial progress, and to secure to the greatest extent possible opportunities for the weaker and underprivileged sections of the people and the balanced development of all parts of the country (Planning Commission: 1956). The priority was shifted from agricultural development to the development of basic and heavy industries. The Plan allocation for industrial development was to the extent of 19 per cent of the total public sector outlay. In terms of growth in national income, the Second Plan envisaged an increase from seven per cent to eleven per cent by 1960-61.

*Third Five Year Plan*

The Third Five Year Plan aimed at achieving self-sustained growth, with five per cent increase in the national income per annum. In order to achieve this goal the Plan laid emphasis once again on increasing agricultural production. However, it called for expansion of heavy and basic industries, for reduction of industrial imports (G o I: 1977 & 78).

Between 1966-69, three annual plans were formulated on an *ad hoc* basis. The planning process and development, however, received a setback due to the Indo-Pak conflict in 1965, famine conditions during 1966-67 and a steep rise in prices.

*Fourth Five Year Plan*

The Fourth Five Year Plan, for the years 1969-74, aimed at accelerating the pace of development in conditions of stability and reduced uncertainties. It reiterated that weakness on the food front and dependence on foreign aid were the basic reasons for the lack of improvement in the economy. One of the important objectives of the Fourth Five Year Plan was creation of more employment opportunities, particularly in rural areas, through labour-intensive schemes. In terms of growth rate the Plan envisaged an overall increase at 5.7 per cent compound rate for the years 1969-74.

### *Fifth Five Year Plan*

The Fifth Five Year Plan was to be effective from April 1974. But, because of the high inflationary trend and severe setback in the balance of payments, the Plan was not finalized. The on-going schemes were executed on an *ad hoc* basis as Annual Plans. Then came suddenly the national emergency. The Prime Minister announced the 20-Point Programme in July 1975, and called it the new economic programme for the welfare of the poor and weaker sections, for the removal of poverty. Top priority was assigned for evolving schemes and their execution under this programme. Subsequently, the draft Fifth Five Year Plan was also finalized keeping in view the policy enunciated under the 20-Point Programme.

One of the distinctions of the Fifth Five Year Plan was that it identified certain areas for development as the country's minimum needs and laid down minimum norms for their fulfilment. These were specified in the areas of primary education, rural health, rural water supply, rural roads, rural electrification, house sites for landless labourers, improvement of urban slums and nutrition.

### *The Rolling Plan: 1978-83*

The scene changed after the March 1977, General Elections. The Janata Party came to power, with the promise of a new deal to the rural masses. The Fifth Five Year Plan was terminated one year in advance at the end of March 1978, to recast the Plan priorities. The new concept of Rolling Plan was introduced to facilitate readjustments of financial allocation after annual reviews.

The strategy of development planning was also shifted from more economic terms to welfare dimension, with the formulation of the draft Five Year Plan for 1978-83. Explaining the new development strategy the Planning Commission observed: "what matters is not the precise increase in the national product that is achieved in five or ten years, but whether we can assure, within a specified time-frame, a measurable increase in the welfare of millions of the poor" (Planning Commission: 1978).

The goals set for achievement by the Government within a period of 10 years were spelt out as:

(a) Removal of unemployment and significant reduction in under-employment;
(b) Appreciable rise in the living standards of the poorest sections of the population; and
(c) Fulfilment by the State of some *basic needs* of the people in these income groups like clean drinking water, adult literacy, elementary education, health care, rural roads, rural housing for the landless and minimum services for the urban slums (Planning Commission: 1978).

The Plan accorded top priority to the sectors which generate maximum employment and which have a significant impact on the standard of living of the people like agriculture and allied activities, village and cottage industries and inputs such as irrigation, fertilizers and power. Simultaneously, the norms of Minimum Needs were also revised to benefit more rural and urban poor.

*Sixth Five Year Plan (1980-85)*

The re-emergence of the Congress Party to power, after the General Elections in 1980, brought once again changes in the approach to the planning process. The Sixth Five Year Plan attached high priority to employment generation and removal of poverty. A substantial increase in Plan allocations was made for Special Area Development Programmes and reducing regional disparities.

*Seventh Five Year Plan (1985-90)*

The poverty alleviation programmes were envisaged during the Seventh Five Year Plan in a much wider perspective of bringing out socio-economic transformation through structural changes in educational development, generation of awareness, change in outlook, attitudes and planned motivation. Cost-effectiveness of the programmes and minimization of leakages were stressed as two guiding principles in the implementation of poverty alleviation programmes.

Keeping in view the limited absorption capacity of the poorest of the poor, the approach to the Seventh Plan also emphasized the need of taking up group-oriented activities for the beneficiaries. In this context it was emphasized that mass media would need to be geared for increasing awareness among the rural poor for dissemination of information and acquisition of skills.

Balanced sectoral coverage was underlined as one of the goals of the Seventh Five Year Plan. To achieve this objective the plan formulators renewed their emphasis on decentralized planning at the district level and identification of potential thrust areas in different areas. In this process it was envisaged to rationalise on-going target group-oriented schemes like Operation Flood II, handloom and sericulture programmes, etc.

It may be summarized that the overall attempt in the Seventh Plan was on achievement of three objectives:

1. Virtual elimination of poverty and illiteracy;
2. Full employment;
3. Securing satisfaction of basic needs, of food, clothing and shelter and provision of health for all.

*Strategy for Rural Development*

Four-fifths of the estimated 683 million population in our country live in villages. Three-fifths of the working force is engaged in farming and allied occupations. One-half of the national income is contributed by those who eke out a living on agriculture (India: 1981). The village community, therefore, forms the base for our development planning. "Village development is the key to India's development" was the slogan of the Father of the Nation, Mahatma Gandhi. The developmental strategies evolved in the successive Plans have not only reiterated the nation's faith in the Gandhian Philosophy and demonstrated that there are no short-cuts to achieve the goals of development other than village development and grass-root planning.

*Community Development Programme*

On October 2, 1952, the Community Development (CD) programme was launched as a national scheme for rural development. The scheme owes its origin to the Village Development Projects run by Gandhiji and his associates during pre-independent days. Each Community Project was planned to benefit 300 villages and an approximate population of two lakhs (Planning Commission: 1952). Simultaneously, the National Extension Service (NES) scheme was sponsored for intensive and coordinated development of rural life as a whole. Explaining the two schemes the First Five Year Plan document observed that Community Development is the method and National Extension the agency through which the Plan seeks to initiate the process of transformation of social and economic life of villages (Planning Commission: 1952).

The main lines of activity in the Community Development programme were agriculture and related fields, health care through Primary Health Centres (PHCs), supplementary employment, housing, training and social welfare. The scheme was, however, drawn up on two optimistic principles; self-help and cooperation.

In 1959, the three-tier Panchayat Raj system was evolved on the recommendation of the Committee on Plan Projects, for the involvement of the village community in developmental planning and execution of schemes. The Panchayat Raj institutions were made responsible for schemes relating to agricultural production, rural industries, health care, maintenance of village roads, and such other development activities.

*Some Specialized Programmes for Rural Development*

As a supplement to the CD scheme, the Union Government sponsored the Intensive Agricultural District Programme in 1961 for achieving self-sufficiency in food. A team of specialists and field workers was attached to each IADP project for the diffusion effort. In 1964-65 this scheme was modified as Intensive Agriculture Area Programme (IAAP) to facilitate concentration in a limited area for popularization or specific crops.

From the beginning of the Foruth Five Year Plan (April 1969) the State Governments were asked to bear the financial responsibility of executing the Community Development Schemes. Commenting on the operation of the scheme, K.P.A. Menon senior development administrator of the Department of Rural Development Government of India, observed: "The State Governments are not paying adequate attention to Block administration. . . . Due to multiplication of Blocks at a faster rate without taking into consideration the financial and organizational resources, the CD Schemes lost a good deal of significance in the process of implementation (Menon: 1979).

### *Small Farmers Development Agency*

The specialized programme of IADP/IAAP yielded encouraging results. However, it was revealed that the benefits accrued mostly to the rich and progressive cultivators. Visualizing the danger of aggravating the disparity between those who have the resources to make use of the new agricultural technology and those who have not, the Fourth Five Year Plan formulated two specialized schemes for small and marginal farmers and agricultural labourers. The schemes known as Small Farmers Development Agency (SPDA) and Marginal Farmers and Agricultural Labourers Development Agency (MFAL) were launched specifically to improve the economic condition of the weaker sections and generate employment opportunities for them. Keeping in view the benefits derived by the target groups the SFDA and MFAL schemes were integrated into a single scheme (SFDA) during the Fifth Five Year Plan period.

Two other distinct programmes specifically drawn to benefit the small and marginal farmers and landless labourers were: The Command Area Development Programme (CAD), initiated during the late sixties, and the Drought Prone Area Programme (DPAP) sponsored during the Fourth Five Year Plan. The CAD scheme was meant for the small farmers for providing on-farm development services (Planning Commission: 1970). The DPAP programme was evolved to improve the economy of the drought-prone areas through a package of infrastructure and on-farm development activities.

### *Minimum Needs Programme*

The strategy aims at fixing minimum norms in respect of certain facilities and meeting them for assuring a minimum level of living to the population.

Norms were specified in the Fifth Plan in respect of seven selected items, viz. elementary education, rural health, rural water supply, rural roads, rural electrification, house sites for landless, environmental improvement in slums, and nutrition programme. The Plan for 1978-83 included Adult Education under the Minimum Needs programme and revised the norms to extend the benefits to a larger population.

### *Integrated Rural Development*

The strategy of Integrated Rural Development was initiated during the year 1978-79. The new approach implies development of all sectors of rural economy and all sections of rural society by adopting a holistic approach. The strategy is advocated as the best means of reaching the goals of self-sufficiency in food production, growth with social justice and full employment in rural areas.

The operation of Special programmes such as Small Farmers Development Agency (SFDA), Drought Prone Area Programme (DPAP) and Command Area Development Programme (CADP) was extended to cover about 3,000 development blocks.

A new scheme, Training of Rural Youth for Self Employment (TRYSEM), was launched in August, 1979, with the objective of providing technical skills to rural youth for undertaking self-employment programmes in the areas of agriculture, industry and services. The Plan aimed to train two lakh rural youth every year at the rate of 40 per cent per development block each year. A minimum of 30 per cent of this target was earmarked for the training of scheduled castes and scheduled tribes and another one-third for the training of rural women.

As the benefits of TRYSEM scheme were not reaching women, as initially conceived, a separate programme, Development of Women and Children in Rural Areas (DWCRA), was launched in September, 1982, on a pilot scale in 50 selected blocks with a view to providing income-generating activities for rural women. Both TRYSEM and DWCRA programmes formed an essential component of the massive Integrated Rural Development Programme.

The National Rural Employment Programme (NREP) was evolved as a new programme to provide direct protection and benefit to the poor through transfer of assets, provision of inputs and training. Subsequently, during 1983-84, the Rural Landless Employment Guarantee Programme (RLEGP) and a separate training and self-employment generation programme for urban youth (SEEUY) were introduced as Plan schemes.

### Magnitude of Underdevelopment

Having indicated the strategies of rural development, in the following paragraphs an attempt is made to analyse some of the factors which explain both causes and effects of underdevelopment, to indicate broadly the dimensions of the problem.

### Poverty

Based on the nutritional norm of 2,400 calories per person per day in rural areas, and 2,100 calories in the urban areas, the poverty line was drawn by the National Sample Survey (NSS). According to the estimate which formed the base for the 1978-83 Plan, the poverty line was calculated at Rs. 61.80, per capita a month in the rural areas, and Rs. 71.30 in urban areas, at 1976-77 prices. According to this exercise about 230 million people, i.e., 47 per cent of the population in rural areas were living below the poverty line in 1979.* Dandekar and Rath (1971) explained that one of the basic reasons for the poverty was the unduly large number of dependents to be supported per earner, particularly among agricultural labourers.

### Small Land Holdings

The base of our economy is agriculture. According to the 1970-71 All India Agricultural Census, as many as 51 per cent of the operational holdings in the country were below 2.50 acres in size; and these farmers hold less than 9 per cent of the total cultivated area. Another 17 per cent of the holdings were between 2.50 and 5 acres; and the area under them amounts to 12 per cent of the total land under cultivation. Thus, about 70 per cent of the farmers in the country are small and marginal cultivators, possessing only one-fifth of the total cultivated land (Menon: 1979). Our yield levels are very low basically due to the uneconomic land holdings and the resultant poor inputs.

### Population Growth

When the resources are limited, rapid increase in population is more a

---

* According to the statement of the Minister of State for Planning in Parliament, *Poona Herald*, dated 23-3-79.

hindrance than a help in raising the standards of living of the people. The population growth during 1971 and 1981 registered at a level of 25 per cent as against 24.8 per cent during 1961-71 and 21.5 per cent during 1951-61. In absolute terms the population increased from 361 million in 1961 to 548 million in 1971 and it crossed 683 million by 1981.

### *Education*

Notwithstanding the educational investments that were made, we are yet to achieve the goal of universalization of elementary education, and the eradication of illiteracy. The literacy rate has gone up from 16.6 per cent in 1961 to 29.5 per cent in 1971 and to 36.2 per cent by 1981. But, in absolute terms the number of illiterates increased because of population growth. Education is a complex issue interlinked with many socio-cultural factors. Whether it is formal, functional, or non-formal, education needs a long time for its country-wide acceptance.

### *Health*

Out of the total 5.76 lakh villages, 1.13 were identified as problem villages from the point of view of drinking water. They fall under one of the following categories: (1) Villages having sources of water supply more than 1.5 km away; (2) Villages having sources of water infested with cholera germs or guinea worms; and (3) Villages having sources of water contaminated with toxic chemicals like flouride, chloride, iron, etc., which are hazardous for health (Menon: 1979).

Diarrhoeal diseases, infectious diseases and nutritional deficiencies are a major cause of mortality of children below five years. Communicable diseases like TB, gastro-intestinal infections, malaria, filariasis, hepatitis, hook worm, rabies, etc., which are interrelated to environmental conditions, account for nearly 21 per cent mortality in the country (Planning Commission: 1978).

### *Social Justice*

Social disabilities like untouchability and exploitation suffered by weaker sections, problems like child labour, bonded labour, differential payment of wages for men and women, child marriages are very deep rooted in our national life. It is necessary to fight a continuous war to establish a just social order free from these evils.

# 2

# COMMUNICATION FOR DEVELOPMENT

DEVELOPMENT IS a qualitative process concerned with people and their vital needs. It presupposes change in the material environment, technology, life-style, attitudes, aspirations and behaviour of the people. These changes are not sought by force; they are planned and won with the involvement of the individual members. The role of communication in this complex process of interaction, culture-change and human behaviour, needs no emphasis. To isolate communication from the process of development is like separating the egg from the chicken. In this chapter, an attempt is made to explain the interlinkages between communication and development, the growing concern for effective development communication for engineering socio-economic change and achieving development.

## What is Communication?

The term 'communication' is used here to denote human interaction. The word is derived from the latin word *"communis"*, which means "to share", "to make common". Any inter-action in which meanings are shared, messages are exchanged and actions are provoked, constitutes communication. It differs from message diffusion or passing of information which does not envisage sharing or obtaining a response. Information delivery is a one-way process; whereas communication is a two-way traffic. As a social process communication involves basically creation of a stimulus and obtaining a response. It is purposeful and ubiquitous. It takes place at every plane, from elimentary units to complex entities, at the individual level in man's inter-action with his environment as well as at the social level, in families, between groups of people, societies and nations.

Several definitions to explain the process of communication are available. But, no single one is comprehensive enough to explain fully its scope and functions. According to Berlo (1960), we communicate to influence, to affect with intent. Raymond Williams (1962) summarised communication as the passing of ideas, information and attitudes from person to person. According to Berelson and Steiner (1964), communication is the act or process of transmission of ideas, emotions and skills by the use of symbols, words, pictures, figures and graphics. Basically communication is understood as the process of transmitting information from the source to receiver with the intention of effecting behaviour change. Hovland (1954), therefore, opined that communication is the process by which we influence others and get influenced in return.

The stimulus and response which constitute the communication process are achieved through a system of components. These are: (1) *Source* from which the messages are released; (2) *Message* or the content of information, coded in verbal or non-verbal language; (3) *Channel* or the message vehicle to carry the input from the source; and (4) *Receiver*, the target for whom the message is intended. Mere movement or release of the message from the source does not complete the communication cycle. The message must be received, understood and responded to by the receiver. Communication is incomplete without feed-back or response to the message, back to the source.

Harold Lasswell (1960) explained the communication process in the popular paradigm: who says what to whom through which channel and with what effect.

Originally, Aristotle defined the study of rhetoric (communication) as the search for all available means of persuasion. By the late 18th century, the scope of communication was broadened to include the art and craft of: (a) information, i.e. providing an appeal to the mind, which is intellectual or cognitive in nature; (b) persuasion which is in the form of appeal to the soul to stir up emotions; and (c) entertainment to provide relaxation (Berlo: 1960). However, the information persuasion-entertainment roles should not be treated as mutually exclusive. Communication could be purely information-oriented, or simultaneously aimed at persuasive behavioural change or it could as well aim at entertainment.

The International Commission for the Study or Communication Problems appointed by UNESCO, under the chairmanship of Sean MacBride, in its Report outlined the functions of communication as:

"Taking the overall approach, communication may be seen alike as a social need, an economic requirement and a political necessity. And it is in this three-fold perspective that its functions can surely be best analysed, whether they be exercised at the individual, social or international levels" (UNESCO: 1978).

The commission distinguished five main functions of communication as under:

1. *Information properly so-called*: This function involves the collection, sifting and processing of data, and its purpose is to guarantee freedom of expression, to ensure dissemination of knowledge, judgement and opinion necessary for understanding society. The function is inseparable from the democratic process as a whole.
2. *Persuasion, motivation, interpretation*: This is linked to the mechanism of social control, organisation of community activities and is inseparable from economic and social development work.
3. *Education, and transmission of social and cultural heritage*: This includes information for awakening curiosity about problems and education for fostering awareness and understanding of and paving the way for a solution to these problems.
4. *Socialization*: This function facilitates involvement of individuals, groups and communities in public life and in decision-making process. This function is an integral part of the process of democratising public life.
5. *Leisure activities and entertainment*: This may be exercised in ways and means varying with the diversity of cultural contexts and development levels, and is bound up with the improvement of the quality of life.

Whatever way the scope and purpose of communication is explained, it permeats our life process. It is fundamental to human existence. Communication system is a vital link through which the individuals of a society are held together, function together and survive together. Communication helps to expand the horizons of people by drawing on the experiences of others. It keeps the life process going, whether it is social organisation or economic activity, or political organisation, or religious activity.

If culture is taken as a totality, the communication system forms an element of the whole. Cultural survival is dependent on the structure and functioning of the communication system. The social, economic, political and other sub-systems are interwoven with the communication system. The elements of the culture whether art or artifacts, beliefs or attitudes are carried as a legacy of the past; down the generations by the individuals of society through the in-built communication mechanism which is explained as enculturation in anthropology.

The whole process of culture-change in which the diffusion and adoption of new culture traits is explained is but another perspective of communication process. The exposure to new ideas, knowledge and skills, and the motivation to seek and acquire the innovations is facilitated by the internal and external communication channels. The extent of adoption or rejection of new traits depends on the strength, vitality and adaptability of the forces of communication. Cultures survive because of communication, cultures grow because of communication and cultures degenerate if there is no communication. Development being a process of planned change, implies exploitation of the communication networks and their potential in the best interests of the people within the frame of the cultural system. As Wilbur Schramm has warned, communication has no life of its own. Human communication is something people do (Schramm: 1973). So, the human element in communication is crucial to the communication process.

**Channels of Communication**

Rogers (1962) classified communication channels into two categories: (1) personal, and (2) impersonal. Personal communication takes place through interpersonal or informal channels and the communicator is face-to-face with the audience. The communication may be directed to an individual or micro-groups. Personal communication sources were again divided into two categories:

1. Personal localite, whose interaction is limited, and
2. Personal cosmopolite, who have wider exposure to outside world.

The channels of personal communication may be listed as under:

1. Non-institutionalised personal channels like informal meetings and discussions within families and friends;
2. Institutionalised personal channels which include:

a. formal and informal meetings and discussions with social institutions like village headman, community leader, etc., either individually or in groups;
b. formal and informal meetings and discussions with non-traditional leaders like elected leaders. Village level Workers and other extension officials, either individually or in groups;

3. Folk channels like:

a. fairs, festivals, weekly markets, etc.
b. performing arts like theatre, singing, dancing, puppet troupes. Falling under this group are art forms like *tamasha*, *Gondhal*, *Bahrud*, etc., in Maharashtra, and
c. other *ad hoc* channels like wandering nomads, religious mendicants, etc.

In pre-literate societies, oral communication takes the function of transmission of knowledge and skills, from one generation to the other. Anthropological and sociological studies in village India by Damle (1955), Dube (1958), Mazumdar (1958) and Agrawal (1978) point out that communication in rural areas is verbal-based with inter-personal and group networks carrying most of the messages.

## Mass Media

Mass Media are the products of technological advancement; and the communication system associated with these man-made channels is impersonal, print, radio, television and film, which constitute the four major elements of mass media are resources devised to reach scattered and heterogeneous audiences. Because of the separated communication, directed to larger audiences, the messages are mostly structured and formal.

Lazersfeld *et al.* (1948) postulated the two-step flow theory, and contended that the messages from the mass media do not directly reach the "masses" they first reach the "opinion leaders", who in turn pass on what they read or hear to "others". Further studies by Katz and Lazarsfeld (1955) also indicated that inter-personal communications play a crucial role in the spread of messages, emanating from the mass media channels. Y.P. Singh (1970) on the basis of the studies on flow of farm information concluded that in rural India information on agriculture and allied aspects generally flows from institutionalised sources such as Government extension agencies to village influentials, and from them through the web of word of mouth to other sections of the farming population.

## Development Communication

The origin of developmental communication dates back to the application of agricultural extension education during 1945-50, launched in most of the developing countries. Initially it was popularised as agricultural communication. Later, when the scope of extension effort was enlarged to include other areas like health, education, etc. it became popular as rural communication. With the emergence of development as a distinct concept in the international areas, communication applied for initiating and accelerating the process of development branched off as a serious study under the discipline of Developmental Communication or Development Support Communication (DSC).

The 1948 U.N. Conference on Freedom of Information which described free and adequate information as the "touchstone of all freedoms" had sown the seeds of developmental communication. Developing countries had set their goals to build infrastructures for free and adequate flow of information without which political articulation, economic growth and social justice cannot be achieved.

The subsequent U.N. General Assembly resolutions of 1953 which emphasised the role of information media in education, economic and social progress, provided a fillip for a faster growth of developmental communication. The idea that development is dependent on effectiveness of communication and is conditioned to a large extent by the character of communication gained momentum. It was widely appreciated that: (a) wherever communication existed on a planned level, development has been accelerated: and (b) that major developmental programmes will not reach their targets without adequate and planned communication inputs.

## Media and Development

Basing on his studies during 1950-51 in the Middle East (covering Iran, Egypt, Turkey, Syria, Lebanon and Jordan) Daniel Lerner (1958) pointed out that "mass communication serves as the great multiplier in development, the device that can spread the requisite knowledge and attitudes immeasurably more quickly and widely than ever before". Lerner's analysis revealed that there is high correlation between media growth and national growth. He argued that the person who changes in a developing society is usually "a mobile personality" who has high capacity to identify with new aspects of his environment, and who can take in his stride the new demands upon himself that are out of his habitual experience. According to lerner, the first element in the social dynamics of development is the infusion of modern or mobile personality, the second element is the mobile multiplier: the mass media.

Lerner and Schramm analysed data for 54 countries and showed the high correlation between the four measures: urbanisation, literacy, media participation and political participation. Schramm and Carter (1959) similarly found correlations of .72 and .74 respectively between the scale of economic development and other scales representing the development of mass media receiving and propagating systems in 100 countries.

Leonard Doob's study in Africa (1961) and Y.V.L. Rao's study in India (1966) are generally cited as further works corroborating Lerner's hypotheses on communication and development. Both the studies explain how extensive exposure to mass media helps to bring about change in the traditional society.

Rao, who studied two villages in Andhra Pradesh in two different settings was convinced that "where the channels of information are varied and broad-based like newspapers, radio, etc., the changes resulting from economic, social or political ideas creeping into the society are smooth. Where the channels of information are tight and controlled by the few, changes are difficult to make and often lead to a worsening of the factions". He argued that the amount of information available and the wideness of its distribution are key factors determining the speed and smoothness of development. While according to Lerner mass communication is the great multiplier of ideas and information, according to Rao it is the great smoother of transition. Finally, Rao concluded that it is futile to attempt to treat the interaction between the communication and development as casual relationship, and isolate the chicken from the egg because the interaction is constant and cumulative.

In his analysis of the role of mass media in the process of change and development in Africa, Doob asserted: "The moment when Africa starts to move out of traditional towards modern society, communication is a critical problem, at the very centre of existence". Doob argued that as more and more of Africans accept the practices and values from the West, they come to be intimately dependent upon the mass media.

Wilbur Schramm's study *Mass Media and National Development* (1964) is the first major treatise on the subject. The analysis in this Report provides the backdrop for the evolution of a distinct philosophy and content for developmental communication. Hence, some of the broad conclusions of this study are reproduced below:

1. Wherever new skills and new attitudes are to be learned, wherever people need to decide new things, wherever traditional society trembles on the verge of modernizing, there a more efficient form of communication can be helpful. . . . Therefore, the efficiency of communication is a consideration in determining the speed and smoothness of national development.
2. The flow of information is sadly inadequate. The situation is particularly cruel for the countries that are in an early stage of development. . . . It greatly thins out as it moves from cities towards the villages, and still more as it feedbacks from the village to the centres.
3. The whole information system not a particular channel or combination of channels needs to be planned to fight the battle of development.
4. Investment in information, in a developing country, is investment in the most essential social and economic changes which make up national development.

Pradipto Roy, Rogers *et al*. (1969) conducted a comparative study on the impact of communication on development in Costa Rica and India. Communication treatment with Radio Rural Forms, Literacy-cum-Reading Forums, and Animation Leadership training was given on 20 selected innovations in agriculture, health and social education. The study revealed a significant correlation between the degree of participation and exposure to the Radio Forum treatment and amount of change in the important variables among the Forum participants. The Radio Forum treatment not only accelerated the growth of knowledge and adoption but also discouraged discontinuance of innovations.

Kivlin, Fliegel *et al.* (1971) conducted another study on the spread of modern agriculture and health practices in India under a three-nation project and concluded among others that villages with greater access to and contact with mass media channels were more likely to score high on agricultural adoption. They also pointed out that mass media channels were widely used and that promotional efforts via them were likely to be successful.

## Communication Tasks in Development

Nora Quebral defined developmental communication as "the art and science of human communication applied to the speedy transformation of a country and mass of its people from poverty to a dynamic state of economic growth that makes possible greater social equality and the greater fulfilment of the human potentialities" (AMIC: 1976). This provides a broad perspective of the communication tasks in development. But, the specific tasks need to be analysed from the practical life situations of developing countries.

Schramm who is considered the father of developmental communication distinguished three kinds of tasks for communication in national development: (1) People must be given information about national development, their attention must be focused on the need for change, the methods and means of change and, if possible, their aspirations must be raised; (2) There must be opportunity to participate meaningfully in the decision-making process, the leaders must have an opportunity to lead and the common people to be heard; information must flow both up and down the hierarchy; (3) The needed skills must be taught, farmers must learn the new methods of farming, adults must be educated, extension workers must be trained (Schramm: 1964).

Developmental communication is not unidimensional. It envisages multi-dimensional linkages for ensuring free and adequate flow of information, and building interaction between the sources and the users of the knowledge. It implies linkages between all agencies involved in development work, such as planners, administrators, subject matter specialists, field workers, local leaders, media representatives, researchers and individuals who constitute the final consumers of the information. Thus, the routes of communication envisaged are not only vertical from top to bottom and bottom to top, but also horizontal between the institutions and personnel connected with developmental work. The net-working also presupposes constant monitoring and redrawing of communication strategy to eliminate seepage in the effort.

John L. Woods (1976) conceived a triangular nexus with three points: knowledge generators, political leaders and development knowledge users as shown below:

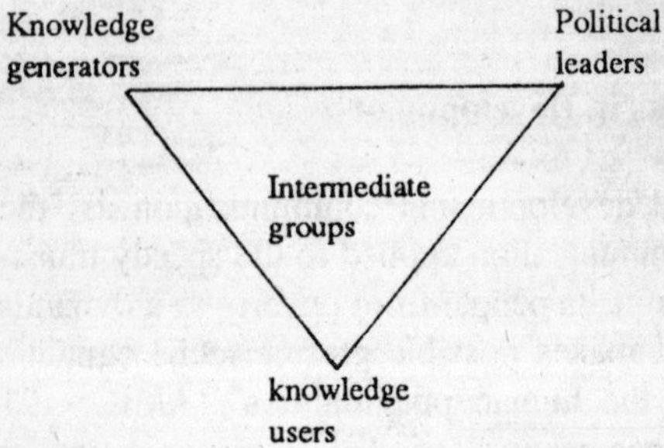


The role of developmental communication, according to him, is to link all the three elements in the development linkage triangle *plus* all the intermediate audience groups. Wood desired emphasis not on pushing the information towards the target audience, but on taking into account the information seeking patterns of the target audience and integrating them into the development planning process.

One essential prerequisite of developmental communication is that it should not be tied to any specific channel or communication technique. It must be able to exploit fruitfully informal and institutionalised networks, for promoting interaction through inter-personal means by word of mouth, by folk and traditional channels as well as mass media. The strategy of integrated communication is gaining momentum. According to this concept integration of communication input is envisaged primarily at three levels: (a) inter-personal; (b) mass media; and (c) in inter-agency and within agency communication. Even though the decisive role in development is played by the inter-personal channels interacting at the point of delivery, the philosophy in this strategy is to evolve a coordinated system to avoid isolated efforts, and divergent messages that are likely to create confusion. The system also envisages selection of right type of a communication channel or channels in combination (which is now popular as media mix) for specific informational input at a right moment.

The AMIC Seminar on developmental communication (1976)

identified two prerequisites: (1) Shift from dissatisfaction to satisfaction; and (2) Psychology of completeness.

1. The first prerequisite stresses that information delivery or transfer is only a prelude. It is a motivation which is the basic citadel of development communication. Without adequate motivation and persuasion it would be impossible to make people move along certain desired lines. Therefore, it is incumbent on development communication to affect the information transfer and behavioural change in a way that the people do not get psychologically imbalanced. The communication input should be tailored in a fashion that: (a) expectations are raised with minimum frustration and maximum satisfaction; and (b) the dynamic equilibrium is maintained between socio-economic and psycho-cultural components. Development effort raises aspirations, calls for new adjustments, implies discarding of traditional modes. Communication effort needs to be geared to minimise the irritants and smoothen the change process.

2. The second presupposition lays stress on the results. Development communication is result-oriented. Response is the indicator of the success of communication effort. But action and application of the message are long-drawn processes. Since seeing is believing and learning is doing, developmental communication has to create adequate opportunities for thinking, seeing and learning new innovations. It may, therefore, be essential to take up only such items which have the backing of the infrastructure, and launch a coordinated strategy to achieve results, to the fullest satisfaction of all.

The Working Group on Autonomy for Broadcasting Institutions in India (headed by B.G. Verghese) was critical of the disorganised growth of broadcasting media and attributed this to the failure to evolve a national communication policy (I & B: 1978). The group felt that "in the Indian situation, the objective of the communication policy must be to awaken the people, inform and educate them to be democratic citizens since eternal vigilance is the price of liberty, ensure equity and equality of opportunity, safeguard national values, preserve both unity and diversity and promote development and accepted national goals". It felt that such a policy may "envisage a web of vertical and lateral communications designed to facilitate the transmission of informal, educational and cultural messages not merely from government to people, people to people, masses to decision makers, rural to urban, the young to the rest, and so on at all levels and as a circular flow with switches for cross-cultural exchange".

The Indian Institute of Mass Communication (IIMC) and the International Institute of Communication (IIC) sponsored jointly a Regional Seminar on Communication Policies and Rural Development in 1979. This seminar outlined the basic objectives of the communication policies as:

promotion of change,
avoidance of alienation,
encouragement of participation, and
fostering of social justice and equity.

**Planning for Developmental Communication in India**

"Reach the common man with the message of development" is the slogan ever since we initiated developmental planning. Our Five Year Plans stress the need for pooling the resources in communication for taking the Plans to the average citizen and carrying back his feelings to the agencies involved in planning and execution of the schemes. The First Five Year Plan *inter alia* observed: "A widespread understanding of the Plan is an essential stage in its fulfilment. . . . The Plan has, therefore, to be carried into every home in the language and symbols of the people and expressed in terms of their common needs. . . . All available methods of communication have to be developed and the people approached through the written and the spoken word and no less than through radio, film, song and drama. Above all steps have to be taken to provide literature and information for the people in simple language on a scale equal to the needs of the country. . . . If obstacles are encountered and things go wrong anywhere, it would be helpful in every sense if information is imparted candidly and the people are acquainted with the steps being taken to set things right" (Planning Commission: 1952).

The National Extension Service (NES) with the village level worker as the king-pin was conceived with a view to reaching every farmer and assist in the coordinated development of rural life as a whole. Extension activity was planned as a continuous process to make the rural people know of their problems, and indicating to them the ways and means by which they can solve them. It was not planned as a mere information transfer process, but as an action-oriented strategy.

The directorate of Field publicity was created under the Ministry of Information and Broadcasting in 1953 primarily to seek public support for national campaigns on planned development. The field units of the organisation were directed to make use of the traditional media and folk formats to propagate the message of the Plan. The primary emphasis in extension education (CD) and Plan publicity was on personalised communication than on mediated communication. But, mass media, specifically radio, was called upon to play a supporting role in reaching the masses with developmental messages.

The Second Five Year Plan reiterated that information links with the people at grassroots are vital for enlisting their confidence and active participation. Even though the individual development departments were given the responsibility to evolve their own methods of extension education (e.g. agriculture departments of the Centre and States taking care of agricultural schemes, health departments executing health education programmes, etc.), it was felt that a coordinated effort is needed to provide support to the development campaigns in totality. The Plan stated: "The programmes of the Ministry of Information and Broadcasting and the State Governments are being carefully coordinated. They have been so framed as to provide effective machinery for the publicity of the Plan, having regard to the relative effectiveness of different media and the necessity of a uniform pattern of publicity organisation in the country through decentralisation and greater coordination with States and participation by non-official bodies" (Planning Commission: 1956).

Soon after the attainment of independence some isolated efforts were made to make use of radio in agricultural extension education. But, this could not sustain mainly because of the limited network and reach of AIR. Initially, therefore, the support of radio in developmental communication was extremely meagre. In February 1956, the Pune station of AIR conducted systematically an adult education programme for the farmers, by organising listening-cum-discussion groups in 145 villages on the Canadian model of Farm Radio Forums. Evaluation of this experiment by Mathur and Neurath (1959) revealed significant knowledge gains and active participation in village development projects by the members. Enthused by the success, AIR launched the countrywide scheme of Radio Rural Forums in November, 1959. The objective of the scheme was to provide linkage through radio between farmers and extension workers.

The scope of these rural-oriented radio programmes was extended to cover other aspects of rural life in 1966, by establishing Farm and Home Units at selected AIR centres. These units manned by trained agricultural extension personnel were created to provide adequate broadcasting support for rural-oriented developmental schemes. The accent continued to be on hardcore agricultural programmes but informational items relating to nutrition, health education, social welfare, etc., were also envisaged along with entertainment on a regular scale. Despite this growth, in terms of the total output of AIR, the share of rural-oriented developmental programmes did hardly exceed six per cent of the total output.

The study team constituted by the Ministry of Information and Broadcasting in the early sixties to evaluate the Five Year Plan publicity programmes observed in its Report that "even though the volume, speed and consistency with which the information services flow to the rural areas offer considerable scope for improvement, there can be little doubt that publicity has been able to generate an interest in certain sectors like agriculture and allied pursuits and major irrigation projects. It has, however, failed in inculcating a desire for an understanding of the wider social and economic aims of the socialistic pattern of society, and of aspects of national life other than those connected with farming and allied activities" (I & B: 1964).

The Committee on Broadcasting and Information Media headed by Ashok K. Chanda was equally critical of the meagre attention paid to rural-oriented developmental programmes by AIR. Their Report commented that: "It (AIR) cannot be allowed to continue to devote its effort and resources to provide information and entertainment to the relatively small urban community: it must be forged into a powerful instrument for bringing social and economic progress to the rural community and contribute towards building now India, self-reliant, self-sufficient, vibrant with new life (I & B: 1966).

Taking into consideration these Reports, the Fourth Five Year Plan stressed the need to coordinate the activities of information services at Centre, State and district levels. It deplored the creation of information personnel and facilities severally and in isolation by development departments and suggested a single integrated servicing agency. Information centres, radio transmitters, film production, mobile cine vans and other media were envisaged as different activities of a single servicing agency established for the use of all other departments and Ministries.

Expressing concern at the imbalance in the spread of information facilities in favour of urban concentrations, the plan stressed that "there is need for a deliberate attempt to inform the people in the rural areas, in particular those in backward areas, about specific schemes in agriculture, forestry, road construction, marketing, supply of credit and other inputs so that the benefits of these programmes are more widely spread (Planning Commission: 1969).

As a policy statement the Sixth Five Year Plan outlined that "the approach in the 1978-83 Plan in regard to sound broadcasting, TV, information and publicity is to give priority to schemes which can assist in promoting rural development as part of an integrated communication policy". Making a remark that "the interlinkages between the broadcasting services and the user agencies at the Central, State and local levels have been minimal, the Plan made it clear that primary support would be for sound broadcasting as the medium is economical, widespread in its coverage and socially acceptable" (Planning Commission: 1978).

Supporting such an approach the Working Group on autonomy for Akashwani and Doordarshan made a strong plea for a well-defined communication policy taking every kind of media from inter-personal to electronic as a resource. It also sounded a note of caution stating "there is danger of confusing the medium for the message and of hardware-led software systems. It has been well said that the issue is not whether the cat is black or white, but whether it can catch mice. Communications are also part of a larger culture and impose certain values" (I & B: 1978).

## Communication Resources

The sphere of communication is much wider. Mass media constitute only a microcosm of the universe, composed of a network of inter-personal and impersonal channels. To understand the specific role of television in the field of developmental communication, a brief outline of the status of other media involved in this task is considered essential.

Ours is a vast country with 800 million people and land area extending to 3.288 million square kilometres. Most of the population is dispersed in about 576,000 villages. The geographical variations, ethno-cultural and linguistic differences are marked as one moves from Kerala in the south to Kashmir in the north, from the Andamans in the south-east to Lakshadweep in the south-west, from Arunachal Pradesh in the north-east to Rajasthan deserts in the west. The Constitution recognises 15 major languages. But, there are numerous conventionally accepted cultural zones and dialectic pockets. It is estimated that as many as 300 languages are spoken in the country. Heterogeneity in languages, dissimilarities in culture and variations in the agro-economic systems due to ecological differences pose a big challenge to our communication planning.

Developmental messages emanate from governmental or non-governmental agencies sponsoring the schemes. These sources may select a personalised media like extension staff, or folk media, or mass media for propagation of the innovations. Traditional inter-personal channels, within families, friends, relatives, etc., assume importance as secondary sources after the receipt of information from the primary sources and play a very vital role in information diffusion. Our main concern is with the sources which originate the messages and initiate the diffusion process. Hence, the discussion is confined here to the institutionalised media.

### Extension Services

There are nation-wide networks of extension services, run by different developmental agencies. But, the infrastructure is considered highly inadequate in terms of the magnitude of the work involved. We may take for illustration the agricultural extension services which have a country-wide network. According to the revised pattern of Training and Visits (T&V) system the jurisdiction of a Village Level Worker extends to 500 farm families in intensive areas and 800 in other areas. He is expected to establish contacts with each family at least once a fortnight. It is physically considered impossible to maintain such a schedule because of the multifarious functions assigned to the VLW (Singh: 1979). The Verghese Panel on Broadcasting Media observed that for about 80 million farm families not more than 15,000 Village Level Workers exist in the country which works out to 5,335 families per worker (I & B: 1978). Even in the case of Community Health Scheme launched in 1978 in selected Blocks, each Health Worker is expected to deliver health care facilities to a population of 1,000 in the rural areas. Quoting an FAO Report, Adivi Reddy pointed out that the number of people served per Extension Worker is 2,700 in our country as against 160 in Israel, 400 in Greece, 730 in Japan and 1,700 in Taiwan (Reddy: 1979).

### Radio

All India Radio is a monopoly organisation run by the Union Ministry of Information and Broadcasting. Its network consists of 85 stations with 155 transmitters. Theoretically 90 per cent of the country's population is assumed to receive satisfactory medium-wave service. But, the transmitter power being weak the effective coverage keeps shrinking because of external interference.

Of the 20 million radio receiver sets in the country (at the end of 1978) not more than 15-20 per cent are estimated to be located in rural areas. In other words there is one set for a population of 125 in villages as against one for 20, the norm recommended by UNESCO. Community listening once advocated for rural audiences does not find favour any more because of the organisational problems and poor utilisation. The SITE social impact studies by Binod Agrawal *et al.* (1977) indicated that 36 per cent males and 65 per cent females in the rural areas had no exposure to radio.

Only 15.5 per cent of rural households own a radio set. Surveys in Andhra Pradesh revealed that while 18 per cent of farming and artisan families owned a radio set, not more than three per cent of the families depending on agricultural labour had a radio (Rao: 1977). Besides the poor ownership of the sets, the programmes with developmental messages hardly exceed 10 per cent of the total output of AIR.

### Print

Print medium is in private hands. It could have grown well but for the poor literacy rate. As less than 30 per cent of the rural people are educated, the circulation of newspapers and other print channels is mostly confined to urban areas where the literacy rate is 60 per cent. In terms of circulation of newspapers the reach of the medium is limited to 20 copies per thousand as against the UNESCO norm of 100 copies per 1,000 people. Binod Agrawal *et al.* (1977) pointed out that 92 per cent of males and 95 per cent of females in rural areas were unexposed to print medium. Another important factor for the poor consumption and intake of the print medium in villages is the meagre coverage of the rural scene. Hardly 10 per cent of the content concerns the rural life.

### Films

India is the largest film producing country in the world with over 500 productions per year. But, the industry being privately managed it is mostly commercial oriented. Nearly 60 per cent of the output constitutes entertainment films. The Films Division of the Government of India originates documentaries and newsreels with developmental messages. During 1976 about 100 such short films were released in regional languages for screening in cinema halls by the Directorate of Field Publicity in the villages (Dharap: 1978).

Besides the low quantum of output relating to developmental themes, another major inhibiting factor is the lack of cinema halls in rural areas. Of the 12,000 cinema halls in the country as many as two-thirds are located in cities and towns. The number of cinema seats per 1,000 population is less than one as against the UNESCO norm of two. With the existing infrastructure in rural areas we cannot expect more than one cinema hall for a population of 1,00,000. A study by the author in Andhra Pradesh revealed that an average villager has to treck 16 km to see a movie. As for the actual exposure, studies by Agrawal *et al.* (1977) indicated that 64 per cent of males and 84 per cent of females in villages have not seen a film. Even those who get exposure, hardly see a movie once in a quarter due to constraints like poverty, poor communication facilities, etc. (Rao: 1977).

**Traditional Media**

We have a rich cultural heritage and our traditional media have a wide reach because of their variety and cultural specificity. However, traditionally they were developed to serve the entertainment and religious communication. But some of the formats like *Tamasha* in Maharashtra, *Burrakatha* in Andhra pradesh and *Jatra* in West Bengal were successfully adapted for propagating nationalist spirit among the masses during the freedom struggle. Encouraged by the popular response, some effort was made to disseminate developmental information through traditional media during the fifties. But, there has been no concerted effort to make use of the traditional media in the developmental communication process: the accent is more on mass media like radio.

**Instructional TV in other Countries**

Having presented a broad spectrum of the linkages between communication, media growth and development, it is proposed to review the literature on some of the important experiments in other parts of the world on the utilization of television for developmental purposes.

Educational Television (ETV), which is basically designed for providing support to formal education, either curriculum-oriented or enrichment type, has not been discussed here, as it is outside the purview of this study. It is confined to experiments in Instructional Television (ITV), aimed at information diffusion and extension education of the adult members of society. ITV is essentially non-formal; it envisages creation of awareness and motivation for overall development of the country. It, therefore, touches all essential aspects such as agriculture and other economic activities, health care and social education for active participation of the individuals in the development process.

**Adult Education through TV in France**

French TV was the first to experiment in instructional television. As a Pilot Project the scheme was sponsored by UNESCO in 1953-54 for the education of the farmers. Small groups were organised around television in the rural districts for discussion and follow-up on farm telecasts. Dumazedier who conducted an evaluation of the Project concluded that television programmes carried information to the members and motivated them to accept new innovations. The Report says, "it was amply demonstrated that the agricultural programmes encouraged the small farmers and workmen to take part in after-telecast discussions. . . The theme of the debates and discussions centred around the subject matter of the telecasts and the participation of the audience indicated that the rural population was keenly interested in the basic problems of its daily life". Another important observation was about the increased effectiveness when the broadcast topics were selected and programmes planned in cooperation with prospective viewers (UNESCO: 1964).

**Telescuola in Italy**

Radio-Television Italiana and the Italian Education Ministry sponsored the Telescuola programme in 1958 for mass education of the illiterate citizens. The series under the title, "It is never too late", was produced in such a way that it contained humour, besides teaching skills in reading and writing. The telecasts were systematically followed with specifically prepared reading material. The results were reported to be highly encouraging (UNESCO: 1964). But, telescuola being basically an adult literacy programme, its achievements were measured in terms of gains in literacy.

**Rural Television in Japan**

Encouraged by the success of the pilot project on Community TV viewing in the rural areas of France, UNESCO sponsored the second project on instructional TV in Japan during 1956-57. Under the auspices of this project the Japan Broadcasting Corporation (NHK) organised teleclubs in 64 villages for group viewing of Social Education and Farm Programmes. The two main objectives of this experimental project were: (a) to find out to what extent television helps to improve the lives of general public; and (b) to assess how useful teleclubs are as means of social education in rural districts.

The important findings of the evaluation report (UNESCO; 1960) on the project are indicated below:

1. Television which combines all the strong points of other media was received with an easiness and readiness that had not been experienced in other cases. To rural people who tend to be suspicious of anything new and are not inclined to enjoy entertainment at their own expense, television brings ample entertainment in an easily acceptable form and provides an extremely convenient and enjoyable pastime.
2. The farmers did not attend the gatherings to be educated, but came to get some recreation and entertainment. However, it was the group viewing that gradually changed their comparatively easy and passive attitude into positive participation.
3. The villagers began to take an interest in more serious subjects than in gossip and idle chatter.
4. The audience wanted to be given definite suggestions on agricultural management and technique. While they wanted to see many examples of modernization, mechanisation and collectivization in advanced villages, they also wanted to be told how to achieve the improvements. Psychological dependence of the villagers on the television as a means of solving their problems was behind this attitude.

### Television in Africa

The growth of television in the African countries has been slow due to financial and other technical constraints. Nigeria was the first to introduce television in 1959, followed by Kenya (1962), Ghana (1965), Egypt (1968) and other countries. However, TV coverage is mostly limited to important urban centres. As such, although a number of items with development messages are included in the regular telecasts, their reach, utilisation and impact are considered to be marginal (CBA: 1976).

The voice of Kenya originates TV programmes covering health, hygiene and adult education and a number of programmes are designed for the women. The service is, however, limited to the areas around Nairobi, Mombasa and Kisumu on Lake Victoria.

Television in Ghana functions with the commitment to assist in social transformation of the country. Hachten (1971), who studied the media in Ghana, observed that among the African nations, Ghana makes the best efforts for utilising TV for instruction and education.

Television services in Nigeria and Egypt also have a mandate to promote national development by originating programmes in support of formal and non-formal education.

But, in none of the African countries there was any major project under which instructional TV programmes were taken up on a country-wide scale (Dua: 1979).

### Television in Latin America

In most of the Latin American countries television service is limited to major cities. Secondly, 70 per cent of the programme output is entertainment-oriented and it is mostly imported from other countries. However, studies in Columbia and Brazil revealed that TV exposure contributes significantly towards rural development.

Everett Rogers (1962) noted that Columbian farmers exposed to TV get the benefit of "increased social status, literacy, cosmopoliteness, innovativeness, political knowledge, achievement motivation and education aspirations". He found a similar situation in Brazil also which is another country making extensive use of television for instruction and social education.

### Television in Asia

Excepting Japan, Television in most other Asian countries like

Singapore, Malaysia, Pakistan, the Philippines, etc., is yet to prove its role as an instrument of rural development. Its avowed objective is to provide to the masses information and entertainment. Even though in many of these countries TV was introduced in the 1960s, due to constraints like lack of infrastructure, finance and technical man-power its actual application for instructional purposes is meagre (UNESCO: 1975).

# 3

# TELEVISION IN INDIA

THE CREDIT for introducing television in India goes to Phillips (India) Company, which exhibited some TV equipment brought from Holland at the annual Industrial Fair at New Delhi in 1955. With a temporary studio and a transmitter complex set up in the exhibition grounds, it made a beginning in TV transmission, with live telecast of programmes. Twentyfive conventional TV receivers (and one with a giant screen 9′ × 12′) were installed at different points within the exhibition premises for public viewing.

This provided a good opportunity for the personnel in the national broadcasting network, All India Radio (AIR), to study equipment and get acquainted with the process and management of TV transmission. Enthused by public response to television an outlay of Rs. 40 lakhs (out of the total outlay of Rs. 9 crores) was included by the Government in the Second Five Year Plan budget (1956-61) towards making a beginning in television (Planning Commission: 1956). Subsequently, in November 1956, UNESCO held its General Conference at New Delhi. It was proposed at this meeting to sponsor, on behalf of UNESCO, a Pilot Project for studying the use of TV as a medium of education, rural uplift and community development (Menon: 1976).

In 1957, Phillips (India) offered for sale to All India Radio the TV equipment that was brought from Holland. The transmitter and the TV camera were purchased for experimental work and in the deal the company gifted the 20 TV receiver sets to AIR. The equipment so acquired was placed under the charge of the Engineering Research Department of AIR for conducting technical investigation, training of personnel, and assessing the value of the medium for mass communication (Ministry of I & B: 1958-59).

In April 1958, this transmitter was installed with an improvised mast. There was no studio facility. Hence, arrangements were made in the Research Laboratory itself to project 16mm and 35mm films, on a movie screen and pick them up by TV camera for transmission. A few TV receiver sets were installed for VIP viewing in the residential quarters of the President, the Vice-President, the Prime Minister, the Minister for Information and Broadcasting, and others. Occasionally, there were also live telecasts like puppet shows of the Song and Drama Division of the I&B Ministry. The Research Unit successfully organised a stall at the India-1958 exhibition where the audiences for the first time had the opportunity to view the experimental telecasts, produced and presented by AIR.

Subsequently, in October 1958, additional TV equipment was received as aid from the United States Information Services (USIS) and UNESCO supplied 20 receiver sets for community viewing in teleclubs. In December 1958, AIR obtained micro-wave link and one camera chain with which the live telecast of January 1959, Republic Day Parade and folk dances from the National Stadium were successfully covered by the Research Department.

**Social Education Programmes**

The regular Experimental Television Services was inaugurated at Delhi on September 15, 1959, by the President, heralding the use of the medium for community education. In pursuance of the agreement signed with AIR, UNESCO provided a grant of 20,000 U.S. dollars for this Pilot Project which aimed at assessing the value of different types of educational TV programmes for group viewing in rural and urban communities in such a way that the result of such an experiment may be useful not only for India, but also other Asian countries (Mathur & Saksena: 1963). The project envisaged:

(a) Production and broadcasting of a series of special educational TV programmes on such subjects as would improve urban and rural conditions, adult and health education, the promotion of recreational community activities and the use of various forms of entertainment for community programmes and in a limited way supplement school education;
(b) Formation of group-viewing centres for the reception and discussion of these programmes; and

(c) Scientific evaluation of the impact of the medium of mass communication upon the rural and urban communities.

With the small improvised studio in Akashwani Bhavan and the transmitter range limited to 25 km the television service was run successfully twice a week (on Tuesdays and Fridays) for a duration of 60 minutes each day. The programmes consisted of about 40 minutes of educational items and 20 minutes of entertainment items, in a variety of formats.

Initially AIR arranged to instal 21 TV sets at selected Community Centres, within Delhi Municipal Corporation limits. At each of these centres a teleclub was organised for viewing and conducting follow-up discussions. The response was encouraging with 150-200 persons attending at each centre.

**Programmes on Citizenship**

The test programmes under the experimental project sponsored by UNESCO, comprising 20 special programmes in citizenship, were telecast from December 28, 1960 to May 1961. The five subjects covered (with four programmes) on each topic were: (1) traffic and the road sense; (2) dangers to the health of the community; (3) adulteration of food; (4) encroachment on public property; and (5) manners of a citizen. In addition to the 21 receiver sets already installed by AIR, UNESCO supplied 45 more sets for installation in schools, where teleclubs were organised for the benefit of school children as well as the adults in the neighbourhood.

After the completion of the test series an evaluation study to assess the nature and extent of the impact of these programmes was jointly conducted by UNESCO, Indian Adult Education Association and the National Fundamental Education Centre of the Ministry of Education. This Report confirmed that TV can be used as a medium for information and mass communication in developing countries. It revealed positive gains in the field of information, even though changes in attitudes and behaviour were not immediately perceptible. (Mathur & Saksena: 1963). In view of the encouraging results AIR arranged to continue five more series (comprising 20 programmes) for the benefit of teleclubs, wherein the viewers' doubts were also removed by the specialists. In the Third Five Year Plan (1961-66), a scheme was included for the expansion of TV by opening another centre at Bombay. An outlay of Rs. 40 lakhs (out of the total outlay of Rs. 10.86 crores on broadcasting) was proposed on this scheme (Planning Commission: 1961). But due to subsequent foreign exchange difficulties due to Chinese and Pakistani aggressions this project could not be taken up.

### School Television

For about 10 weeks during January-March, 1960, lessons for school children were telecast on Tuesdays from 3 to 4 p.m. on an experimental basis. The Delhi Administration made arrangements for taking batches of students from various schools to the nearest Community Centre for exposure to these programmes. In early 1961 AIR signed a new agreement with the Ford Foundation for a four-year Project in Educational Television. This Project envisaged supply of necessary technical equipment, training of AIR personnel, deputation of educational television experts from the USA and installation of 600 TV sets in the secondary schools in Delhi. Marking a beginning in regular Educational Television (ETV) this Project was launched on October 23, 1961. Initially, TV sets were installed in 146 higher secondary schools in Delhi to facilitate group viewing.

The subsequent landmark was the installation of a 5 kW transmitter in September 1962 (in replacement of the old 500 watt transmitter) which was acquired under the aid agreement with the Ford Foundation. An additional consignment of 150 TV sets was also received for placement in schools. By early 1965 the ETV programmes were made available to 233 out of the 366 higher secondary schools in Delhi.

After running the ETV project for four years, an evaluation study was entrusted to Paul Neurath by the Ford Foundation. His Report, among others, substantiated that: (a) students learn better with the aid of TV than without it; (b) even some of the good schools in Delhi do not have facilities to show the experiments as shown in the ETV programmes; (c) TV is good for equalising educational opportunities; and (d) the process of change in teaching methodology and administration of teaching was noticeable after the ETV programmes. AIR was commended by international organisations for sound planning, integration of lessons with the school syllabus and coordinating with the user departments (Menon: 1976).

AIR prepared a master plan in the early sixties for the development of TV, envisaging an outlay of Rs. 10 crores, spread over a period of

25 years and submitted this to the Government for consideration. The objective of this long-term plan was to avoid haphazard growth.

**General Service**

A significant step in the growth of Indian TV was the receipt of West German gift of equipment in 1965, under which AIR's auditorium was converted into a studio and on August 15, 1965, the daily general service of one hour duration was inaugurated. This facilitated transmission of both entertainment and informative programmes for all categories like children, women, youth, etc. The earlier information-oriented programmes for teleclubs were made a part of the general service. Thus, the viewers could have varied fare with news commentaries, social education programmes, entertaining feature films, music, etc. Consequently, the number of TV sets which were only 551 in 1963 increased to 4,500 in 1966.

**Krishi Darshan**

The pioneering efforts of Dr. Vikram Sarabhai of the Atomic Energy Commission and Dr. M. S. Swaminathan of the Indian Agricultural Research Institute (IARI) were instrumental in launching the Krishi Darshan service with effect from January 26, 1967.

The primary objective of these programmes was popularisation of improved agricultural practices with telecasts twice a week for 20 minutes each. In 80 selected villages (60 drawn from the Union Territory of Delhi and 20 from adjoining U.P. and Haryana States), "Farm Teleclubs" were organised and community TV sets installed for group viewing. So great was the enthusiasm of Dr. Sarabhai that he personally gifted TV sets for the experimental extension communication in villages. In close coordination with the subject consultants from the Agricultural Research Institute and the extension agencies of the State departments concerned, the service was maintained with need-based instructional programmes on not only agriculture but also allied subjects.

The first evaluation report on the service was prepared by the National Council of Educational Research and Training and it revealed significant knowledge gains in farm technology (NCERT: 1968). However, a study by Jagadish Singh (1971) indicated that a majority of the farmers considered the programme more suitable to the "educated urbanites" than to the "average ruralite". Shingi and Mody (1974) who studied the knowledge gaps similarly found media concentration with the better educated farmers getting more exposure to TV than the small farmers.

**Expansion Proposals**

During the *ad hoc* Plan years 1966-69, there was no expansion of TV excepting increase in the transmission time of the Delhi centre from seven to 11 hours per week. But, one of the significant developments was the recommendation of the International Advisory Panel on Communication, sponsored by UNESCO, which met at Paris on March 23, 1967, that India would be best suited for a pilot project on satellite-based educational TV.

For many years, the Government of India resisted the demand for opening of more TV centres arguing that the country could not afford to invest on this costly medium ignoring other essential development needs. But, the results of the pilot experimental projects, on the use of TV for Social Education (1959), School Education (1961) and Agricultural Extension (1967) being favourable, there has been persistent demand for expansion of TV network in the country. It was convincingly argued that if television is efficiently used for instructional purposes, many of the communication needs in respect of developmental efforts could be met in the areas of agricultural extension, population control, health and nutrition, etc.

The Committee on Broadcasting and Information Media headed by Ashok K. Chanda recommended an independent Television Authority for extensive development of television communication by terrestrial network (I&B : 1966). The Committee observed, "we are firmly convinced that the time has come when its essentiality should no longer be questioned and its introduction on a massive scale no longer deferred. We envisage and recommend a plan to give country-wide coverage by a television network in a period of about seven years". The Committee examined the Master Plan prepared by AIR and recommended opening up of TV centres in all towns with a population of 100,000 or over, setting up production facilities and mother stations in all State capitals and relaying centres in other areas. Justifying its proposal the Committee stated "one of our primary considerations in recommending the introduction of television on a country-wide scale was the benefit it would bring to our rural areas.

The Ministry of Information and Broadcasting appointed in June 1965, a technical Committee headed by Dr. S. Bhagavantam to examine separately the Master Plan prepared by AIR for TV expansion. This Committee recommended that as a first step TV centres be created in all State capitals. Taking note of the rapid advances in the field of electronics, specifically in satellite communication, the Committee favoured experimentation with satellite-supported TV transmission for wider diffusion. But, the Chanda Committee ruled out its feasibility and preferred localised coverage through conventional terrestrial expansion (I&B : 1966).

**Decision to Expand TV Broadcasting**

Finally in 1968 the Government of India announced its decision to expand television broadcasting. The basic objective was to use the medium for both school and out-of-school education, with special emphasis on the field of agricultural development, health and family planning (UNESCO: 1969).

Subsequently it requested the United Nations Development Programme (UNDP) to depute an expert mission to study and recommend plans for television development and help initiate necessary training programmes in software (programme generation) and hardware (engineering) aspects. In pursuance of this request a six-member mission under the leadership of John Willings was deputed in May 1969, by UNESCO/UNDP with the following assignment:

(a) to examine with Indian authorities the whole range of educational effort both for formal education and for general and specialised adult education aiming at the economic and social development of the country and to determine what parts of the total teaching process would lend themselves to televised communication;
(b) to work out a realistic phased development programme; and
(c) to suggest concrete plans for the training of the personnel.

The Willings Mission submitted a comprehensive report in November 1969, recommending development of TV for formal education at primary and secondary levels and as a medium of non-formal instruction for health education including family planning, agricultural extension and farmers' training. It observed that "the essence of communication process in India as between media producers and village users will depend upon thoroughly informed and sympathetic grasp of village life" (UNESCO: 1969).

Meanwhile in pursuance of the earlier recommendation of the International Advisory Panel on Communication (1967), the Department of Atomic Energy of Government of India (ISRO), signed an agreement, in 1969, with the National Aeronautics and Space Administration (NASA) of the USA for availing, on loan, their Applications Technology Satellite (ATS-6) for one year, for the purpose of Satellite Instructional Television Experiment (SITE). This project, however, became operational after six years in August 1975.

Concrete proposals were drawn for the expansion of ground TV network during the Fourth Five Year Plan (1969-74). The Plan envisaged strengthening of the existing facilities at Delhi and constructing of five more centres at (1) Bombay with a relay centre at Pune, (2) Srinagar, (3) Calcutta, (4) Madras and (5) Lucknow with a relay centre at Kanpur (Planning Commission: 1970). The budgeted outlay on TV was Rs. 32 crores as against Rs. 45.1 crores on radio.

To train the programme and technical staff for these new stations, the Government of India approached the UNDP, in pursuance of the Willings Mission report, for assistance. Accordingly, a Television Training Centre was initially established in 1971 at Delhi and later shifted to Pune in 1974 as a wing of the Film Institute.

## Philosophy of TV Communication

As a policy the Government declared that the medium would be used as an instrument for accelerating socio-economic change. It was stated that in developing the TV network the guiding principle would be how best the medium could be harnessed to the requirements of education and development. Concluding on the basis of various official statements Mehra Masani observed: "From the start the Government's proclamations indicated that TV would be used as a weapon against illiteracy and ignorance; it would bring about awareness among people of sociological problems and make them conscious of national goals; it would create a sense of participation in India's efforts to usher in a new social order; it would play a vital role in cultivating civic consciousness and respect for law and order, public morality and so forth and, in the field of entertainment, it would mould public taste to higher aesthetic levels" (Masani: 1976).

In 1973 fresh proposals were drawn up by AIR for a countrywide terrestrial TV network, in preference to satellite coverage proposing an outlay of Rs. 308 crores. This scheme envisaged installation of a mother TV transmitter in each State capital with production facilities and auxiliary relay transmitters at a few centres in each State for wider diffusion. It was argued that such a system would facilitate presentation of programmes with specific regional approach which is not possible in satellite system, designed for very large coverage. According to this Plan, TV centres were to be linked by micro-wave for inter-state communication and for national hook-ups.

A seminar on software objective of TV held under the aegis of AIR in February, 1973, reiterated that "television must be used in the development process as an instrument of social change and national cohesion by unhesitatingly upholding progressive values and involving the community in free dialogue. Indian TV has to shun an elitist approach and consumer value system and evolve a true national model (Masani: 1976).

**Development during Fourth Five Year Plan**

The transmission time of the Delhi centre was gradually increased to about 25 hours per week, introducing more of popular entertainment items and news and current affairs programmes. The frequency of farm programmes (Krishi Darshan) was increased to three programmes per week, each of 30-minute duration. Consequently the number of TV sets in Delhi and around increased from 12,000 in 1969 to 38,000 in 1971. Before the end of the Plan, the inauguration of four TV Centres at Bombay (October 1972), Srinagar (January 1973), Amritsar (September 1973) and Pune (October 1973) was completed.

Till 1970 TV receiver sets were mostly imported. But, after the constitution of the Electronics Commission in early 1971, their indigenous production was encouraged mainly in the small scale sector. However, with high production costs and taxation the total number of sets at the end of 1973 in the country stood only at 160,000.

**Telecasts for Primary School Children**

One significant development towards the end of the Fourth Five Year Plan was the commencement of the telecasts for the primary school children from the Delhi Centre in March 1974, in pursuance of the

Willings Mission recommendation. These telecasts were planned for general enrichment, unlike the earlier ETV programmes which were syllabus-oriented.

**Progress in Fifth Five Year Plan**

The inauguration of the Satellite Instructional Television Experiment (SITE) on August 1, 1975, was the most significant landmark in the history of TV, not only in India but also the world over. The ATS-6 satellite loaned to India was used most successfully for direct reception of telecasts on community sets. The whole experiment was conceived for reaching the rural audience with developmental messages. TV sets were placed in 2,330 villages dispersed in six backward clusters, identified in Andhra Pradesh, Karnataka, Orissa, Bihar, Madhya Pradesh and Rajasthan States. There was also one experimental centre at Pij in Kheda district near Ahmedabad. This communication experiment, the first of its kind in the world, ended on July 31, 1976.

Simultaneously with SITE, the strengthening of the ground TV network was also planned. The budgeted Plan outlay for 1974-79 was Rs. 50.98 crores for TV expansion, as against Rs.37.63 crores for radio (Planning Commission: 1976). Before the end of 1975, three more TV centres were commissioned at Calcutta and Madras in August 1975, and Lucknow in November, 1975. The production of TV sets meanwhile increased to about 75,000 per year. But, the growth of TV receivers within the country was only marginal with 479,000 as on December 31, 1976. (due to lack of internal market most of the sets were exported to other countries).

**TV Commercials and Delinking of TV from Radio**

With a view to having commercial earnings, advertisements were introduced on TV from January 1, 1976. Subsequently, on April 1, 1976, TV was delinked from AIR creating a separate Directorate for Doordarshan under the Ministry of Information and Broadcasting.

**Post-SITE Centres for Rural Coverage**

After the termination of SITE at the end of July 1976, for some time the villages covered under the experiment did not have telecast facilities. For continuing exposure of these villages to TV and supplementing the extension education, six SITE continuity terrestrial centres were set up during 1977-78 at Jaipur (Rajasthan), Raipur (Madhya Pradesh), Gulbarga (Karnataka), Hyderabad (Andhra Pradesh), Sambalpur (Orissa) and Muzaffarpur (Bihar). The potential coverage of these centres is 12,000 villages out of which 967 were earlier exposed to TV under the SITE programme.

Jaipur, Raipur and Muzaffarpur centres were been provided with separate production facilities. For these centres the programmes were centrally-originated at the Base Production Centre, Delhi, in Hindi language. Similarly the programmes for the Gulbarga centre were produced at the Hyderabad centre in Kannada language. For Sambalpur the production centre was located at Cuttack. In addition to these six centres, the Ahmedabad centre, which was earlier set up for experimental station at Pij, continued to function under the SITE continuity scheme. These seven centres were telecasting programmes primarily for rural audiences covering mainly agriculture, animal husbandry, dairy farming and allied subjects, rural industries, nutrition, health care, family welfare and welfare of weaker sections, with a mix of instructional and entertainment formats.

In March 1977, there was change of Government at the Centre with the Janata Party coming to power. However, making a statement in Parliament the Minister for Information and Broadcasting announced: "The Government is definite about making the TV programmes positively rural-based so that development in rural areas could be initiated at a fast pace.[1]

The Government, in August 1977, announced the appointment of a Working Group (headed by Shri B. G. Verghese) to suggest an appropriate autonomous structure for Akashvani and Doordarshan. The expert panel recommended the establishment of a single National Broadcast Trust (NBT) for both AIR and Doordarshan (I&B: 1978). Some of the important observations of the Committee are given below:

1. If broadcasting is to receive a high place in the Nation's scale of priorities, it can do so only if it is seen to be playing a vital and essential supportive role in the development goals of the nation. For the next two decades among the most important of the goals must be rural development. The purpose of radio and television is to inform, educate and entertain people. As mass media they must truly be made of and for the masses rather than retain a

predominantly class or urban elitist bias, which is largely the case today, some 'popular' instructional and rural programming notwithstanding.

2. Both in terms of physical presence and programme content the emphasis of broadcasting will have to shift from its largely elitist moorings to the rural and semi-urban areas and to the urban poor. The quality and proportion of its instructional content will likewise have to increase. The NBT must bridge the urban-rural divide and combine modernity with relevant tradition.
3. While we acknowledge that television is a powerful and effective medium, India should give first priority to the development of densification of radio for at least the next 10 to 15 years.

**Expansion in Urban Areas**

One relay centre was commissioned at Mussoorie in August 1977, to carry the telecasts from Delhi. Subsequent additions were the relay centre for Lucknow at Kanpur in January 1979, and the permanent studio complex at Jullunder in April 1979.

Initially it was proposed to set up TV centres at all State capitals by 1983. But, the Planning Commission had approved three centres during the Sixth Five Year Plan (1978-83) for location at Bangalore, Trivandrum and Ahmedabad. However, nine more relay centres were planned at Vijayawada, Jammu, Cuttack, Ajmer, Madurai, Varanasi, Asansole, Murshidabad and Panaji during this period. About expansion for rural coverage the Planning Commission categorically stated: "Until the ongoing programme for rural TV has been fully evaluated and its cost effectiveness as a channel for rural development established no major extension of rural TV is envisaged during 1978-83".

**No Major Expansion of TV during 1978-83**

Apart from making some provision for on-going programmes and setting up of TV transmitters at six centres — Jaipur, Hyderabad, Raipur, Gulbarga, Sambalpur and Muzaffarpur — under the SITE continuity programme, a few new schemes were approved. For this, Rs. 50 crores was earmarked for TV, out of which Rs. 32 crores was

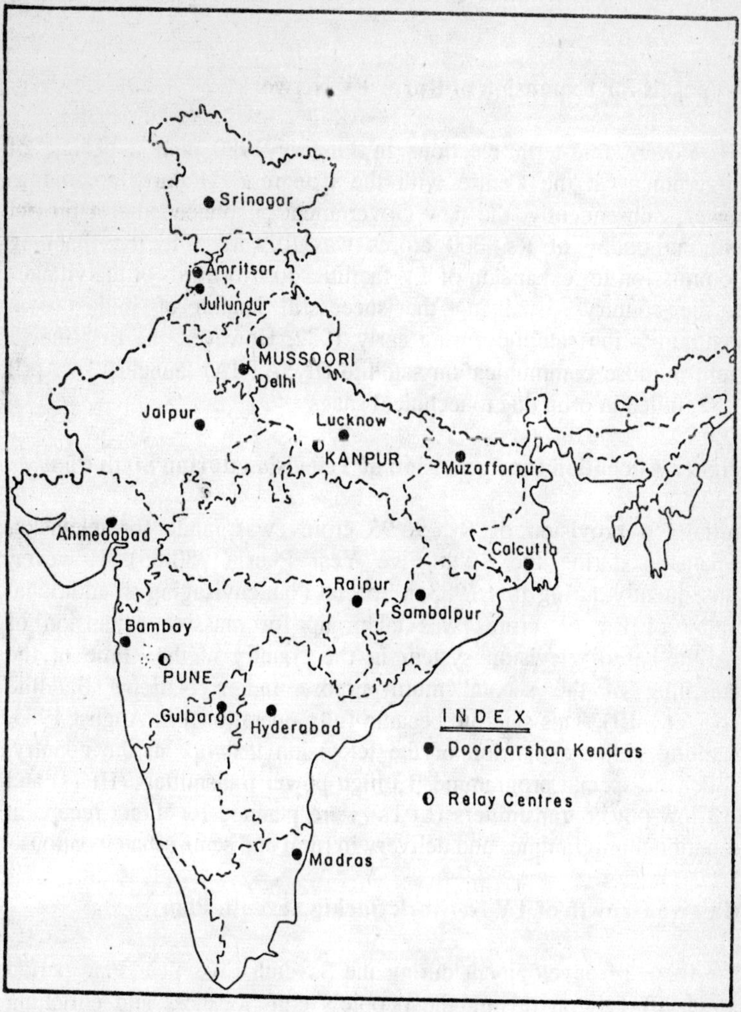


MAP 3.1: India : Doordarshan Kendras and Relay Centres

meant for new schemes and Rs. 18 crores for spillover schemes during 1978-83.

### Proposals for Expansion of Rural TV Network

There were mid-term elections in January 1980, and a change of Government at the Centre with the Congress (I) Party coming to power. Subsequently, the new Government announced that a project with an outlay of Rs. 300 crores was forwarded to the Planning Commission for expansion of TV facilities to two-thirds of the villages in the country visualising the successful launch of India's own communication satellite during early 1982. However, the first Indian multi-purpose communication satellite (INSAT-IA) launched in April 1982, failed in orbit due to technical snags.

### Higher Allocation for Expansion of Television during Sixth Plan

Initially a provision of Rs. 96.95 crores was made for television expansion during the Sixth Five Year Plan (1980-85). However, subsequently during July 1983, a Special Plan envisaging an additional outlay of Rs. 68 crores was taken up for massive expansion of satellite-based television system in the country at the time of the launching of the second multi-purpose Indian National Satellite (INSAT - IB). This satellite became fully operational in August 1983, enabling major expansion of the television network in the country. Under the special programme, 13 high-power transmitters (HPTs) and 118 low-power transmitters (LPTs) were planned for direct reception of national programmes and delivery in rural and semi-urban locations.

### Massive Growth of TV Network during Seventh Plan

The focus of development during the Seventh Five Year Plan period (1985-90) was on raising the people's consciousness and enriching their cultural and social life with a view to making them better informed citizens. It was envisaged that instruments of mass media would be developed to act as vehicles of education and extension to narrow down the informational gaps of the people.

The Plan document stressed the key role of mass media in the development process. A large-scale TV expansion plan was drawn up, justifying the potential and utilisation of television as a medium for development communication, particularly in agriculture, rural development, adult education, protection of environment, preservation of ecological plans and energy management.

The Plan laid stress on increasing productivity and consolidation of hardware infrastructure. More than 400 low-power transmitters (LPTs) were planned to be installed to provide communication support to the massive development programmes. Limited production facilities were also envisaged at the LPTs to have community participation in generating local specific programmes.

The Seventh Plan made a provision of Rs. 700 crores for expansion of Doordarshan. This included Rs. 145 crores for spillover schemes and Rs. 75 crores for replacement and modernisation of equipment.

## SITE — A Perspective

The Satellite Instructional Television Experiment (SITE) which is heralded as the world's largest project in development communication was hosted by our country during 1975-76. It was the vision and foresight of Dr. Vikram Sarabhai, the pioneer in space science, who conceived the project for taking television to Indian villages, to spread the gospel of development.

### *Satellites in Communication*

With a man-to-man communication link via artificial satellites becoming an operational feasibility in the early sixties,[2] high hopes were held out by the applications of space technology for the betterment of mankind. Continuous efforts were made to put into use communication satellites for receiving, amplifying and transmitting voice, music, television, telephone, telegraphic and data signals, from one point to another point on the globe.

The multi-purpose Applications Technology Satellite (ATS) was the most complex in communications satellites developed by the National Aeronautics and Space Administration (NASA) of the United States, in 1966. It was primarily intended for experiments in the application of satellite communication technology for educational purposes. NASA was interested in testing the capabilities of the sixth and last in the series, ATS-6, in mass instructional broadcasting.[3]

Appreciating the potentialities of the Applications Technology Satellite, in reaching the remote and underdeveloped areas in India, by

Direct Broadcast System (DBS), Dr. Sarabhai approached NASA for loaning ATS-6 for joint experiments in Instructional Television. He had a firm conviction that in the absence of any satisfactory terrestrial communication network the best alternative to reach the remote areas in India is to make use of the modern communication satellites. Dr. Sarabhai was confident that television could be meaningfully developed for instruction and education. He convincingly argued that: "In any developing country one of the prime ingredients of development is the dissemination of information — information about fertilizers, seeds, insecticides, cropping patterns, new goods and services, new living patterns, etc. The process of education is basically related to an information dissemination/transfer process. For the rapid and sustained growth of developing countries the urgent need to disseminate information to masses is obvious. Mass media are clearly the main components in this system of information transfer. . . . Television is ideal as a medium to convey information and news to the masses of people, particularly to the segment of population on whom such an audio-visual medium would have profound impact.(Agrawal: 1978).

The Government of India appointed the National Satellite Communication Group (NASCOM) under the chairmanship of Dr. Sarabhai, with representatives drawn from the Ministry of Information and Broadcasting, Agriculture, Health to consider the proposal of making use of the satellite. This group recommended the conduct of the experiments in instructional television for a year in our country availing of the ATS-6. Thereupon Dr. Sarabhai, on behalf of the Department of Atomic Energy (DAE), Government of India, signed an agreement with NASA, on September 18, 1969, for the India-U.S. ITV Satellite Experiment Project, which became popular later as SITE.

Even though both the countries initiated preliminary studies, following the signing of the memorandum of understanding, due to technical problems and budgetary constraints the launching of the satellite was delayed by about three years and till mid 1973 the pre-project operations could not be taken up.

ATS-6 was finally rocketed into space on May 30, 1974.[4] Up to the middle of 1975, it was used for the relay of Instructional/Educational Television messages in the rocky mountains, Alaska, and the Appalachian areas of the USA, which were not adequately covered by the ground TV system. After the experiments in the United States, the satellite was repositioned 35° East longitude over lake Victoria in

Kenya with its antenna pointing towards Nagpur, providing an operational view of India.[5]

*Execution of SITE*

SITE became finally operational with effect from August 1, 1975 and lasted for one year up to July 31, 1976. Major responsibility for the operational part of the experiment rested with the Space Applications Centre (SAC) of the Indian Space Research Organisation (ISRO). Besides, planning and management of the hardware aspects like earth stations, installation and maintenance of television sets and similar other electronic equipments, SAC was also made responsible for the software social research for the formative and summative evaluation of the Experiment. All India Radio/Doordarshan[6] had taken the software responsibilities of originating video and film programmes for telecast. Part of this requirement was also shared by ISRO. Other participants in the programme were the Central and State organisations connected with developmental activities.

*Objectives of SITE*

The general objectives of the Experiment were:

1. To gain experience in the development, testing and management of a satellite-based Instructional Television System, particularly in rural areas, and determine optimal system parameters;
2. To demonstrate the potential value of satellite technology in the rapid development of effective mass communication in developing countries;
3. To demonstrate the potential value of satellite broadcast TV in the practical instruction of village inhabitants; and
4. To stimulate national development in India with important managerial, economic, technological and social implications.

In specific terms the Indian instructional objectives were outlined as:

I. *Primary*

1. Contribute to family planning objectives,
2. Improve agricultural practices, and

3. Contribute to national integration.

II. *Secondary*

1. Contribute to general school and adult education,
2. Contribute to teacher training,
3. Improve other occupational skills, and
4. Improve health and hygiene.

**Coverage of SITE**

Twenty districts were selected from six States, referred to as clusters — Andhra Pradesh, Bihar, Karnataka, Madhya Pradesh, Orissa and Rajasthan — on the basis of their backwardness, contiguity, common agro-socio-economic conditions and availability of infrastructure (Map 3.2). Initially, 2,400 villages were selected at the rate of 400 from each cluster, adopting the stratified random sampling method. For stratification, factors like power supply, all-weather roads and population were taken into consideration. However, 70 of the selected villages had to be dropped for operational reasons, and 2,330 only could be covered finally.

In each of the SITE villages, one augmented TV set, capable of receiving TV signals direct from the satellite, was installed for community viewing. In addition, 504 more conventional TV sets were installed in 355 villages of Kheda district in Gujarat for studies in controlled situations. Thus, the benefit of the experiment was extended to 2,834 villages in the country. The distribution of TV sets in SITE clusters is indicated in Table 3.1.

**Location of TV Sets**

TV sets were placed in public places, mostly either Primary schools or Panchayat offices. This was purposely done to facilitate community viewing, assuming that visitors would have an easy access to the public institutions and would gather without any social inhibitions or constraints.

**Maintenance of Sets**

Altogether 26 maintenance centres were set up by SAC for the

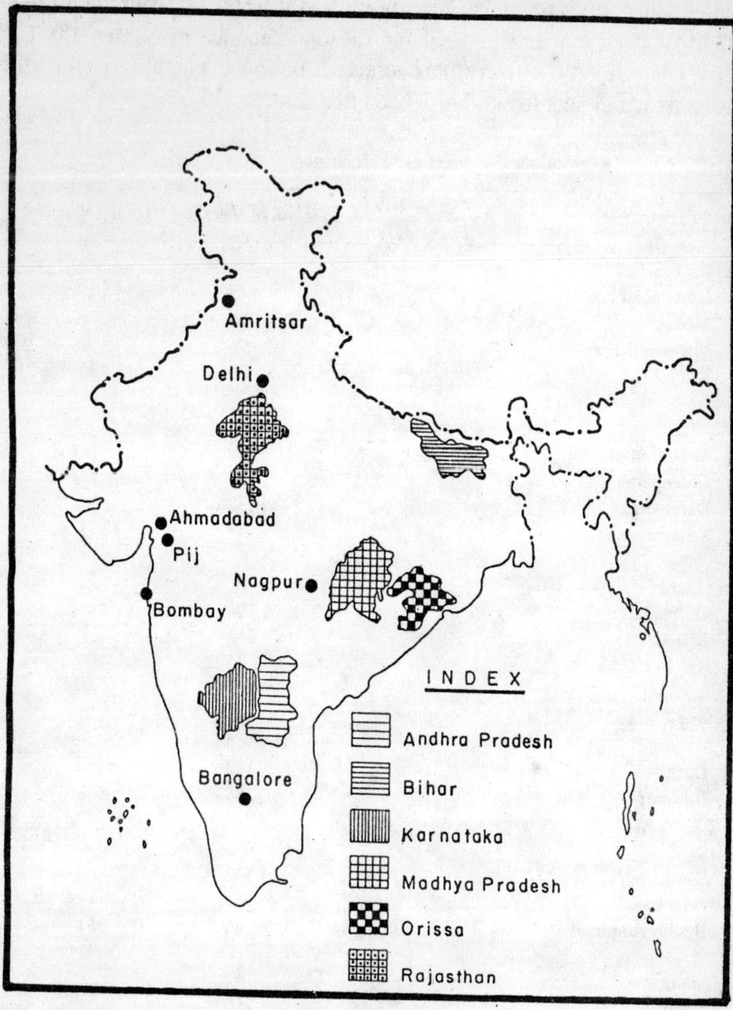


MAP 3.2: SITE Clusters

maintenance and repair of community TV sets. At each centre, a technical person was stationed for the maintenance of about 100 TV sets. The Gujarat Government created its own machinery for the maintenance of sets located in Kheda district.

TABLE 3.1: Distribution of TV sets in SITE clusters

| Cluster/District | No. of Villages | Total TV sets |
|---|---|---|
| *Andhra Pradesh* | | |
| Hyderabad | 148 | |
| Medak | 66 | |
| Mahboobnagar | 96 | |
| Kurnool | 90 | 400 |
| *Bihar* | | |
| Muzaffarpur | 139 | |
| Champaran | 89 | |
| Darbhanga | 132 | |
| Saharsa | 33 | 393 |
| *Karnataka* | | |
| Gulbarga | 109 | |
| Bijapur | 215 | |
| Raichur | 76 | 400 |
| *Madhya Pradesh* | | |
| Raipur | 168 | |
| Durg | 142 | |
| Bilaspur | 88 | 398 |
| *Orissa* | | |
| Sambalpur | 142 | |
| Dhenkanal | 163 | |
| Boudh Kondmal | 46 | 351 |
| *Rajasthan* | | |
| Jaipur | 269 | |
| Sawai Madhopur | 62 | |
| Kota | 57 | 388 |
| *Gujarat* | | |
| Kheda Villages | 355 | 504 sets |
| Grand Total | 2,685 | 2,834 |

**Formative Research**

The Space Application Centre of ISRO created its own Research and Evaluation Cell towards the end of 1973. This Cell was entrusted with the responsibility of the selection of villages and later the preparation of Audience Profiles, Need Assessment Reports and pilot-testing of a few programmes.

The Audience Profile Reports were prepared on the basis of secondary data and some field-based interviews to provide information on socio-economic profiles of the targeted audience, their life-style, economic structure of the cluster, communication patterns, etc. Supplementing this information, background data were collected on the development activities in each cluster and presented as Need Assessment Reports. Thereupon, specific studies to test the villager's response to different television formats, their perception and comprehension of visual images, understanding of the television grammar were taken up both by SAC and the Audience Research Unit of AIR. These pilot tests revealed that in some clusters the rural audiences were not exposed to moving images and were, therefore, not able to comprehend the gimmicks and grammar of TV like flashbacks, dissolves and graphics, models, etc. The results of the formative research exercise were made available to the programme generators before the commencement of SITE.

**Programme Generation**

The programmes for SITE were produced by Doordarshan at three Base Production Units (BPUs) located at Cuttack, Delhi and Hyderabad. However, the science education programmes for children and Gujarati programmes for the Kheda area were originated by the Space Application Centre at its Ahmedabad/Bombay studios. The National Programmes, which were shared by all areas, were produced by the Delhi Base Production Unit.

For the purpose of programme production, the target audiences in different clusters were grouped under four language heads as under:

| *Language* | *Cluster* |
|---|---|
| Hindi | Madhya Pradesh, Bihar and Rajasthan |
| Oriya | Orissa |
| Telugu | Andhra Pradesh |
| Kannada | Karnataka |

While the Educational Television (ETV) programmes for school children were generated in all the four languages, for a duration of 22.5 minutes each, the adult audience Instructional TV programmes were split into two parts as: (a) National Programmes and (b) Cluster Programmes. The National Programmes in Hindi with a duration of 30 minutes were common to all clusters. The time earmarked for each cluster being 20 minutes the three Hindi-speaking clusters – Bihar, Madhya Pradesh and Rajasthan – together had 60 minutes of programmes. Orissa had 20 minutes and Andhra Pradesh and Karnataka combinedly had 40 minutes of programmes. For the Kheda region 60-minute programmes were prepared for telecast over Pij transmitter with 30 minutes of National Programmes and 30 minutes of programmes in Gujarati.

## One Video – Two Audio Transmission

One of the objectives of SITE was to explore the possibility of accompanying a single video with two separate audio channels, in bilingual situations. The selection of contiguous clusters with different languages was made primarily for this purpose. The two-audio transmission was initially envisaged in Orissa-Madhya Pradesh clusters and Andhra Pradesh-Karnataka clusters. But, after the first quarter, this transmission was given up in Orissa-Madhya Pradesh clusters. From November 1, 1975, Madhya Pradesh was combined with other Hindi-speaking clusters and programmes in Oriya were originated and telecast separately. The one video-two audio experiment, however, continued in Andhra Pradesh-Karnataka clusters throughout SITE.

## Telecast Pattern

The programmes were telecast daily for a duration of four hours, divided into two transmissions. The duration of ETV programmes was 90 minutes, with transmission during school hours. The programmes for adult audience (ITV) were telecast for 150 minutes during the evening transmission. The morning and evening telecast schedules are given in Table 3.2.

TABLE 3.2: (a) Telecast Schedule of ETV Programmes

| Cluster | Language | Timings |
|---|---|---|
| | | From August 1, 1975 to July 31, 1976 |
| Karnataka | Kannada | 10.00 to 10.22½ a.m |
| Orissa | Oriya | 10.22½ to 10.45 a.m |
| Andhra Pradesh | Telugu | 10.45 to 11.7½ a.m |
| Bihar, Rajasthan and Madhya Pradesh | Hindi | 11.7½ to 11.30 a.m |

(b) Telecast Schedule of ITV Programmes

| Name of the cluster | Video (Picture) | Audio (Language) | Timings |
|---|---|---|---|
| *August 1, 1975 — October 31, 1975* | | | |
| Andhra Pradesh-Karnataka | One | Telugu/Kannada | 6.20 p.m. — 7.00 p.m. |
| National Programme | One | Hindi | 7.00 p.m. — 7.30 p.m. |
| Orissa-Madhya Pradesh | One | Oriya/Hindi | 7.30 p.m. — 8.10 p.m. |
| Rajasthan-Bihar | One | Hindi | 8.10 p.m. — 8.50 p.m. |
| *November 1, 1975 — March 31, 1976* | | | |
| Rajasthan-Bihar-Madhya Pradesh | One | Hindi | 6.00 p.m. — 7.00 p.m. |
| National Programme | One | Hindi | 7.00 p.m. — 7.30 p.m. |
| Orissa | One | Oriya | 7.30 p.m. — 7.50 p.m. |
| Andhra Pradesh-Karnataka | One | Telugu/Kannada | 7.50 p.m. — 8.30 p.m. |
| *April 1, 1976 — July 31, 1976* | | | |
| Orissa | One | Oriya | 6.40 p.m. — 7.00 p.m. |
| National Programme | One | Hindi | 7.00 p.m. — 7.30 p.m. |
| Bihar-Rajasthan-Madhya Pradesh | One | Hindi | 7.30 p.m. — 8.30 p.m. |
| Andhra Pradesh-Karnataka | One | Telugu/Kannada | 8.30 p.m. — 9.10 p.m. |

## Special Sessions

As part of SITE two special courses were conducted for the training of science teachers and agricultural Extension workers. Both the courses adopted the multi-media strategy, for delivering a package of messages through television, supplemented by radio, print and interpersonal channels.

## Training of Science Teachers

The course was conducted twice during SITE – in October 1975, and in July 1976. It covered all the six clusters, and was designed and executed by the Centre for Educational Technology (CET), an associate of the National Council of Educational Research and Training (NCERT), with ISRO, for the benefit of in-service primary teachers. The main objectives of the course were to familiarize the teachers with the pedagogy associated with science education and to upgrade the teacher's knowledge of modern science, included in the primary school syllabus.

Each time the duration of the course was 15 days. The multi-media package consisted of nine radio programmes of 30-35 minutes and 12 TV lessons of 22.5 minutes each. To facilitate presentation in four languages, the lessons were filmed adopting the voice-over technique. It was estimated that in each course about 24,000 teachers in primary schools were trained under this package programme.

## Training Programme for Extension Workers

During the summer of 1976 when there were no ETV programmes, with a view to making use of the available transmission time, a special course (limited to Andhra Pradesh-Karnataka clusters) was conducted from May 24 to 16 June to prepare the farmers and Extension workers for the agricultural operations during Kharif.

The course was a joint venture of ISRO, Doordarshan, Farm and Home Unit of AIR, and the Information Unit of the Directorate of Extension, New Delhi. As part of the training 12 hard-core programmes (with some entertainment items) were presented on TV from 10.00 to 10.30 in the morning. Four of them were designed for the Extension workers and eight were meant for the ordinary farmers. It was so arranged that each TV programme would be followed by a 30-minute radio programme on the same subject.

## Programme Content

The Adult Programmes were aimed at providing information relating to the following fields:

1. *Improved Agricultural Practices:* Better methods of cultivation, use of improved implements, pesticides, fertilizers and other inputs.
2. *Family Planning:* Methods and practices as well as creation of awareness for adoption of small family norm.
3. *Health, Hygiene and Nutrition:* Preventive as well as curative measures for diseases, care to be taken for infants, children, pregnant and nursing women and supplementing their diet with nutritious food.
4. *National Integration:* Popularizing the idea of unity in diversity of India and acquainting the people with the life and culture of other regions.

The total spread of SITE evening transmission was estimated to have lasted for about 900 hours. The content of the programmes (average for all centres) distributed under major subjects is indicated in Table 3.3.

TABLE 3.3: Content of SITE Instructional Programmes

| Broad area | Percentage to total |
|---|---|
| 1. Agriculture | 10.7 |
| 2. Animal husbandry | 2.8 |
| 3. Family planning | 4.2 |
| 4. Health, hygiene & nutrition | 11.3 |
| 5. National Integration | 2.4 |
| 6. Informative and instructional other than SITE objectives | 22.2 |
| 7. Entertainment | 46.4 |
| Total | 100.0 |

Source: Agrawal et al : 1977: *Social Impact of SITE on Adults*, Part II, p. 368.

**Evaluation of SITE**

SAC sponsored a number of social studies for the feedback on programmes and overall assessment of SITE. The major studies are: (1) Survey of the social impact of SITE on Adults; (2) Holistic study of seven selected villages; and (3) Utilization of SITE. The results of these three studies have been released. As in-house evaluation reports they are, however, subject to the criticism of subjectivity and lack of critical analysis. Notwithstanding this limitation, a brief review of the important conclusions of SAC studies is made in the following paragraphs. Simultaneously, the available literature on SITE evaluation studies conducted by external agencies is also reviewed for drawing some lessons from SITE.

Even though numerous organizations were engaged in short-term observation and feed-back studies on SITE Instructional programmes, only a few agencies sponsored comprehensive assessment studies. Prominent among them are:

1. Planning Commission, Government of India, New Delhi.
2. Communication Department, University of Bangalore, Bangalore.
3. Doordarshan, for the Communications Policies Division, UNESCO, Paris.
4. National Institute of Rural Development, Hyderabad.
5. Evaluation Cell of the Indian Institute of Mass Communication, New Delhi.
6. Council for Social Development, New Delhi.
7. A.N. Sinha Institute of Social Studies, Patna.

Unfortunately, some of these organizations have not made their findings public. But there is adequate material to draw broad conclusions.

Summarizing the results of SITE, Prof. Yashpal, Director of SAC, observed: "As a system test of satellite broadcast technology, the experiment was a singular success. The NASA satellite, ATS-6, worked without fault. All the ground equipment designed and built by the Indian Space Research Organization performed exceedingly well. The reliability of earth stations was higher than 99.8 per cent. The community sets received a picture quality better than the normal VHF receivers in cities. The reliability of the receiving equipment coupled with the efficiency of the maintenance system was sufficient to keep 90 per cent of the sets working at any time. The research and development capacity generated during the setting up of the equipment was an invaluable spin-off." (Agrawal *et al*: 1977). But, Prof. Eapen of Bangalore University basing on his studies in the Karnataka cluster concluded: "SITE hardware proved a great success. This cannot be said of the programmes, and what they are supposed to achieve." He was particularly critical of the change in the objectives of SITE and the drawing of the evaluation criteria to suit the revised objectives. "SITE goals as detailed in the 1969 Indo-U.S. agreement were intended to bring about change in various developmental fronts such as agricultural modernization, family planning and national integration. . . . The goals were later interpreted as creation of the climate for change rather than change itself" (Eapen: 1979). There are, thus, divergent views on what was expected of SITE.

The Study on the Social Impact of SITE on Adults by Agrawal *et al* (1977) was an extensive survey conducted in 12 experimental and six control villages in each of the six clusters, with a total coverage of 7,776 respondents – 72 from each of the 108 SITE villages. Some of the main findings of this study are:

1. Males in the age-group of 15-24 years, middle-aged women and persons belonging to lower socio-economic levels formed the prime constituents of "core-viewers" who watched the programmes at least four times a month.
2. Majority of the viewers had very little exposure to mass media before SITE. One-third of the viewers were first generation media participants.
3. TV attracted more people in smaller villages than in big or medium-size villages.
4. Statistically significant and unexpectedly large gain was noticed in information and knowledge in areas such as health and hygiene, political consciousness, overall modernity and family planning. In the field of agriculture and allied areas, as well as nutrition, there was no significant gain.

When TV was placed in the villages, it was hoped that most of the inhabitants would avail of the facility and get the exposure to the medium. But, fairly a substantial proportion kept away from TV. This study does not say about the extent of non-viewing in the villages, and their distribution according to various socio-economic variables. It also fails to explain the reasons for "rare" viewing (those who watched TV less than once a month), among 51.6 per cent of women and 18.5 per cent of men. The study was equally silent on the physical and human constraints in the context of the existing realities in the villages, the loose ends in the distribution system like the irregularity of the custodian, inflated audience figures, and the contribution of these elements towards the loss in communication.

The study conducted by Bangalore University in the Karnataka cluster revealed that the TV custodian plays a very crucial role in its utilization (Ahmed: 1977). Similarly the study sponsored by Doordarshan in the Andhra Pradesh-Karnataka clusters indicated that the custodians specifically the non-resident custodians were irregular and indifferent. Their commitment was found to be one of the major determinants of audience build-up and exposure to the medium (Rao and Ramachandra: 1976).

SITE was described by some researchers as the "poor man's medium" and satisfaction was expressed with the reports that the rich and the landlords kept away from the riff-raff in the community viewing situation (Bhatia: 1979). But, the results of the SITE social impact study on adults indicate that even though in absolute terms more people from lower socio-economic levels watched TV, both by status as measured by the educational level or type of house, it was positively associated with the TV viewing behaviour. Thus, the higher the status the higher was the viewing behaviour. SITE holistic studies also indicated that the core viewers were either the educated unemployed youth who had no work, or the middle-aged women from high caste well-to-do families with free time, or adult males from non-agricultural families like labourers, traders, etc.

The holistic studies in seven villages by anthropologists sponsored by SAC (Agrawal: 1978) revealed some very interesting social phenomena relating to television use and its impact:

1. The comparison of the language spoken in village and TV programme language suggests loss of message comprehension, especially in the Hindi-speaking areas. SITE Hindi programmes were common for audiences in three States, viz. Rajasthan, Bihar and Madhya Pradesh. This suggests that in the absence of a local touch, satellite-based communication to larger areas would be less effective.
2. The village cultural and development communication system suggests "class difference" in the communication pattern. Any effective communication should be tailored to suit these class differences. Future rural TV should, therefore, treat the landless small farmers as a distinct class.
3. Attendance at television watching is closely related to the agricultural and religious activity. So, important programmes should be avoided during peak agricultural seasons.

4. Audience in the southern clusters followed the traditional castewise groupings in the sitting pattern while watching the TV. But they were not rigid in the HIndi-speaking clusters.
5. Innovations requiring little or no external help and additional expenditure stand a good chance of adoption. If the innovation requires only alteration in the existing practice, it has a better chance of adoption. Small cultivators who adopted innovations on watching TV do not disclose the results if not rewarding due to fear of redicule.
6. Those who reside more than half a kilometre away from the place where TV is located find it difficult to watch the programmes.
7. The special telecasts with multi-media approach received poor response from farmers due to organizational problems as well as inadequate planning.

The in-depth study conducted by Bangalore University on the Farmers Training Course indicated major shortcomings in execution. Repetition of programmes, irrelevance to the local audience, and unsuitable telecast timings were cited as the main reasons for the non-participation of the farmers. It was pointed out that the multi-media strategy did not work in a number of villagers (Umadevi: 1977).

Studies conducted by other agencies, however, corroborated the findings of SAC that by and large the audience appreciated and understood the hard-core, message-oriented programmes and general informative programmes, better than the entertainment items. But, instructional programmes constituted only 30 per cent of the total transmission, while the entertainment programmes constituted the main bulk. Simultaneously, these studies indicate that the overall comprehension of evening programmes was low in relation to the amount of information disseminated, thus suggesting "communication over-kill" (Shanmugam: 1977).

The Utilization Cell of SITE conducted a study to evaluate the impact of utilization activity and follow-up in six selected Blocks, each covering five villages. A Research Assistant was posted at the Block level to organize the follow-up discussions, meetings, field demonstrations, etc., on five programmes each month, in the five villages under his observation. The findings of the study were as under (Bhatia and Chauhan: 1978):

1. If utilization activities in the form of group discussions, demonstrations, etc., accompany the community viewing television programmes, it significantly enhances the knowledge of the participants.
2. Though all strata of the farming community learnt more due to the utilization activity, "small" farmers appear to have gained more than the other sections, thus suggesting that utilization helps the small farmer.
3. The role of VLW at the trial stage is very important and about 20 per cent of the farmers discussed with him before trying.

**Cost-effectiveness of SITE**

Notwithstanding the encouraging results from the otherwise unexposed sleepy villages to the television medium, and the promising future of satellite-based communication in the country, SITE has proved to be a costly exercise. Considerable amounts of resources were directed for the experiment with the hope of generating maximum social benefit. It was estimated that in terms of the total hours of programming, one minute of transmission had cost the exchequer about Rs.3,000 (Shanmugam: 1977). According to SAC, the following was the break-up of the expenditure incurred by the participating agencies on the ground system.

TABLE 3.4: Expenditure on SITE

| Agency | Rupees in crores |
|---|---|
| Indian Space Research Organisation (ISRO) | 10.0 |
| Ministry of I&B, Govt. of India | 3.5 |
| United Nations Development Programme (UNDP) | 1.5 |
| National Council of Educational Research and Training (NCERT) | 0.5 |
| State Governments | 0.5 |
| Total | 16.0 |

Of this expenditure incurred by ISRO, it was estimated that about 80 per cent was spent on the hardware elements, 15 per cent on social evaluation and 5 per cent on overall systems management and support (Sampath: 1977).

SITE evaluation reports list out the benefits accrued to the rural population, specifically the poor and underprivileged, who would not have otherwise got this advantage in the near future. But, one basic issue raised by the Planning Commission was whether SITE was cost-effective. Even though the gains in human value and social benefits cannot be measured in absolute monetary terms, the following issues warrant attention while assessing the potential of television for rural development:

1. Can television meet the basic communication needs of the villagers in terms of help in achieving more food production, health care and other necessities which are primary to their existence?
2. Have the existing resources been fully exploited and utilized to warrant large-scale expansion of a new medium?

In the foregoing chapters an attempt has been to search for some satisfactory answers to these questions on the basis of field inquiries in five villages in Pune district of Maharashtra.

**Working Group on Television Software Planning**

The Ministry of Information and Broadcasting appointed a Working Group on Doordarshan's soft-ware planning in December 1982. This Group headed by Prof. P. Joshi of the Institute of Economic Growth, Delhi, submitted its Report in April 1984. The Panel raised some fundamental issues of priority with regard to the basic policies and approach of television and was highly critical of the Government for the glamourisation of the medium. The Working Group stressed the need for shift in Doordarshan's programming culture from commercial-oriented entertainment fare to creative areas of education and development. It felt that at least one-half of the telecast time should be devoted to developmental and educational programmes.

The Panel also suggested giving the pride of place to community viewing to promote viewership in rural areas. The basic thrust of the soft-ware Working Group was directed towards evolving a new personality for Indian television to that the medium could fulfil the primary task as a live instrument of communication and socio-economic change. In fulfilment of this task, the Panel laid stress on the need for demystifying and deglamourising the programme content of Doordarshan.

Analysing the pattern of expansion of television and the availability of receiver sets, Prof. U.K. Srivastava of the Indian Institute of Management, Ahmedabad, observed that hardly two per cent of the population would have accessibility to the medium despite the ambitious expansion of the network. To increase the reach of the medium to the targeted population in rural areas, he felt that there was no other way but to organise Community TV on a large scale at public cost (Srivastava : 1974).

Delivering the Sardar Patel Memorial Lectures organised by All India Radio in October 1985 Prof. P.C. Joshi made a scathing criticism of television for its bias in catering to the rich and elite and neglecting its role in promoting development and education in the country. He remarked: "Having sought legitimacy for its introduction and subsequent vast expansion in the name of development education, Television had departed from its objectives and had become a factor in distorting social consciousness by catering to the psychology of the neo-rich and elite stroking the fires of consumerism through commercially-sponsored programme." Prof. Joshi made a fervent appeal to make the best use of television for correcting imbalances. He felt that the modern technology was exploited to create an island of affluence in a country of poor people. "While television created titillating entertainment to a few, it eroded national, cultural identity and destroyed social outlook and consciousness."

Studies on the performance of Doordarshan, with focus on its contribution after the large-scale expansion of the network with the LPT boom during the eighties, are few and far between.

The monograph on *Television in Kheda*, based on an anthropological study of a village covered under the 1 kW Pij transmitter in Kheda district of Gujarat, by B.C. Agrawal and M.R. Malek (1986) has not documented any far-reaching changes in terms of development achievements. It is rather distressing to note that instead of reducing the conflicts and tensions based on traditional rivalries of caste and class differentiations, television has accentuated the deep-rooted antagonism among various groups of the people.

Exposure to the medium has led to higher expectations from the existing facilities in the areas of health, education and other developmental activities. But the programming input and extension support on the television has not been beneficial to the small and marginal farmers. The agricultural labourers, similarly, disliked, with a sense of threat, the recommendations in respect of labour-saving devices for improving the productivity in the large farms.

Frequent power failures, unsuitable telecast timings and family restrictions have emerged as the major contributing factors for non-viewing and low exposure to the medium. The study once again confirmed the crucial role of the TV custodian in the flow of developmental information from the television set to the potential audience.

The study on *Media, Communication and Development* by S.C. Sharma (1987) in four villages drawn from Jaipur and Tonk districts of Rajasthan attempted a comparative analysis of different communication channels and their contribution to the process of development. The exposure and utilisation of the mass media sources was found to be closely associated with the pattern of living of the higher socio-economic sections, and the people belonging to the lower socio-economic sections depended mostly upon traditional media. Thus, the deprived sections remained unreached by the television medium. Similar was the observation of R.K. Paliwal (1987). His work on the *Impediments to Rural Communication* in Ghaziabad district of Uttar Pradesh, highlighted that communication consciousness has not affected the possible articulative behaviour of the rural masses. Substantive gains from the mass media accrued to the dominant castes and classes. The benefits of television communication to the poor and middle class household remained marginal. Radio, on the other hand, commanded a significantly wider reach with higher set ownership among the middle class villagers.

The study on *Impact of Television on Viewers* by Andal Narayan (1987) was restricted to the Bombay city audience. It was designed to assess the influence of Bombay Doordarshan programmes on the social life of the urban audience, mainly women and children. The main findings of the study relate to a higher patronage for entertainment programmes, reduction of social activities and increase in the habit of silent observation. But, these findings are irrelevant to the subject of Television for Rural Development under review. Hence, not discussed further.

## NOTES

1. *Indian Express*, Bombay, dated June 24, 1977.
2. Man's first communication satellite was the moon. In the early 1950s, the United State's army used it for radio contact between Washington and Honolulu (Hawaii). The first artificial passive satellite (Echo x) which relayed radio and TV signals was launched by the United States in August 1960.

3. According to Mr. Bernes, Director, International Affairs, NASA, by this time in the USA, there existed a highly developed terrestrial broad-based communication network and, therefore, there was very little interest on the part of large communication users in such capacity (Agrawal *et al.*, 1977).
4. ATS-6 weighing about 1,500 kg was located at a height of 35,680 km, as table space craft platform, at a synchronous altitude. The satellite carried two high-powered TV transponders.
5. The footprint produced by parabolic reflector covered a major part of India, enabling the Experiment to be carried out in remote Indian villages far away from each other.
6. Both radio and television were under All India Ratio till March 31, 1976. Subsequently, television was bifurcated and Doordarshan was created as a separate Directorate, under the Ministry of I & B.

# 4

# METHODOLOGY AND STUDY DESIGN

THE PRECEDING three chapters were in the nature of backgrounders for adequate understanding of the expectations from television, as a means of communication for rural development. The following four chapters were devoted to the presentation and analysis of the data relating to the people, their informational needs, the status and role performance of television in meeting these needs and the strengths and weaknesses of the medium in fulfilling the expectations in respect of rural development. This Chapter explains the methodology adopted for the collection and interpretation of the data.

In the past, most of the studies on television were in the nature of quantitative sample surveys for the evaluation of the effects of exposure. The basic objective of these studies was measurement of the impact of specific programmes (like social education, agriculture, health, etc.) on the audience, in terms of changes – positive or negative – in knowledge, attitudes and practices. As such, they were designed to measure the levels of knowledge and attitudes, initially before the exposure of the people to the programmes, and later after the exposure (or "treatment"). Such surveys, based on what are popularly known as "experimental designs", speak generally in terms of computed figures and lack sufficient qualitative supporting information to explain television communication as a human problem and as a social process.

This study was not designed for impact measurement. It was planned as a feed-forward study to understand the position of television as a social institution *vis-a-vis* the rural people and their human problems. Its objective was to understand the potentialities of television, in the context of ground realities, instead of estimating precisely how much it was able to contribute in specific areas.

In drawing up the methodology for the study was guided by the traditional anthropological dictum that a "social scientist must avoid indiscriminating and uncritical fact finding on the one hand and the pursuit of abstractions remote from reality on the other" (Piddington: 1957).

**Working Hypotheses**

Being a status study, aimed at understanding the existing realities, there were not *a priori* conceptualizations. However, in broad terms the working hypotheses were drawn, in accordance with the scope and objectives of the study outlined in Chapter One. The research hypotheses were considered essential for giving a direction to the fieldwork. As Malinowski has pointed out "the more problems he (the researcher) brings with him into the field, the more he is in the habit of moulding his theories according to facts, and of seeing facts in their bearing upon theory, the better he is equipped for the work. Preconceived ideas are pernicious in any scientific work, but foreshadowed problems are the main endowment of a scientific thinker, and these problems are first revealed to the observer by his theoretical studies" (Malinowski: 1922).

The following were the working hypotheses drawn for the study:

1. Most of the communication needs of the masses in villages can be effectively met by extension of TV coverage to rural areas.
2. The availability of television in villages would facilitate leap-frogging, cutting across the conventional media.
3. Illiteracy is no barrier for TV communication.
4. Community TV in the villages in a boon to the underprivileged sections, who suffer the most from lack of communication.
5. Community TV is an equalizer of opportunities, and it narrows the gap between "media haves" and "media have-nots".
6. Television helps in political socialization of the illiterate audiences.
7. Television sustains popular support in villages for its instructional value, rather than for the entertainment programmes.
8. In view of its social benefit, the villagers as well as the village institutions would take interest in the affairs of TV and make best use of the medium for developmental purposes.

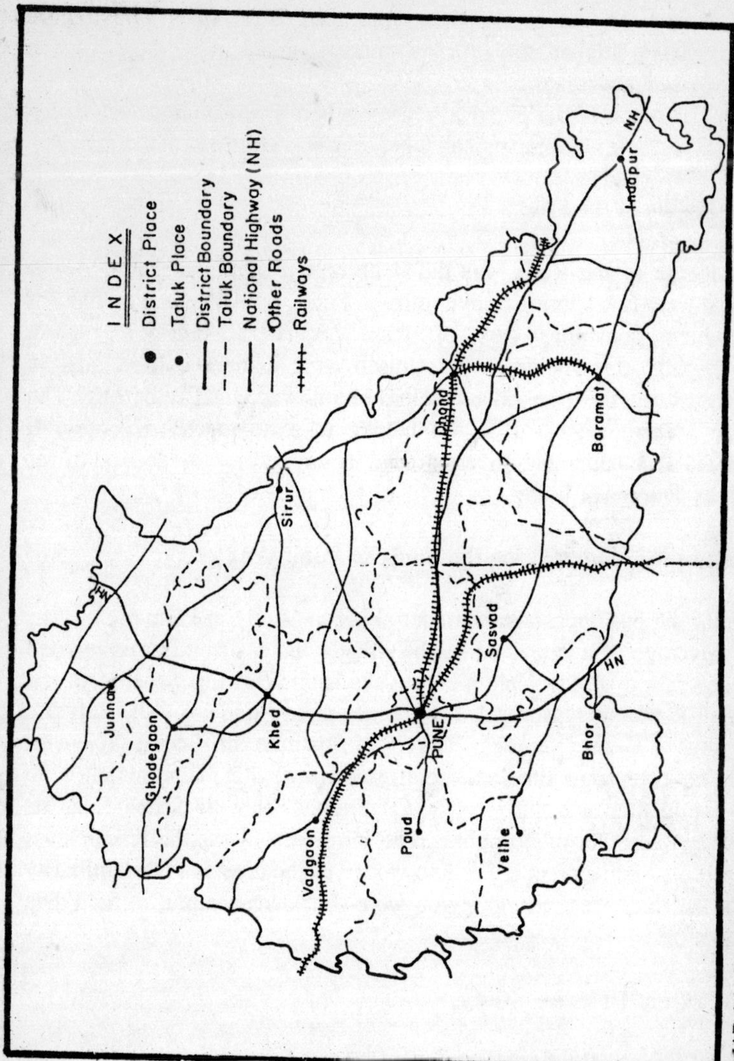


MAP 4.1: Pune District : Communication

9. Being an audio-visual medium, television does not require another "human animator" to stimulate the change process, it will be self-generated.
10. The reach of the personal channels being very limited, television is the best alternative channel of communication in the villages.

### The Locale of the Study

The locale of the study was the Pune region of Maharashtra. It was spread over two administrative units — Pune and Ahmednagar districts – which constitute part of the Western Maharashtra region. Historically this region is recognised as a distinct culture area in Maharashtra, the two others being Marathwada and Vidarbha. The study area, however, does not belong to a homogeneous entity. It manifests considerable diversity and heterogeneity in geography as well as patterns of living.

### Reasons for Undertaking the Study in Pune Area

One of the basic reasons for undertaking the study in Pune region was the coverage of a large number of villages under TV transmission and the operation of the Community Television Viewing Scheme in the area. The second reason was the absence of any studies on the response to rural TV programmes. The Tata Institute of Social Sciences, Bombay, was some time back, entrusted by the State Government with the conducting of a study on the Community Viewing Scheme, but its findings were not made public. The third reason was the researcher's operational convenience. His knowledge of the area and the familiarity with the rural scene in the region were considered helpful in field data collection.

### Selection of Units for Study

Pune TV transmitter covers whole of Pune district (except some parts in Indapur and Junner talukas) and some portions of Satara and Ahmednagar districts. Therefore, it was decided to select one taluka from Pune district and another from the adjoining Ahmednagar district. In view of the large number of TV villages in Pune district it was decided to select four villages from Pune district and one village from Ahmednagar district.

Within Pune district, the choice fell on Ambegaon taluka for the following reasons:

1. It is wholly rural in composition with no urban area.
2. It is located about 80-90 km. away from Pune, thus not very much subjected to city influence.
3. It is one of the most backward areas with poor communication facilities and no assured irrigation.
4. It has 25 per cent of the tribal population in the district.
5. Nearly one-third of the villages are provided with community TV sets, and some of them have been specially installed under the tribal sub-plan in tribal villages.

In Ahmednagar district, Parner taluka is the best covered by TV transmission and it has the highest number of community TV sets. It also lies adjacent to Pune district and shares the same culture. In view of these considerations it was decided to select one village from Parner taluka.

**Selection of Villages**

The next step involved selection of villages. Keeping in view the study requirements and the operational constraints, it was decided to select purposively the five villages adopting the following criteria:

*I. From Ambegaon Taluka*

1. One non-tribal village with satisfactory communication facilities and fairly good exposure to developmental activity.
2. One semi-tribal village which is little isolated and under-developed but having the potential for development.
3. One predominantly tribal village exposed to developmental activity.
4. One backward tribal village not exposed to developmental activity.

*II. From Parner Taluka*

5. One small but well-exposed village, which has good scope for assimilation of developmental messages. This is to facilitate comparison with villages located in Ambegaon taluka, which is essentially a tribal block.

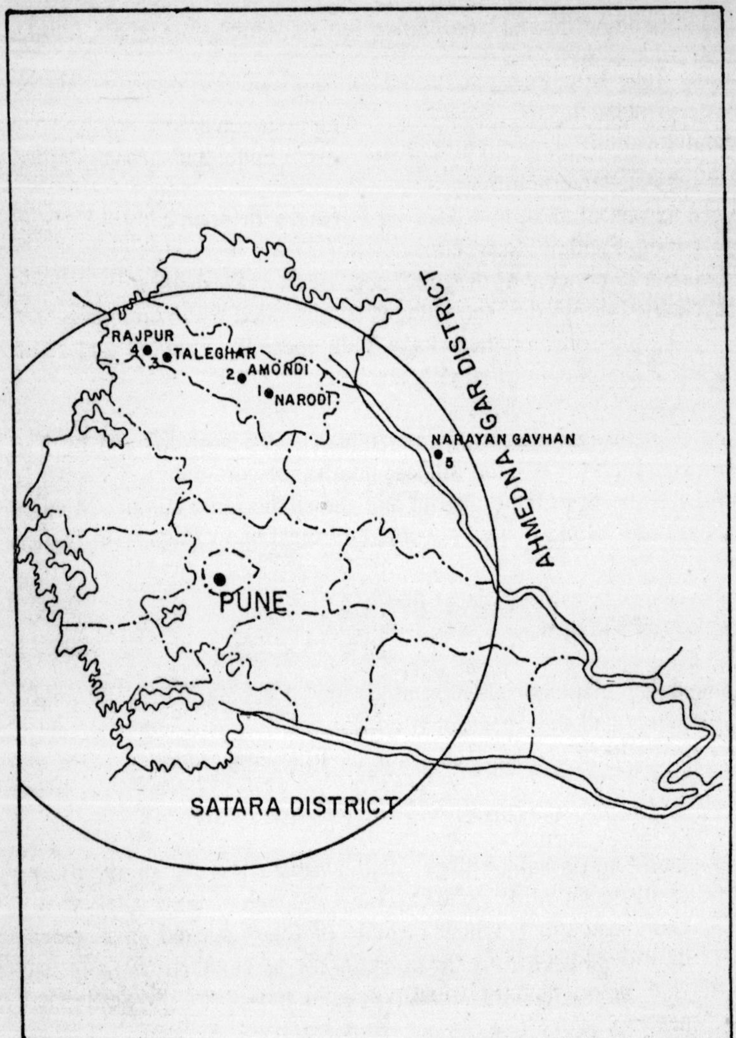


MAP 4.2: Location of Selected Villages

**Preliminary Visits**

During June-July 1978, about 20 villages with community TV sets were visited in the selected talukas. Basic data on Census, communication facilities, developmental schemes and village institutions was collected from the functionaries. Later, informal discussions were also held with extension workers, panchayat officials and school teachers to find out the socio-economic condition of the villages. On the basis of these exercises the following five villages were selected purposively for the study:

*I. Ambegaon Taluka*

1. Narodi : Progressive non-tribal village with substantial developmental activity.
2. Amondi : Semi-tribal village, with poor communication facilities, not very much exposed to developmental activity.
3. Taleghar : Tribal village, exposed to developmental activity.
4. Rajapur : Tribal village not exposed to developmental activity.

*II. Parner Taluka*

5. Narayan Gavhan : Village with substantial exposure to outside world, with potential for development.

**Interviews with Respondents**

Keeping in view the operational constraints and the objectives of the study, it was decided to have a sample of 250 adults for individual interviews, drawn in proportion to the population size of the village. The sample distribution in the selected villages was as under:

| Village | Population | Sample size |
|---|---|---|
| Narayan Gavhan | 1,536 | 50 |
| Narodi | 2,838 | 100 |
| Amondi | 1,633 | 55 |
| Taleghar | 504 | 20 |
| Rajapur | 587 | 25 |

For the selection of the respondents a simple but systematic method was adopted. As the proportion of the sample was approximately in the ratio of 1: 30 population, taking the average size of a village household as six members, it was decided to contact every sixth house. After identifying such houses, a request was made for individual interviews with any person above the age of 14 years.

To provide equal representation for females, in every alternate selected household a female member was interviewed. However, when it was not possible for any reason the interview was conducted with any male member available in the house at the time of the visit. The problem of interviewing females was faced only in middle class and upper middle class Maratha households where the women customarily do not come out and talk to outsiders. In field conditions, the author had to adopt a flexible approach and in the final sample, the proportion of females was limited to 35 per cent instead of 50 per cent.

## Case Studies

A number of case studies were made for analysing the specific communication needs and information-seeking behaviour of the individuals. They were based on in-depth interviews and keen observation of the individual's interaction with personal and mediated channels. The case study method was found to be very useful for understanding the people's perception and image of different channels in meeting their informational needs. Similarly, it was also found to be very useful, in giving a broad perspective of the life pattern of the people, in concrete terms.

## Observation

The observation technique was particularly resorted to for observing facial expressions and behaviour of the audience while watching the television programmes. Similarly a number of persons, both men and women, were observed closely while they were talking among themselves. Considerable time was spent sitting in the Gram Panchayat Office, tea shops and grocer's shop to match people as to how they exchange information on various matters. The process of interaction with personal and mass media channels was based more on observation than on questioning. The data collected through observations was also used to check the information gathered during individual interviews.

**Feedback on Selected Programmes**

The facilities for play-back of the video programmes available with the Film and TV Institute of India, were utilised for obtaining feedback on selected rural-oriented programmes. In-depth interviews were conducted with the viewers, soon after the play-back, to ascertain their reactions on the content and presentation aspects and their perception and comprehension levels.

The qualitative analysis of the feedback was found essential as hardly anybody could recollect specific programmes and give an assessment of the programmes in terms of their relevancy and utility. By arranging the play-back of selected programmes in various formats, the researcher was able to gather information on the type of programmes that generates interest among the rural audience and on those that do not sustain their interest.

**Operational Definitions**

The following are the operational definitions adopted for the study:

*Village*: Refers to the entire revenue village, including the hamlets *(Wadas)*. It was not restricted to the settlement where TV was located, for the reason that the coverage (or potential benefit) is generally estimated for the village as a whole.

*Household*: This refers to the family members living and eating together. Thus, it includes both nucleus and extended type of families, and denotes *Ghar* in the local terminology.

*Harijans*: Persons belonging to Mang, Maher and their equivalent *Jatis* (Castes), who are locally considered as "untouchables" were classified under this category.

*Adivasis*: Persons belonging to the aboriginal communities and listed under the Scheduled Tribes were included under this category.

*Economic level*: Based on the author's own observation, a rough estimate of the income of the household as a whole from various sources was made for economic classification of the respondents under three categories:

*Poor*: Those having income less than Rs. 300 per month.
*Average*: Those having income between Rs. 300 and Rs. 600 per month.

*Upper middle class*: Those having income more than Rs. 600 per month.

## Participation in Media

The operational definitions for indicating the frequency of exposure to different media use were evolved according to the local understanding were as follows:

(a) *Newspapers*:

| | |
|---|---|
| Daily | : Reading of any daily newspaper at least once in two days. |
| Sometimes | : Reading of any paper at least twice a week. |
| Rarely | : Reading of any paper once a week or so. |

(b) *Radio listening*:

| | |
|---|---|
| Frequently | : Listening to radio anywhere at least twice a week. |
| Occasionally | : Listening to radio at least once a week. |
| Rarely | : Listening to radio not even once a week. |

(c) *Exposure to Film/Urban Area/Block headquarters/VLW*:

| | |
|---|---|
| Frequently | : At least once a month. |
| Occasionally | : Once in three months or so. |
| Rarely | : Once or twice a year. |

(d) *Exposure to Television*

| | |
|---|---|
| Frequently | : At least once a week or four times a month. |
| Occasionally | : Two-three times a month. |
| Rarely | : Once a month or so. |

## Sample Composition

The quantitative data presented in the following chapters is based on responses collected from 250 individuals. The composition of the sample in terms of different socio-economic variables is presented in Table 4.1. It may be noted that there is no imbalance in the structure of the sample except in the case of the proportion of the females. As explained earlier, due to practical constraints, the male-female ratio could not be maintained at 50: 50 level. However, since there were as many as 88 females constituting 35.2 per cent of the sample, the results of the analysis are fairly representative.

TABLE 4.1: Composition of the sample

| Category | Number | Percentage |
|---|---|---|
| *Sex:* | | |
| Male | 162 | 64.8 |
| Female | 88 | 35.2 |
| *Age:* | | |
| 15-30 years | 83 | 33.2 |
| 31-45 years | 88 | 35.2 |
| 46-60 years | 57 | 22.8 |
| Above 60 years | 22 | 8.8 |
| *Education:* | | |
| Illiterate | 103 | 41.2 |
| 1-7th std. | 109 | 43.6 |
| 8-10th | 31 | 12.4 |
| College | 7 | 2.8 |
| *Occupation:* | | |
| Agriculture | 154 | 61.6 |
| Labour | 42 | 16.8 |
| Trade & Traditional services | 26 | 10.4 |
| White-collar workers and others | 28 | 11.2 |
| *Social Status:* | | |
| Non-Harijans | 161 | 64.4 |
| Harijans | 25 | 10.0 |
| Adivasis | 64 | 25.6 |
| *Economic Status:* | | |
| Poor | 89 | 35.6 |
| Average | 125 | 50.0 |
| Upper Middle | 36 | 14.4 |
| All categories | 250 | 100.0 |

It may be noted here that in the occupationwise analysis, with a view to minimising the categories, traders, artisans and those depending on traditional services (like washermen, barbers, oilmen) have been clubbed together. By and large, all these groups have been observed to have better resources for media participation than others. Similarly, under the white-collar workers, all the village functionaries, teachers and army personnel have been grouped together to form a single category. Instead of having a separate category for students and dependants, they have been combined with white-collar workers because all of them enjoy conservatively more leisure time than other categories.

In the communitywise analysis, all those enjoying a higher social status have been grouped together as non-Harijans. This also includes a negligible percentage of muslims, who do not suffer from any social disabilities like the Harijans.

# 5

# THE AUDIENCE – A PROFILE

MAHARASHTRA STATE forms a major part of the peninsular India with the Vindhyas as the dividing line between the northern and southern States. Roughly it represents one-tenth of the country, with 0.3 miilion square kilometres of area and 50 million population.

Geographically it has two main natural divisions: the *Konkan* in the west and the *Desh* (plateau) in the east. Konkan is the narrow stretch of land adjoining the Arabian sea coast. The Sahyadri mountains run parallel to the coast, extending southwards. To the east of this chain of mountains lies the tableland, popular as *Desh*. While the Mahadeo and Ajanta ranges stretch eastwards of Sahyadris, the Satpura hills form a chain in the north. The important river basins lying in between are: Krishna in the South, Bhima covering the central parts and Godavari towards the west of the Sahyadris.

## Culture Area

The State is divided into 26 districts for administrative purposes. But, the cultural history divides it into three distinct regions as under:

| Region | Districts covered |
|---|---|
| 1. Western Maharashtra | : Greater Bombay, Thane, Kulaba, Ratnagiri, Nashik, Dhule, Jalgaon, Ahmednagar, Pune, Satara, Sangli, Solapur and Kolhapur. |
| 2. Vidarbha | : Buldhana, Akola, Amaravati, Yavatmal, Wardha, Nagpur, Bhandara, and Chandrapur. |
| 3. Marathwada | : Aurangabad, Parbhani, Bhir, Nanded and Osmanabad. |

For administrative convenience the State is divided into four divisions. The Western Maharashtra region is split into two divisions – Pune and Bombay: Vidarbha constitutes Nagpur division; and Marathwada forms the Aurangabad division. Pune division comprises five districts namely Pune, Ahmednagar, Satara, Sangli, Solapur and Kolhapur.

## Physical Variations

The coastal districts of Thane, Kulaba and Ratnagiri and the Western Ghats receive very heavy rainfall touching in some places 300 cm per year. Tropical wet green forests are found along the ghats. While the eastern side of Maharashtra is mostly covered by the thorny shrub forests, the thick forests of Chandrapur are a wealth of treasure, with plantations of commercial and medicinal value. the best known hey lands lie north of Bombay, in the area between the sea coast and the Western Ghats where the average rainfall is 20 cm. The major part of the State, however, lies in the rain shadow of the ghats, with rainfall averaging 60-75 cm and in some areas even less than 50 cm. These include the districts of Nashik, Pune, Ahmednagar, Dhule, Jalgaon, Satara, Sangli, Solapur, and parts of Kolhapur. While in Marathwada the rainfall varies from 75-100 cm, in Vidarbha region it varies between 100-150 cm.

## Demographic Variations

The density of population per square kilometre ranges from 9,900 in metropolitan Greater Bombay to 64 in the hilly Chandrapur district, with an average of 164 for the State as a whole. The urban segment constitutes 31 per cent of the total population, as against the national average of 20 per cent. One of the recent developments is the fast growth of small and medium-scale industries, particularly in the southern region, which has become popular as the "beehive" of Maharashtra. The working force, therefore, consists of relatively more persons engaged in industry. Those dependent on agriculture constitute about 65 per cent and this includes about 30 per cent of those who subsist on labour. Because of the urbanisation, education has spread and the proportion of literates is higher with 39 per cent, as against 29 per cent for the country as a whole. The influence of the educated urban middle class on the socio-cultural life of society is considered to be remarkable throughout the history of Maharashtra (Maharashtra: 1977).

The cultivators who constitute nearly 36 per cent of the working force belong to mostly what are considered as the "high castes" (like Marathas, Malis, etc.). The "low caste" Harijans (like Mhang, Mahar Chambhar, etc.) together with the Adivasis (Scheduled Tribes) constitute about one-eighth of the total population. The tribals preponderate the Sahyadri and Satpura ranges. Among the main communities are: Warlis, Katkaris and Thakkars of Thana and Kulaba districts; Bhils of Dhule; Korkus, Gonds and Madias of Vidarbha region. With 2.95 million they account for nearly 6 per cent of the total State population.

**Agriculture Base**

Approximately two-thirds of the people are engaged in agriculture and allied occupations. But, the income from these sources hardly constitutes one-third of the Net Domestic Product of the State. The average cultivated area per worker approximates 3.75 acres and there is heavy dependence on monsoon. Of the total cropped area less than one-tenth is estimated to get assured irrigation. As much as one-third of the cropped area is exposed to frequent droughts.

*Jowar* is the principal food crop grown extensively in Vidarbha, Marathwada and parts of Western Maharashtra. Bajri is the second important food crop cultivated on the dry lands of Western Maharashtra where the rainfall is scanty. While rice is the important crop in Konkan, wheat forms a major crop in the Vidarbha region. Among the cash crops, groundnut is cultivated in Marathwada and cotton is grown extensively in the northern districts. Sugarcane is popular in the southern districts like Satara, Kolhapur, Sangli, and parts of Pune and Ahmednagar districts. In the urban fringe fruit orchards and vegetables constitute important commercial crops.

**Infrastructure in Rural Areas**

About one-half of the 35,780 villages are electrified. Communication facilities in the rural areas are, however, inadequate. Village roads (with about 35,000 km length) are mostly unsurfaced *kutcha* link roads.

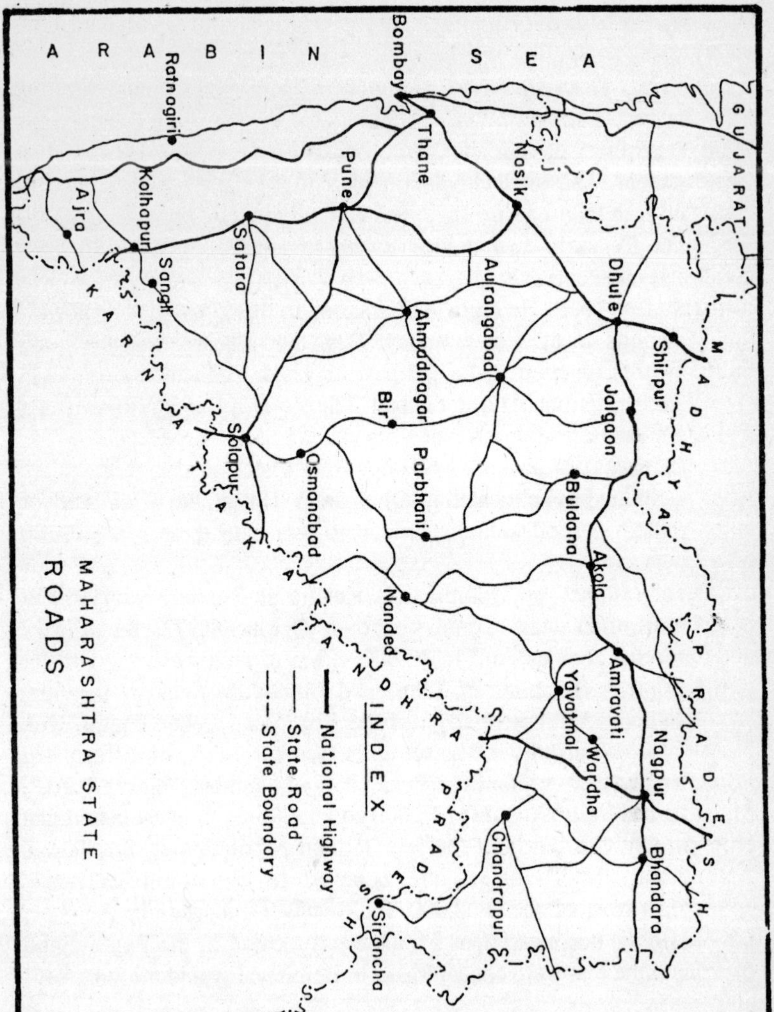


MAP 5.1: Maharashtra : Communication

## Mass Media

(a) *Print*: The state has as many as 1950 newspapers which is the largest number in the country. Out of these 130 have been registered as dailies.* But, most of them are non-Marathi papers. The total circulation of Marathi dailies is estimated to be less than one million. The *Loksatta* and *Maharashtra Times* are the only two dailies having a circulation of more than 1,00,000 copies.*

(b) *Radio*: There are eight AIR stations in the State, of which three stations located at Bombay, Pune and Nagpur are the main centres functioning for the past 25 years. The centres located at Sangli, Parbhani, Aurangabad, Jalgaon and Ratnagiri are recent additions. The number of licensed radio sets (Broadcast receiver Licences) is around 2,60,000. But, three-fourths of them are estimated to be located in urban areas. Hence, the availability of radios in rural areas is limited to less than three sets for 100 persons.

(c) *Television*: The Doordarshan Kendra at Bombay with 10-kW transmitter was commissioned in October 1972. Its primary service zone extends to 10,000 sq km of area, covering Greater Bombay and parts of Thane and Kulaba districts. Its potential audience is essentially urban. The Pune relay centre with 0.6-kW transmitter was set up in October 1973, for diffusion of Bombay programmes in Pune city and neighbouring rural areas. Its coverage extends to 15,000 sq km of area. It is estimated that nearly two-thirds of the four million population is rural-based. About 1400 villages are believed to be within its reach. However, of the 3,68,000 TV Receiver Licences in the State (1979), not more than 21,300 were located in the Pune region and the rest were concentrated in Bombay city and the suburbs.

In Table 5.1 the growth of Television Receiver Licences in the State (1973-79) is indicated.

## Community TV

The Directorate of Rural Broadcasting, Government of Maharashtra,

* Newspaper statistics relate to 1976.

has been executing the Community TV scheme in villages and slums for the benefit of the poorer sections since 1972-73. Under this scheme 380 sets were installed in Bombay Division and 460 in Pune Division by the end of 1979. Most of the Community TV sets in Pune Division are located in villages.

TABLE 5.1: Growth of Television Receiver Licences in Maharashtra

| Category | Number as on 31-12-1973 | Number as on 31-12-1976 | Number as on 31-12-1979 |
|---|---|---|---|
| Domestic | 51,958 | 199,447 | 364,897 |
| Community | 51 | 469 | 451 |
| School | 266 | 356 | 587 |
| Commercial | 531 | 1,547 | 1,696 |
| Others | 98 | 243 | 298 |
| Total | 52,904 | 202,072 | 367,929 |

In the following paragraphs a brief account of the two talukas wherein the selected villages are located is given. Later, an outline of the individual villages is given to facilitate better appreciation of the informational needs of the potential audience.

## Ambegaon Taluka

Ambegaon is one of the 13 talukas in Pune district. It constitutes an important segment of the area covered under the Tribal sub-plan, which includes parts of Junner and Khed talukas. The headquarters of the taluka and the Development Block, which is coterminus with the taluka, are located at Ghodegaon, a big village in the area with a population of nearly 10,000. The Development Block, initiated in 1963, covers 100 villages, out of which 56 are located in tribal area. The tribal population accounts for nearly 20 per cent of its total coverage and the important communities are: Mahadeo Kolis, Thakkars and Katkaris.

The communications facilities are poor except for the surfaced road connecting Manchar with Bhimashankar shrine located on the Sahyadri ranges. Bhimashankar is a popular pilgrim centre worshipped by not only the Mahadeo Kolis but also the non-tribals in the area. It attracts large numbers of tourists from all over the State. But, because of heavy rains during the monsoon, traffic on the ghat section remains dislocated during the rainy season. Otherwise, State Transport (ST) buses run regularly to Bhimashankar covering the tribal area from Manchar, Pune, Ahmednagar and Bombay.

There are no assured irrigation facilities. But, the Dimba irrigation project under construction, on Ghode river (near Shinoli under Ghodegaon Block) is expected to benefit not only some parts of the taluka but also the drought-prone area of Shirur. The tribal villages on the hills receive heavy rainfall (around 300 cm) and the important *kharif* (summer) crops are rice and millets like *Nachni (Eleusine Coracana), Varai (Coix Barbata)* etc. During *rabi* (winter) pulses are grown in some area. In the foot-hills *jowar, bajri* (millets) and groundnut are the main crops during Kharif, and potato and wheat during Rabi. In the plains which lie near Manchar, cash crops like onion, garlic, vegetables and flowers are grown as commercial crops under lift irrigation. The inputs on land in terms of fertilizers, pesticides, etc., are very meagre in the tribal area but in the plains the non-tribal cultivators use them extensively on irrigated crops and hybrid *jowar*. Due to the cultivation of commercial crops the land prices sometimes exceed Rs. 20,000 per acre but in the tribal area it hardly exceeds Rs. 3,000.

One of the important sources of income for the tribals is collection of *Hirada (Terminalsa Chebula)* which has medicinal value. It is harvested twice in a year – once in November-December and again in April-May months. The tree grows extensively in the forest area and the tribals have their own demarcations and ownership rights.

The infrastructure in the tribal area particularly is under-developed. Although 66 of the 100 villages are electrified, the use of electricity for agriculture and small-scale industries is very little. During the agricultural season the tribals have no employment opportunities.

One of the major problems of the area is lack of drinking water facilities. Even though the hills receive excessive rain, during summer the hill streams dry up and the tribals face acute shortage of drinking water. Due to the rocky mountainous terrain there are very few wells. Hence, the Zilla Parishad takes up construction of percolation tanks to store rainwater. It also arranges to supply water in mobile tankers to problem villages during the summer months.

Due to unsatisfactory and inadequate drinking water facilities many persons in the tribal areas suffer from water-borne diseases. There are only three Primary Health Centres in the area, of which two are located in the tribal area. In addition, however, three Ayurvedic dispensaries are run by the Zilla Parishad for the benefit of tribals.

There is only one college in Ambegaon taluka and it is located at Manchar. The whole area is served by 200 primary schools and about 15 high schools. This includes three Ashram schools with boarding and lodging facilities, run exclusively for the benefit of tribals.

The facilities for community viewing are made available in 33 out of 100 villages covered by the Block. But, most of them are located in non-tribal habitations. Only seven villages in the tribal area have been recently covered under the tribal sub-plan.

**Parner Taluka**

Parner is one of the 13 talukas in Ahmednagar district. It covers about 17,900 sq km of area and 154,000 population which is wholly rural. There are 114 villages and 90 per cent of the population subsists on agriculture and allied occupations. The dependence on labour is heavy and about 15 per cent eke out living as agricultural labourers.

The district is one of the worst hit by frequent droughts and Parner as part of it experiences scarcity conditions once in three-four years. The area receives hardly 50-60 cm of rain annually. In the absence of irrigation projects, only dry crops are grown and *jowar* and *bajri* are the main *kharif* crops. Wheat and pulses are grown in *rabi* in a limited area if soil conditions are favourable. Otherwise, most of the area is single-cropped. Irrigation by private sources like wells, etc. is limited to rich land-owners possessing 25-30 acres of land. Due to poor soils and low productivity the land prices vary between Rs 1,000 and 3,000 per acre. Under the circumstances even cultivators having 6-8 acres of land also cannot make both ends meet.

In the absence of industries and avenues for supplementary occupations, many people migrate to other areas during off-season and when the monsoon fails. Ahmednagar being an important military centre attracts many from the poorer sections to get enlisted in the Army for earning a living.

A number of Rural Works Programmes are sponsored in the area to generate employment under the Drought Prone Area Programme (DPAP) and Employment Guarantee Schemes (EGS). Assistance to small and marginal farmers and landless labourers is provided for taking up dairy and poultry farming.

Communications-wise, Parner is more developed than Ambegaon. State highway as well as inter-district roads pass through the taluka connecting Ahmednagar city. Like Pune, Ahmednagar city is an important educational centre and an army base. State transport buses ply regularly on different routes and the flow of traffic is heavy.

In Table 5.2 the demographic profile of the State and selected talukas is presented.

TABLE 5.2: **Demographic Profile of the Study Area**

| Sl. No. | Item | Maharashtra State | Pune district | Ahmednagar district | Ambegaon taluka | Parner taluka |
|---|---|---|---|---|---|---|
| 1. | Population ('000) | 50,412 | 3,178 | 2,269 | 139 | 155 |
| 2. | Percentage of Rural population | 68.8 | 58.2 | 88.9 | 100.0 | 100.0 |
| 3. | Percentage of workers | 36.5 | 32.3 | 35.4 | 35.2 | 38.2 |
| 4. | Percentage of workers subsisting on agriculture, etc. | 64.8 | 52.3 | 76.9 | 87.5 | 90.1 |
| 5. | Percentage of Scheduled Castes | 6.0 | 5.5 | 9.3 | 2.5 | 6.0 |
| 6. | Percentage of Scheduled Tribes | 5.9 | 3.4 | 6.4 | 19.8 | 3.5 |
| 7. | Literacy percentage | 39.2 | 44.6 | 36.2 | 33.0 | 32.0 |
| | Males | 51.0 | 56.3 | 49.0 | 47.4 | 46.0 |
| | Females | 26.4 | 32.1 | 22.9 | 18.9 | 18.4 |
| 8. | Inhabited villages | 35,778 | 1,482 | 1,321 | 100 | 114 |
| 9. | Villages with Community TV sets (as on 1.12.79) (Approximate) | 680 | 285 | 50 | 33 | 32 |

## An Outline of the Villages

1. *Narayan Gavhan*: Is a small but well-connected village with a population of 1500, located on the Pune-Ahmednagar highway. It lies very close to Shirur town (10 km) on the border of Pune-Ahmednagar districts. As such the villagers have more links with Shirur than with their taluka headquarters 16 km away, except for administrative work. Being situated on the highway, it enjoys good transport facilities towards Pune as well as Ahmednagar cities.

As a revenue village it consists of four hamlets *(wadis)* and the main village has approximately 200 out of the total 320 households. About two-fifths of the population is in working force and nearly 75 per cent of the workers are cultivators. There is heavy dependence on labour and the construction work of the canal near the village provides employment for a number of families. Majority of the cultivators are small farmers with land holdings between 5 and 10 acres. There are no industries and the agriculture is mostly rain-fed.

*Jowar* and *Bajri* are the main *kharif* crops. Varieties of gram and groundnut are grown on the uplands. Wheat is the only *rabi* crop grown on a limited scale. The rich farmers, however, have orchards like lemon and grow cash crops under well irrigation. There are four-five families who own 80-100 acres of land. They are the progressive farmers possessing resources and equipment like electric motors, pump sets, irrigation wells, sprayers, improved ploughs, etc. In the absence of irrigation facilities small and marginal cultivators are not in a position to make use of fertilizers, pesticides, etc.

Under the DPAP, a milk chilling plant with a capacity of 4,500 litres was commissioned in the village in 1977. A dairy cooperative was formed and the farmers are keen in taking up cross-breeding of cows for supplementing their income. There are no poultry farms in the village and only recently an ex-Army man has started a small farm on his own.

There is no high school and the middle school runs classes up to Standard VII with a strength of about 350 students. However, many children from the village go to the high school at Vade Gavhan, located 2 km away. Five-six boys are attending college at Shirur.

The village has an ANM (Auxiliary Nurse Midwife) Centre and the B.J. Medical College, Pune, runs a part-time OPD in the sub-centre twice a week with student interns. But, the facilities being irregular and unsatisfactory, the villagers prefer to go to Shirur to consult private doctors.

The Gram Panchayat got a borewell and constructed a tank for piped water supply. However, the facilities in the hamlets are inadequate.

There is unity among the Marathas who constitute the majority community but their relations with the Harijans are strained. In view of this the Harijans do not participate in the village affairs and actually voted against the local Surpanch in the 1979 Zilla Perishad elections.

The Gram Panchayat has a community radio set in the main village and it is tuned in regularly in the morning and evening for farm programmes. Even though there is no organised listening, because a number of persons sit around the *Wada* which houses the Panchayat office there is sizable listening of the programmes, particularly in the evenings. It is roughly estimated that there would be about 75-80 domestic radio sets and the programmes on dry farming and dairy are said to command wide listening in the houses.

The Gram Panchayat gets four Marathi newspapers daily and two of them are district newspapers. These are widely shared by the literates in the village. In addition, the hotel owners and shop keepers and a few individuals also subscribe to daily papers. The total inflow of daily newspapers is around 15 for the village as a whole. There is a small library run by the Gram Panchayat with 200-300 books and it was observed that a number of housewives take advantage of the facility.

The community TV installed in December 1974, in the Gram Panchayat building is placed in a small temple-like structure outside facing the main village road. The open ground in front can accommodate 300-400 people in the fair weather. However, the set is not switched on daily. The Panchayat peon, who acts as the custodian, has been instructed to keep the set open on Thursdays, Saturdays and Sundays for the popular film-based entertainment programmes. Therefore, many of the villagers have no idea of the Farm Programmes or other Rural Programmes. The Gram Sewak (VLW) who stays next door does not take any interest. He keeps mostly busy with administrative work as Secretary of the Gram Panchayat.

2. *Narodi*: This is a progressive village with a population of about 3,000 located one and half kilometres off Manchar-Bhimashankar road, in the non-tribal segment of Ambegaon Block. Because of its proximity to Manchar (8 km) and Ghodegaon (6 km) it enjoys good communications facilities by road. One noteworthy facility is the direct State Transport service from the village to Bombay city, daily in the morning.

As a revenue village it consists of four major hamlets; one of which is inhabited by the Mahadeo Koli tribals. But, it is located about 5 km from the main village with very little contact. Most of the houses in the close by hamlets are also scattered.

The village has a history in development and has to its credit some remarkable achievements through public cooperation. In 1961 it was awarded the Ideal Village Prize by the Zilla Parishad and the Gram Sewak of the village received several prizes as the best worker at Block and district levels. The Gram Panchayat successfully tapped external funds from institutions like the Maharashtra Arogya Mandal, Lions Club, Pune, Terres-des-homes, Kasturba Trust, etc., to finance its development projects. One of the remarkable features is the convention that all those who go out and work should donate monthly a small amount of half-a-rupee as minimum contribution towards the Village Development Trust. This is well planned and fruitfully utilised by the dedicated leadership in the village. As such, it attracts a number of voluntary organisations for sponsoring welfare schemes.

The village has all the institutional facilities and these include a branch of the Bank of Maharashtra, a High School run by the Ryat Sikshan Samstha, Cottage Hospital with six beds and an orphanage run by the Maharashtra Arogya Mandal, a Balwadi sponsored by the Kasturba Trust and lift irrigation projects financed by the Maharashtra Bank. The villagers have executed on their own the surfaced link road from the main road and the piped water supply schemes.

In the agricultural front, about one-third of the 2,000 acres of the cultivated land is irrigated by private sources. Taking advantage of its location on the banks of Ghode river, the villagers executed two lift irrigation schemes with the assistance of the Maharashtra Arogya Mandal and Bank of Maharashtra. *Jowar*, *Bajri* and groundnut are the important *kharif* crops. During *rabi*, potato, onion and garlic are mostly grown. Those who have adequate irrigation facilities cultivate vegetables, fruits and flowers and export them to Bombay city.

There is widespread awareness of the modern methods of cultivation and animal husbandry. Available facilities in the village like the veterinary sub-centre, multi-purpose credit society, dairy cooperative, etc., are fully utilised. But, the land prices being prohibitive, most of the cultivators are marginal farmers possessing one-two acres of land. Farmers having 8-10 acres of land with irrigation facilities are very few in the village.

There are no industrial units at present except a few flour mills. Many educated and uneducated people, therefore, migrate to Bombay. Land holdings being small, there is locally no scope for absorption of the surplus manpower. The villagers are, therefore, planning to set up an Onion Dehydration Plant as a cooperative unit to generate employment for the landless and small farmers.

The Gram Panchayat has a community radio set in the main village which is regularly tuned in for the agricultural programmes. This has wide listening and people gather round the Panchayat building in small groups during the evenings when they come to the nearby temple. There are two more community radio sets in the hamlets but they are not in working condition. It is estimated that there would be about 80-90 radio sets in individual houses on a permanent basis and an equal number of sets on a temporary basis with those who come often to the village from places like Bombay. Thus, the exposure to radio is substantial.

The Youth Club sponsored by the Gram Panchayat runs a Reading Room and subscribes for four dailies and 10 magazines. There are about 1,300 books in its Library. In addition, individual subscribers receive 10-15 daily newspapers. It was observed that as a routine many people come and sit either at the Panchayat Office or nearby hotels daily in the morning to read newspaper and discuss about the weather, market rates and local politics for some time before they go to the fields.

The community TV set was installed in the village in November 1975, and placed in the Panchayat Office near a window facing the open ground outside. It can accommodate 400-500 people and even indoors about 100 can watch the programmes comfortably. However, the set was found to be out of order during the period of study and the Gram Panchayat reported that many times the set was repaired but it frequently developed trouble. It was gathered that for about two months the set was not in working order. Even when it was in good condition it was switched on only on Thursdays, Saturdays and Sundays for the more popular film-based programmes and occasionally was for agricultural and other programmes. If on reading newspapers people find an item of relevance to village is scheduled, they request the custodian and on such occasions a few persons gather around the set. Thus, the exposure to the medium is otherwise limited.

3. *Amondi*: Is a semi-tribal village with a population of 1,600 out of which nearly 300 belong to the Scheduled Tribes – Thakkars and Mahadeo Kolis. It is located in the foothills 4 km away from the main road, off Shinde Wadi near Ghodegaon on the Manchar-Bhimashankar route. Being located on the northern bank of the Ghode river, communication facilities are very poor. The fair-weather link road is not suitable for vehicular traffic. During the monsoon when the river is full, one has to take a boat to cross the river or go by a circuitous routs via Gangapur where there is a bridge across the river. Besides this problem, there is a small *nallah* just near the village which overflows during the monsoon and floods the entire area.

The Revenue village consists of five hamlets of which two are inhabited by the tribals and three are shared by the non-tribal communities. All of them lie scattered and separated by gorges and forest growth. The hamlet where the Mahadeo Kolis live is situated on top of the hill more than 5 km away and its contact with the main village is limited. But, the Thakkar hamlet lies close to the main village and one of the Thakkars – an educated young man was recently appointed as Police Patil of the village. Therefore, their contact is more with the main village.

The village has 4,500 acres of land but one-half is uncultivated forest land. Most of the area, except for a small portion irrigated by wells and river water, is rain-fed and single-cropped. Because of the poor soils and low productivity cultivators having 6-8 acres of land also are considered as poor farmers. The price of land (not having irrigation facilities) varies from Rs. 1,000 to 3,000 per acre.

*Jowar* and *bajri* are the main *Kharif* crops. Groundnut is also cultivated in small patches. Those who possess lands on the river side (non-tribals) grow onion and chillies in a limited area. As such, the intake of fertilisers and pesticides is low. The tribals mostly follow the primitive methods. The villagers are, however, hoping for canal irrigation under the Dimba project. A part of the village land is expected to receive canal water but most of it will remain unirrigated.

There are no industrial units excepting two flour mills. Due to constraints like transportation across the river, people are hesitant to take up dairy and poultry keeping.

The main village has a common well which is adequate for the local residents. In the Thakkar hamlet recently the Block provided a bore-well. But, in other hamlets there are no satisfactory facilities for drinking water and people face acute shortage during the summer months.

An Ayurvedic dispensary with a qualified doctor is being run by the Zilla Parishad, particularly for the benefit of tribals. But, the response from them is very poor. They depend mostly on their traditional system of cure. The non-tribals mostly prefer allopathic medicines and are not very much keen to make use of the locally available facilities excepting under an emergency. They go to Ghodegaon and consult private doctors. Malaria is said to be endemic in the area and there are about 10 lepers living as social outcasts without regular treatment.

The main village does not have a community radio set, but one of the hamlets where the non-tribals live has a set, but it is not in working order. It is estimated that there would be about 40-50 domestic radio sets mostly owned by the non-tribal cultivators.

The Gram Panchayat subscribes for only one daily newspaper and a few magazines. These are mostly read by the village functionaries. However, in fair weather as most of the people visit Ghodegaon, they either read them at tea shops or purchase one occasionally. During the monsoon when the village remains almost cut off, the reach of newspapers is almost negligible.

A community TV set was installed in the village in January 1977, under the Tribal sub-plan. It is placed in the school building located in the centre of the main village. As such the beneficiaries are mostly non-tribals. Only occasionally, the Thakkars come to watch TV. The Mahadeo Kolis and other non-tribals living in far-off hamlets do not find it convenient to come during the night time due to fear of snakes and wild animals.

One of the primary school teachers is given the responsibility of the TV set. But, he hardly takes any interest. He has handed over the key to one of the unemployed youths who stays near the school. It was gathered that this boy is regular in switching on the set daily as he himself finds it a good pastime. But, the set was found to be not in good working order at the time of the Study as both sound and picture were found to be of poor quality.

Seldom Extension officials visit the village because of poor communication facilities. The Gram Sewak posted in the village resides at Ghodegaon and does not normally visit the hamlets except for collection of house tax, etc. His interaction with the tribals is minimal.

4. *Taleghar*: Is a small but important tribal village, inhabited by the Mahadeo Kolis, on the Ghat section of the Manchar-Bhimshankar route, about 15 km ahead of Bhimashankar. It serves as the main centre for the Mahadeo Koli habitations, which are usually located on hill-tops, for marketing and other facilities. It has institutional facilities like a middle school, post office, police out-past, credit and consumer cooperative etc. Recently a Primary Health Centre (PHC) and a veterinary clinic were set up under the Tribal sub-plan. But, the two doctors do not stay in the village as there are no staff quarters. Even the VLW stays outside.

Being located on the hills, the village gets heavy rainfall during the monsoon. Of the total 1,800 acres of land belonging to the village only one-fourth is under cultivation. *Nachni*, *Varai* (millets) and rice are the important *kharif* crops. During *rabi* wheat is grown in small pockets. Otherwise, there is no second crop. In the absence of cottage industries, there is no employment for the tribals during off-season, except for the collection of *Hirada* during April-May and November-December months. Cattle-rearing and breeding of goats is traditional but not for selling milk. Dairy farming is yet to become popular with the tribals. It was gathered that the cross-bred varieties do not survive in the locality and the local varieties do not yield much milk.

One of the major problems of the village is lack of adequate drinking water facilities. During the summer months the only well in the village dries up and the people have to trek long distances to fetch water or depend on the mobile tankers operated by the Zilla Parishad.

It was gathered that the school in the village was established as long age as 90 years and it was upgraded as middle school in 1962. But still, it does not have proper accommodation. There are about 150 students on the rolls and most of them are boys. The drop-out ratio is very heavy after Standard IV. Early marriages of girls and other socio-economic conditions are the main constraints. However, there are a few boys from the village attending the Ashram School at Gohe Budruk, down the hills.

Being connected with State Transport facilities, a number of Extension officials visit the village but hardly anybody makes a night halt.

The Gram Panchayat subscribes for two dailies and they are mostly read by the school teachers and other functionaries. There is no community radio set, either in the village or in the hamlets. The number of domestic radio sets also does not exceed 15 for the whole village.

The community TV set was installed under the Tribal sub-plan in March 1978. It is kept in the temple which houses the school as well as the Panchayat office. Its custody is entrusted to a local boy who owns a shop opposite the building across the road. The set was found to be in good condition at the time of this study. But it was gathered that it is switched on only on three days in the week for the popular film-based programmes on Thursdays, Saturdays and Sundays. The Panchayat officials or non-officials do not take any interest and it is mostly left to the village youth who make use of it.

5. *Rajpur*: It is a predominantly tribal village, with a population of 600 and just 3 km away from Taleghar on the Bhimshankar route. As it is situated off the main road it does not have much exposure. Its hamlets particularly remain isolated.

Mahadeo Kolis and Neo-Buddhists are the two communities

sharing the village. During the summer months a few families of Katkari tribals come and stay in temporary huts for *Hirada* collection. The relations between the communities are said to be cordial. But, there is no unity among the Mahadeo Kolis who constitute the main group. Due to internal rivalries, there is very little development activity.

Of the 2,800 acres of land belonging to the village less than one-third is cultivated. The rest is either under forest or hilly terrain not suitable for cultivation. The village has a natural tank with a perennial spring, but it is not exploited for irrigation purposes. *Nachni* and rice are the important crops during *kharif*. There is no crop during *rabi*. *Hirada* collection is an important activity during November-December and April-May months. The intake of fertilizers and pesticides is minimal and the traditional primitive methods of cultivation are mostly followed. Some of the families also resort to shifting cultivation on the hill slopes for growing minor millets. Poultry, goat-rearing and cattle-breeding are traditional, but not popular for earning a living.

There is an Ashram School in one of the hamlets of the village but the people are unhappy with its functioning. Similar is the case with the single-teacher Zilla Parishad school.

There is a branch of the Adivasi Maha Mandal (Tribal Development Corporation) which runs a Consumers Cooperative store. But, the villagers mostly depend on the weekly market at Ambegaon and a private shop in the village run by one of the tribals.

The Gram Panchayat does not have a building and the Gram Sewak also does not stay in the village. His interaction with the local villagers, particularly those who live in the hamlets, is minimal.

There is no community radio in the village and the Panchayat does not subscribe to any paper. The TV set installed in the village in March 1977, under the Tribal sub-plan was initially placed in the house of the Sarpanch as there was no other suitable accommodation. He was using it according to his convenience. Later, some villagers protested and the set was shifted to the temple opposite his house which has power supply.

The villagers to keep the power bill to the minimum decided to switch on the set only on three days, for the film-based items only. As it was kept in a private building, the villagers were given to understand that they would have to share the bill by raising contributions. The sarpanch does not take any interest as the set was removed from his house. Since nobody was nominated as the custodian by the Gram

Panchayat or the Rural Broadcasting Department, whoever goes to the temple early switches on the set on the three days decided by the villagers. There is no lock and key and mostly it is used by the Harijans who live close by. As the tribals do not understand Hindi, they do not show much interest in the Hindi film programmes. Only children and youngsters watch such programmes, though they do not understand the language. It was observed during the period of study that the set was defective with poor picture quality.

In Table 5.3 a statistical profile of the selected villages is presented for ready reference.

TABLE 5.3: (a) Statistical Profile of the Villages

| Sl. No. | Item | Narayan Gavhan | Narodi | Amondi | Teleghar | Rajpur |
|---|---|---|---|---|---|---|
| 1. | Population | 1,536 | 2,858 | 1,643 | 504 | 587 |
| 2. | Males | 737 | 1,386 | 792 | 275 | 292 |
| 3. | Females | 799 | 1,472 | 851 | 229 | 295 |
| 4. | Percentage of workers | 43.1 | 31.6 | 39.3 | 45.2 | 60.8 |
| 5. | Dependents on agriculture, etc. | 93.5 | 90.9 | 92.2 | 93.8 | 97.8 |
| 6. | Literacy: Total | 33.1 | 30.5 | 35.2 | 26.6 | 26.1 |
| | Males | 46.3 | 46.4 | 50.9 | 40.0 | 31.5 |
| | Females | 21.0 | 15.6 | 20.7 | 10.5 | 8.8 |
| 7. | Percentage of Scheduled Castes | 2.5 | 3.3 | 1.1 | nil | 10.6 |
| 8. | Percentage of Scheduled Tribes | 1.0 | 8.6 | 16.8 | 93.3 | 89.4 |
| 9. | Cultivated area (acres) | 3,736 | 1,968 | 2,357 | 468 | 829 |
| 10. | Irrigation area | 400 | 437 | 95 | 4 | nil |

(b) Other Facilities in the Selected Villages

| Sl. No. | Facility | Narayan Gavhan | Narodi | Amondi | Teleghar | Rajpur |
|---|---|---|---|---|---|---|
| 1. | Distance from the town/Main market centre (km) | 10 | 8 | 20 | 50 | 55 |
| 2. | Health facilities | Dispensary | Hospital | Dispensary | Hospital (PHC) | Nil |
| 3. | Educational Facilities | Middle school | High school | Middle school | Middle school | Middle school |
| 4. | Community Radio | Available | Available | absent | absent | Absent |
| 5. | Number of domestic radio sets (Approx.) | 75 | 160 | 40 | 15 | 5 |
| 6. | Flow of daily newspapers | 15 | 15 | 5 | 2 | Nil |
| | Date of installation of the TV set | 3-12-74 | 28-11-75 | 24-1-77 | 20-3-78 | 26-3-77 |

# 6

# THE STATUS OF THE MEDIUM

IN THIS chapter, the reach and utilization of the media and the villagers' exposure to other informational channels has been analysed. The basic objective is to find out the status of television as an instrument of development *vis-a-vis* other available channels. The information is presented first in relation to the pattern of exposure to the mass media – newspapers, radio, films and then to other personal media.

## Newspapers

The data collection on newspapers was restricted to dailies only. Periodicals and such other channels were excluded assuming that the pattern of consumption of all print channels would be more or less similar.

The analyses presented in Table 6.1 indicate that the regular exposure to daily papers in villages is restricted to 16 per cent. Nearly 60 per cent of the population remain completely untouched by the medium due to illiteracy. It was observed that illiterates getting information from newspapers read out to them was a very rare phenomenon. There were only seven persons in the sample (2.8 per cent) getting news from newspapers read out to them or conveyed to them almost on a regular basis. All of them happened to be *Karbharis*, leaders of some position in village politics. Illiterate ordinary villagers, representing the most common denominator, do not have any exposure to print channels.

TABLE 6.1: Pattern of Exposure to Daily Papers

| Frequency of reading | Narayan Gavhan % | Narodi % | Amondi % | Tale-ghar % | Rajpur % | All Villages N | All Villages % |
|---|---|---|---|---|---|---|---|
| Regular (at least once in two days) | 28 | 16.0 | 12.7 | 15.0 | - | 40 | 16.0 |
| Sometimes (2-3 times a week) | 8 | 20.0 | 9 1 | 10.0 | 12.0 | 34 | 13.6 |
| Rarely (once a week or so) | 20 | 5.0 | 20.0 | - | 20.0 | 31 | 12.4 |
| Never | 44 | 59.0 | 58.2 | 75.0 | 68.0 | 145 | 58.0 |
| Total | 50 | 100 | 55 | 20 | 25 | 250 | 100.0 |

For obvious reasons, villages with better communication and education facilities like Narayan Gavhan and Narodi had a better exposure to newspapers than the interior tribal villages like Rajpur where not a single newspaper reaches.

Analyses by different social characteristics (presented in Appendix 1) revealed that less than four per cent of the females read the daily newspapers and 76 per cent of them get no exposure to the medium. Among men while about 48 per cent never read newspapers, only 23 per cent reported regular reading. The habit of newspaper reading was more widespread among the following categories:

- males
- youngsters below 30 years of age
- those who are educated beyond high school level
- white-collar workers and unemployed youth

Among the different occupational groups, those depending on trade and traditional occupations like artisans were found to be better exposed to newspapers than cultivators. Apparently due to lack of education, the exposure was minimal with 14 per cent in the case of labourers. None in this category was found to read a daily paper on a regular basis.

(a) *Place of Reading*

There were only six persons in the sample (2.4 per cent) subscribing to the daily papers and all of them happened to be from Narayan Gavhan, the roadside non-tribal village. While 43 per cent of the readers were found to depend on newspapers subscribed to by the Gram Panchayat, another 20 per cent depended upon the tea shops and *Kirana* (general) stores.

It was noted that newspaper reading was mostly a shared phenomenon. Individual reading was observed to be limited to persons like Government servants, retired officials and such other persons who do not normally mix with other villagers. One important observation was that where Gram Panchayats were sponsoring reading rooms and contributing to newspapers, there was wider exposure. In villages where the Gram Panchayats did not have such a facility (due to financial or other constraints) comparatively less exposure was observed. Purchase of newspapers was found to be regarded as a style associated with modern living. The medium, however, is not considered a status symbol like radio, to be exhibited in the house.

Since women do not normally visit public places like tea shops, Panchayat office etc. their exposure is wholly dependent on the occasional purchase of papers by the better-off educated men-folk when they go on errands to the town/market-place. This habit being limited to economically well-off families, women from poor and lower middle class families normally do not get the benefit of exposure even if they are educated.

TABLE 6.2: Place of Reading of Newspapers

| Place of of reading | Narayan Gavhan | Narodi | Amondi | Taleg-har | Rajpur | All Villages | |
|---|---|---|---|---|---|---|---|
| | % | % | % | % | % | N | % |
| Relevant sample (N) | 28 | 41 | 23 | 5 | 8 | 105 | 100.0 |
| Subscribes | 21.4 | - | - | - | - | 6 | 5.7 |
| Occasional purchase | 3.6 | 9.8 | 17.4 | 20.0 | 37.5 | 13 | 12.4 |
| Gram Panchayat | 25.0 | 58.5 | 56.5 | 20.0 | - | 45 | 42.9 |
| Hotel/stores | 28.6 | 14.6 | 26.1 | - | 12.5 | 21 | 20.0 |
| Friends/Relatives | 17.8 | 4.9 | - | - | 12.5 | 8 | 7.6 |
| Other institutions | 3.6 | 12.2 | - | 60.0 | 37.5 | 12 | 11.4 |

## (b) *Selection of Newspapers*

The exposure to national newspapers was found to be practically nil, as the knowledge of English/Hindi languages was inadequate. The readership was, therefore, limited to local Marathi dailies. The analyses of the data relating to selection of newspapers (presented in Table 6.3) indicate that one-half of the readers were not selective. "Beggars cannot be choosers" was the explanation of the readers. Except the small percentage who reported reading the daily papers as a matter of routine, others, who occasionally glance through the papers as and when they go to the Panchayat office or a nearby tea shop, indicated that they read any piece that is readily available. They would not also mind even if it were an old paper.

TABLE 6.3: Selection of Newspapers

*(Multiple response)*

| Newspaper | Narayan Gavhan % | Narodi % | Amondi % | Tale-ghar % | Rajpur % | All Villages N | All Villages % |
|---|---|---|---|---|---|---|---|
| Relevant Sample (N) | 28 | 41 | 23 | 5 | 8 | 105 | 100.0 |
| No selection | 39.3 | 61.0 | 43.5 | 80.0 | 75.0 | 56 | 53.3 |
| Sakal | 46.4 | 31.7 | 43.5 | 20.0 | 25.0 | 39 | 37.1 |
| Kesari | 21.4 | 14.6 | 13.0 | 20.0 | - | 16 | 15.2 |
| Sahyadri | 7.1 | 10.1 | 17.4 | - | - | 13 | 12.4 |
| Tarun Bharat | 7.1 | 12.2 | 17.4 | 40.0 | - | 13 | 12.4 |
| Lok Satta | 7.1 | 2.4 | - | 20.0 | - | 4 | 3.8 |
| Prabhat | - | - | 4.3 | - | - | 1 | 0.9 |
| Other locals | 10.7 | - | - | - | - | 3 | 2.9 |

Some of the progressive farmers and school teachers in non-tribal villages were observed to be very particular in reading current affairs as well as farm features and market rates almost daily before going out for work. They invariably shared this information with other adult male members in the house at the time of lunch and with fellow farmers when they assembled near the temple/Panchayat office in the evening.

Wide disparity was noticed in the ownership of radios in the villages. In Narayan Gavhan, the roadside, non-tribal village, as many as 48 per cent of the respondents reported own radio sets in their houses. In the interior tribal villages, radio ownership was confined to 15 per cent of the households. Taken the sample as a whole, 30 per cent of the households possessed their own radio sets. Villagewise information is presented in Table 6.4.

PLATE 6.1: Sharing of Newspapers

PLATE 6.2: Domestic Radio Listening

## Radio

TABLE 6.4: Radio Ownership in the Villages

| Village | | Per cent |
|---|---|---|
| Narayan Gavhan | .. | 48.0 |
| Narodi | .. | 29.0 |
| Amondi | .. | 27.3 |
| Taleghar | .. | 15.0 |
| Rajpur | .. | 16.0 |
| All villages | .. | 30.0 |

Data relating to ownership of radios was analysed by economic and social variables and is presented in Table 6.5. It reveals that the proportion of radio ownership is relatively more among traders, artisans, etc., with 42 per cent closely followed by white-collar workers with 39 per cent. Among agricultural families the ownership is limited to 32 per cent and among labourers it is hardly 10 per cent.

The data suggest that among the weaker sections, Adivasis are a better lot than Harijans, so far as radio ownership is concerned. But, it may be noted here that the sample consists of mostly Mahadeo Koli tribals whose economic condition is better than that of the Harijans. Among Mahadeo Koli tribals, land ownership is relatively higher than among the Harijans who mostly depend on labour.

TABLE 6.5: Radio Ownership by Occupation and Social Status

| Category | All villages % |
|---|---|
| *Occupation*: | |
| Agriculture & allied occupations | 31.8 |
| Labour | 9.5 |
| Trade and traditional services | 42.3 |
| White-collar workers, etc. | 39.3 |
| *Social Status*: | |
| Non-Harijans | 37.9 |
| Harijans (S.C.) | 12.0 |
| Adivasis (S.T.) | 17.2 |
| *Economic status*: | |
| Poor | 9.5 |
| Average | 36.8 |
| Upper middle class | 51.2 |
| All categories | 30.0 |

Analyses by economic status revealed that among families with income less than Rs. 300 per month (categorised as poor) radio ownership is limited to 10 per cent. Even among those whose incomes were estimated to exceed Rs. 600 per month (categorised as upper middle class) possession of a radio was restricted to 51 per cent of the families.

It was observed that by and large, farmers do not attach weightage to radio as an essential household item. In their scales of value, land, cattle and ornaments seem to weigh more heavily than house and material goods like radio, furniture and even dress.

### (a) *Frequency of Radio Listening*

Despite the poor ownership, exposure to the medium was found to be significantly high, with as many as 80 per cent having access to the medium and getting the benefit of exposure to the broadcasts.

The data presented in Table 6.6 indicate that the non-tribal villages (Narodi and Narayan Gavhan) having more domestic radio sets as well as Community listening facilities enjoy wider exposure to the medium than the tribal villages like Taleghar and Rajpur where a large percentage of population depend on external sources.

TABLE 6.6: Frequency of Radio Listening

| Frequency | Narayan Gavhan | Narodi | Amondi | Taleg-har | Rajpur | All Villages | |
|---|---|---|---|---|---|---|---|
| | % | % | % | % | % | N | % |
| Frequently (at least twice a week) | 54.0 | 43.0 | 27.3 | 15.0 | 24.0 | 94 | 37.6 |
| Occasionally (at least once a week) | 16.0 | 27.0 | 23.6 | 40.0 | 20.0 | 61 | 24.4 |
| Rarely (less than once a week) | 20.0 | 14.0 | 10.9 | 20.0 | 36.0 | 43 | 17.2 |
| Never | 10.0 | 16.0 | 38.2 | 25.0 | 20.0 | 52 | 20.8 |
| Total | 30 | 100 | 55 | 20 | 25 | 250 | 100.0 |

Analyses of the data by different socio-economic variables (Table A-2) revealed that one-third of the females remain out of reach of radio while 86 per cent of the males get the benefit of exposure. It was observed that, as a social tradition, women do not go to public places. Hence, among those who do not own a set, there is hardly any scope for exposure unless there is a set within the next three-four houses.

Agewise not much difference in the pattern of exposure was noticed. But, direct association was observed with education; the higher the education the more the frequency of radio listening. The maximum exposure was noticed in the case of white-collar workers and such other categories among whom as many as 68 per cent reported frequent listening to the broadcasts. In the case of labourers only 12 per cent were found to enjoy regular listening facilities.

### (b) *Place of Listening to the Broadcasts*

Those who reported listening to the broadcasts but did not possess a set of their own were asked to indicate where they normally listened to the programmes. There were altogether 123 such persons in the sample (49.2 per cent) and their responses are presented in Table 6.7.

TABLE 6.7: Place of Listening to Radio in the Case of Non-owners

(*Multiple response*)

| Place | Narayan Gavhan | Narodi | Amondi | Taleg-har | Rajpur | All Villages | |
|---|---|---|---|---|---|---|---|
| | % | % | % | % | % | N | % |
| Relevant sample (N) | 21 | 55 | 19 | 12 | 16 | 123 | 100.0 |
| Neighbours | 38.1 | 34.5 | 78.9 | 41.7 | 81.3 | 60 | 48.7 |
| Community set | 52.4 | 54.5 | no facility | - | - | 41 | 33.3 |
| Hotel/shop | 14.3 | 14.5 | 31.6 | 58.3 | 25.0 | 28 | 22.8 |
| Other places | 4.8 | 5.5 | - | - | - | 4 | 3.2 |

The data suggest that nearly one-half of the persons depending on external sources for radio listening avail of the facility visiting friends or relatives in the neighbourhood. In the non-tribal villages Narayan Gavhan and Narodi, where the community radio sets were functioning, the men-folk assemble there to avail of the facility. In Narodi, the community radio set with the Gram Panchayat was attracting large audiences during the evening for the rural programmes. In the absence of such a facility (in the tribal villages and scattered hamlets of non-tribal villages) the sharing of the private sets was noticed to be quite high.

### (c) *Selection of Programmes*

All those who had the benefit of exposure to radio were asked to indicate the type of programmes they prefer to listen. The data presented in Table 6.8 shows that about one-fifth do not have any selection. They listen to any programme that comes on the air when they happen to be with the set.

TABLE 6.8 Pattern of Exposure to the Programmes

| Programmes | Percentage |
|---|---|
| No Selection | 21.2 |
| Rural/Agriculture | 37.9 |
| News (Marathi) | 36.4 |
| Film songs | 29.3 |
| Devotional songs | 26.8 |
| Plays | 21.2 |
| Folk formats (Tamasha, etc.) | 17.2 |
| Programmes for women and children | 10.6 |
| Others | 8.1 |

It is encouraging to note that the villagers attach high importance to the listening of rural programmes. The Pune station of All India Radio transmits daily about 60 minutes of farm programmes and has been able to establish itself as an important source of agricultural information. Its Radio Rural Forum programmes received worldwide attention during 1956.[1]

One of the significant observations was the wide inter-village disparity in the pattern of listening to the programmes. In Narodi which has irrigation potential and grows commercial crops, wide listening was noticed for farm broadcasts. Narayan Gavhan, located on the roadside and more exposed to political influence, reflected more news consciousness. In tribal villages, where cultivation is rainfed, entertainment programmes like film songs, plays and devotional songs commanded more listening. It was revealed in the discussions that the agricultural broadcasts have a bias towards commercial crops and hybrid varieties which cannot be grown in the hilly areas. It was pointed out that very little coverage is provided for dry crops and hardly any mention is made of millets which are widely grown in the Ambegaon region.

(d) *Awareness of Agricultural Broadcasts*

All those who reported exposure to radio were asked if they were aware of the rural broadcasts, irrespective of their choice of the programmes. It was revealed that on the average about 75 per cent of the persons were aware of the rural broadcasts (see Table, Appendix 3). However, it varied from 58 per cent in the backward semi-tribal village Amondi to 86 per cent in the highly exposed non-tribal village Narayan Gavhan.

Analyses by the socio-economic variables revealed that awareness was positively associated with education and negatively with age. Excepting labourers among whom awareness was limited to 62 per cent, in other occupational groups it was high, ranging between 73 and 82 per cent.

(e) *Specific Recollection of Programmes*

Despite the wide awareness and exposure to rural broadcasts, specific recollection of programmes was poor. The respondents were requested to recall the items listened to during the preceding one week of the interview. Nearly two-thirds failed to recollect any item. The response of the remaining one-third showed that broadcasts of specific relevance to self get mostly registered. For example, it was observed that in Narodi where vegetables are grown, many respondents growing vegetables could recollect broadcasts on vegetable cultivation. Similarly, in Rajpur and Taleghar where rice crop is popular, nearly one-half could recall line sowing and other transplantation methods suggested for rice. In Amondi where hybrid jowar is grown, as many as one-fourth could recollect listening to the broadcasts on hybrid jowar. The programmes on cotton, sugarcane, etc., which went on the air during the period were cited by only a negligible percentage. These crops are not grown in the area.

On the basis of these findings two broad generalisations could be made:

1. The recollection of programmes is mostly confined to hard-core agricultural items with very few citing social education and health programmes that are included in the rural broadcasts; and
2. The recollection of hard-core items is linked to the farmers' cultivation of the specific crops.

**Films**

Cinema being an audio-visual medium is expected to command a bigger clientele than print or radio. As a source of entertainment, films draw large crowds in urban areas and, therefore, high exposure to the medium is assumed in villages also. In spite of the widespread awareness and interest in the medium, actual exposure to films in villages was found to be severely restricted due to poor accessibility. In the entire Ambegaon taluka there is only one cinema hall located at Manchar in the plains, on the Pune-Nasik national highway. The tribal and semi-tribal villages were thus found to have practically no access to the medium with the distance from the cinema hall to the interior villages like Rajpur exceeding 45 km.

The frequency of exposure to films among the sample respondents is given below:

TABLE 6.9: Pattern of Exposure to Films

| Frequency of movie-going | Narayan Gavhan | Narodi | Amondi | Taleg har | Rajpur | All villages | |
|---|---|---|---|---|---|---|---|
| | % | % | % | % | % | N | % |
| Frequently (at least once a month) | 2.0 | 5.0 | 1.8 | - | - | 7 | 2.8 |
| Occasionally (once in three months or so) | 20.0 | 8.0 | 1.8 | - | 4.0 | 20 | 8.0 |
| Rarely (once or twice a year) | 24.0 | 23.0 | 16.4 | 15.0 | 8.0 | 49 | 19.6 |
| Never | 54.0 | 64.0 | 80.0 | 85.0 | 88.0 | 174 | 69.6 |
| Total | 50 | 100 | 55 | 20 | 25 | 250 | 100.0 |

The data presented in Table 6.9 reveal that, on an average, as many as 70 per cent of the people in villages have no exposure to films. In the interior tribal villages as many as 80-85 per cent remain untouched by the medium. In Narayan Gavhan which has the benefit of having a cinema hall 10 km away, about 46 per cent of the respondents reported seeing films. But, in Rajpur which is located 45 km away from the cinema hall, not more than 12 per cent were found to be exposed to the medium.

Frequencywise analyses indicated very meagre exposure even in roadside non-tribal villages. Taken the sample as a whole, less than three per cent were found to see a movie once a month or so which was considered to be frequent viewing according to the villagers' own norms. There was not even a single person in the category of frequent viewers in the tribal villages of Rajpur and Teleghar. Even in the well-exposed Narayan Gavhan, there was only one person in the sample of 55. The maximum response was from Narodi (having a cinema hall at a distance of 8 km) where five per cent reported frequent viewing. Approximately, two-thirds of the filmgoers were found to be rare viewers having as exposure of not more than twice a year.

Analyses of the exposure pattern by social variables presented in Appendix 4 revealed that sexwise there was hardly any marked difference. But, the extent of exposure decreased with the increase in age. Among persons in the age-group of 15-30 years the exposure was maximum with 43 per cent viewers. In the above 60 years age-group, the viewers constituted only 14 per cent.

Contrary to the popular assumption that films are more often viewed by illiterates than the educated people, it was found that the exposure to the medium was highest among those who had college-level education and minimum among the illiterates. The data indicate direct relationship between frequency of viewing of films and the educational level of the respondents.

Occupationwise it was found that while white-collar workers and traders have better chances of exposure, with at least one-third in the category seeing the films rarely, if not frequently. In the case of farmers and labourers the exposure was limited to 30 and 12 per cent respectively.

(a) *Reasons for Lack of Exposure*

In the sample only 7 out of 250 reported viewing of films on a frequent basis. The rest 243 were either non-viewers, or occasional viewers. The reasons for their non-viewing or infrequent viewing were ascertained and presented in Table 6.10.

TABLE 6.10: Reasons for lack of frequent exposure to films

| Reason | Narayan Gavhan | Narodi | Amondi | Taleg-har | Rajpur | All villages | |
|---|---|---|---|---|---|---|---|
| | % | % | % | % | % | N | % |
| Relevant sample | 49 | 95 | 54 | 20 | 25 | 243 | 100.0 |
| No facility | 34.8 | 23.2 | 38.9 | 60.0 | 68.0 | 89 | 36.6 |
| No interest | 36.7 | 36.8 | 13.0 | 25.0 | 12.0 | 68 | 28.0 |
| Poverty | 16.3 | 15.8 | 27.8 | 5.0 | 12.0 | 42 | 17.3 |
| No time | 10.2 | 22.1 | 11.1 | 5.0 | - | 33 | 13.6 |
| Old age, etc. | 2.0 | 2.1 | 9.2 | 5.0 | 8.0 | 11 | 4.5 |

The data reveal that the main inhibiting factor for the unsatisfactory exposure is the poor screening facilities. The distance from the cinema hall is found to be one of the basic factors. Related to this is the problem of communications. In Amondi village, which is located at a distance of 20 km from the cinema hall, one-half reported that they never find it convenient to see films because of problems like crossing the river, etc.

On the whole while nearly 37 per cent gave lack of facilities as the main reason for their non-going/rare going to the movies, lack of interest was cited by 28 per cent. Most of the persons in the latter category happened to be illiterate. Only 17 per cent stated poverty as the reason and most of them were found to be struggling for survival.

(b) *Selection of Films*

All the 76 respondents who reported exposure to films sometime or the other were asked to indicate the type of films they normally feel like seeing. The response indicates that 55 per cent have no selection, they watch any film when they happen to go to the town. Particularly women do not seem to have any choice. Of the rest 45 per cent, while 25 per cent indicated preference for social films, 20 per cent indicated liking for mythological and historical films.

Languagewise the first preference was for Marathi, followed by a small proportion for Hindi films. Those who expressed liking for Hindi films wee mostly persons with urban influence, working at Bombay or reading in colleges.

It was revealed in the discussions that films mean only commercial cinema to most of the villagers. The apparent reasons is the negligible reach of short films with development messages sponsored by Government agencies. Except three-four respondents from Narodi who had seen a film on animal husbandry during a cattle fair, others could not recall having seen any short film in their village. Short films exhibited in cinema halls were mostly taken as advertisement/newsreel programmes and only a negligible proportion could recall the topics.

**Exposure to Personal Media**

(a) *Contacts with Urban Area*

With a view to finding the villagers' exposure to urban influences the respondents were asked to indicate how often they visit the district town or the nearby city (or in the absence of it the nearby market centre). The response is presented in Table 6.11.

TABLE 6.11: Contacts with Urban Area

| Frequency of contact | Narayan Gavhan | Narodi | Amondi har | Taleg- | Rajpur | All villages | |
|---|---|---|---|---|---|---|---|
| | % | % | % | % | % | N | % |
| Frequently (at least once a month | 42.0 | 70.0 | 25.5 | 15.0 | 20.0 | 113 | 45.2 |
| Occasionally (at least once in 3 months) | 20.0 | 11.0 | 21.8 | 10.0 | - | 35 | 14.0 |
| Rarely (at least once a year) | 20.0 | 9.0 | 10.9 | 25.0 | 16.0 | 34 | 13.6 |
| Never | 18.0 | 10.0 | 41.8 | 50.0 | 64.0 | 68 | 27.2 |
| Total | 50 | 100 | 55 | 20 | 25 | 250 | 100.0 |

The data suggest that on an average one-fourth of the villagers do not have any contact with urban area. Majority of those who maintain contact however, visit the urban centres "frequently", which, according to village norms, is explained as at least once a month.

Among the five selected villages, maximum exposure was noticed at Narodi from where many people regularly go Bombay for work and remain in touch with the village. As many as 70 per cent of the respondents in this village reported frequent visits to either Pune or Bombay cities. In contrast minimal interaction was noticed in Rajpur, located in the interior tribal belt, where as many as two-thirds had no contact with any town.

Further analysis of the persons who maintained frequent contacts with the urban centres and also of those who had no exposure whatsoever was attempted to have a profile of the two categories. Data presented in Appendix Table 5 suggest that the people having maximum exposure fall under the categories mentioned below:

- males
- those who are above 45 years of age
- those who have at least high school education
- those who are either traders or are engaged in traditional occupations or white-collar workers

Those who have no exposure to urban area are mostly from the categories of:

- females
- persons below 30 years of age
- illiterates
- labourers

Among the cultivator category, exposure to urban centres was noticed to be quite substantial, with as many as one-half visiting the town or market centre frequently on some work or the other.

(b) *Contacts with Block Headquarters*

Narodi and Amondi villages drawn from the Ambegaon Panchayat Samiti are located with 8 km from their Block Headquarters at Ghodegaon. Regular bus service between Narodi and Ghodegaon being available, exposure to Block-level staff was found to be very high. Data presented in Table 6.12 reveal that as many as 70 per cent of the respondents from Narodi frequently visit the Block Headquarters. But, most of these visits are for marketing purposes. However, informal meetings with Block officials and non-officials during those visits were said to be quite frequent.

TABLE 6.12: Contacts with block headquarters

| Frequency of contact | Narayan Gavhan | Narodi | Amondi | Taleg-har | Rajpur | All villages | |
|---|---|---|---|---|---|---|---|
| | % | % | % | % | % | N | % |
| Frequently | 28.0 | 71.0 | 85.5 | 40.0 | 32.0 | 148 | 59.2 |
| Occasionally | 44.0 | 6.0 | 3.6 | 10.0 | 16.0 | 36 | 14.4 |
| Rarely | 6.0 | 8.0 | 1.8 | 20.0 | 16.0 | 20 | 8.0 |
| Never | 22.0 | 15.0 | 9.1 | 30.0 | 36.0 | 46 | 18.4 |
| Total | 50 | 100 | 55 | 20 | 25 | 250 | 100.0 |

Amondi is situated very near to Ghodegaon right across the river. During fair weather there is frequent interaction between the village and Block Headquarters, which serves as their main marketing place. A large proportion of the people walk daily or go on cycle if the water level is low in the river.

In the case of interior tribal villages, Taleghar and Rajpur, the data reveal that a substantial proportion (nearly 30-35 per cent) never maintain contact with the Block Headquarters due to the long distance even though bus facilities are available. Their market needs are mostly served by the weekly market at Ambegaon. As such, the tribals do not feel the need to visit the Block Headquarters. Those who go out from the village to Ghodegaon were found to be either Gram Panchayat members or village functionaries.

Narayan Gavhan has a unique position. It comes under the administrative control of the Block office located at Parner, 16 kms away. But Shirur town, which is only 10 kms, away also happens to be another Block Headquarters (within Pune district). Hence, most of the people from Narayan Gavhan find it convenient to go to Shirur instead of Parner, except for some administrative work in the Block/Taluka office. Hence, the interaction of the people with the Block Headquarters was found to be meagre, with less than 30 per cent reporting frequent contacts.

Data presented in Appendix Table 6 suggest that the most frequent visitors to the Block Headquarters are farmers. Obviously they go for acquiring seeds, fertilizers, etc. Since these responsibilities are mostly taken by elderly males in the household, the exposure of females and youngsters to the Block Headquarters is practically nil. Another observation is that the interaction is not influenced by education, but is basically dependent on the occupation of the person.

(c) *Contacts with the Village Level Worker*

All the five villages happen to be VLW headquarters and the Gram Sewaks were expected to stay there. But, in reality, except for Narayan Gavhan, in the other four villages the incumbents were found to be staying elsewhere.

The person posted in Narayan Gavhan has a house in the village. But his relations with the Sarpanch and other villagers being cold (if not strained), he avoids staying in the village as often as possible. When he is in the village, he keeps busy with record work and maintains a distance with the villagers. The data presented in Table 6.13 reveal that 62 per cent of the respondents have no interaction with the VLW.

The VLW posted in Narodi was staying at his native place 4 kms away from the village. The commutes daily on bicycle. Though he has to his credit awards as the best Gram Sewak in the Block, his

TABLE 6.13: Contacts with the Village Level Workers

| Frequency of contact | Narayan Gavhan % | Narodi % | Amondi % | Taleg-har % | Rajpur % | All villages N | All villages % |
|---|---|---|---|---|---|---|---|
| Frequently | 18.0 | 19.0 | 20.0 | 60.0 | 16.0 | 55 | 22.0 |
| Occasionally | 6.0 | 15.0 | 9.0 | 5.0 | 4.0 | 25 | 10.0 |
| Rarely | 14.0 | 2.0 | - | - | 4.0 | 10 | 4.0 |
| Never | 62.0 | 64.0 | 71.0 | 35.0 | 76.0 | 160 | 64.0 |
| Total | 50 | 100 | 55 | 20 | 25 | 250 | 100.0 |

interactions were found to be mostly confined to those who have land with irrigation facilities and who use improved seeds, fertilizers and pesticides. His contacts with people in the scattered hamlets, particularly the Mahadeo Koli tribals, were found to be very rare, as he seldom visited them for purposes like collection of house tax, etc. On the whole only one-third of the respondents from the village reported some interaction with the VLW and the rest two-thirds have no contact whatsoever.

In Amondi the Gram Sewak was found to be staying at Ghodegaon and came daily on cycle. He admitted that during the monsoon months his visits became irregular because of poor communication facilities. Even otherwise, his interest and knowledge of agriculture were reported to be limited. His interaction with the poor farmers, particularly the tribals, was found to be rare as he seldom visits their hamlets. It was not surprising, therefore, that 70 per cent reported no contact with the VLW in the village.

The Gram Sewak posted in Taleghar has not been provided with any accommodation even though it comes under tribal area. As such, he stays at his native place and commutes daily by bus. His relations with the residents of the village were, however, found to be very cordial, with as many as 60 per cent reporting regular contact with him.

The VLW posted in Rajpur hails from Narodi village which lies 40 kms away. His relations with the Sarpanch and other villagers were found to be very strained and, therefore, he avoids staying in the village as much as possible. The tribals were found to have very little faith in him as a development worker. There were many complaints and the Sarpanch was found to be very serious about his transfer from the village on grounds that he does not take interest in the development work. On the other hand, the VLW complained of group rivalries in the village and lack of interest among Panchayat members in village improvement. Nearly 80 per cent of the respondents in the village reported no interaction with the VLW. Practically his contacts were nil in the hamlets. Only the Gram Panchayat members and teachers maintain some contact with him. Otherwise, he was found to be hardly known in the village.

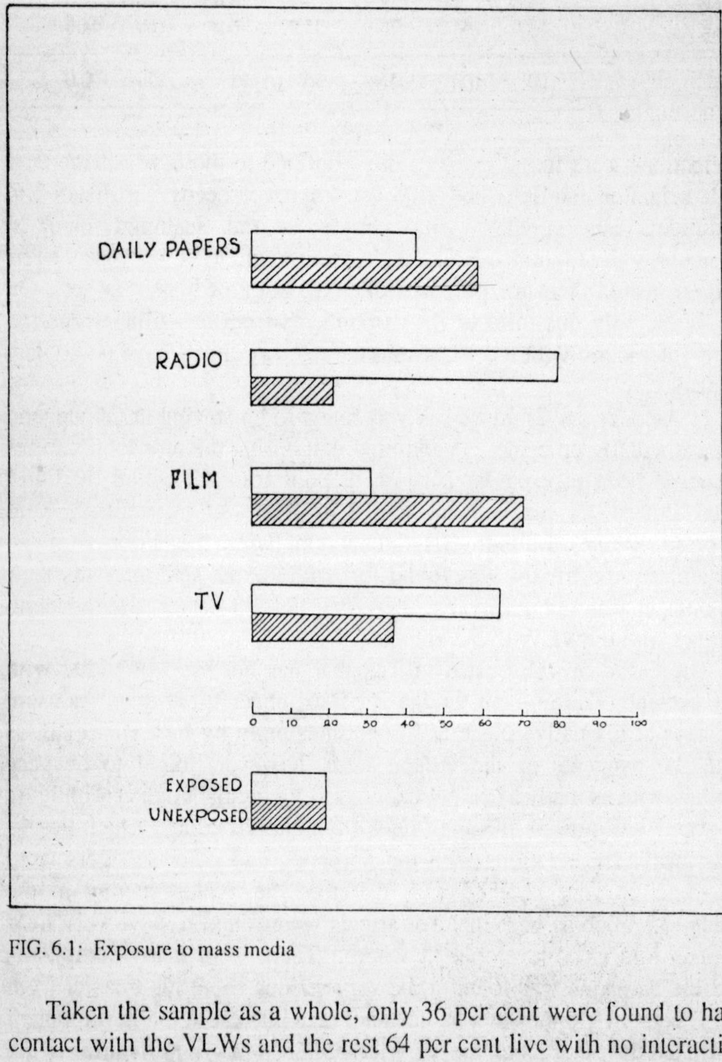


FIG. 6.1: Exposure to mass media

Taken the sample as a whole, only 36 per cent were found to have contact with the VLWs and the rest 64 per cent live with no interaction with him. Regular contact with VLWs was observed onl· ·he case of about one-fifth of the respondents. Data analysed in Appendix Table 7 suggest that these persons belong mostly to the following categories:

— males
— those who are above 45 years of age
— educated at least up to primary level
— farmers and white-collar workers.

As many as 80 per cent of the females, illiterates and labourers have no interaction with the VLW. Similarly, his contact with persons in occupations like trade, traditional service, etc., was found to be nominal.

**Exposure to Television**

(a) *Frequency of viewing*

The community viewing sets were installed in Narayan Gavhan and Narodi villages four years back during 1974-75. In the tribal villages – Amondi, Taleghar and Rajpur — the sets were installed under the Tribal sub-plan scheme during 1977-78.

In spite of the structural differences in location, their distinctive socio-economic characteristics and the consequential variations in exposure to other media, no wide variance was noticed in the pattern of exposure to television in the selected villages. The data indicate that despite availability of the community TV, only two-thirds avail of the viewing facility with some regularity. While approximately one-third of the respondents reported watching TV frequently, i.e. at least once a week, another one-third constituted occasional or rare viewers and the remaining one-third were found to be non-viewers.

Diagramatically the frequency of TV viewing is represented in 6.2.

In Table 6.14 villagewise data regarding frequency of TV viewing is indicated.

For a comparative analysis the findings of the studies conducted by the ISRO and Planning Commission during the Satellite Instructional Television Experiment (SITE) are presented in Table 6.15. It may be noted that in the ISRO studies non-viewers were not shown separately. Their operational definition of rare viewing included non-viewers as well as those who watched TV less than once a month.

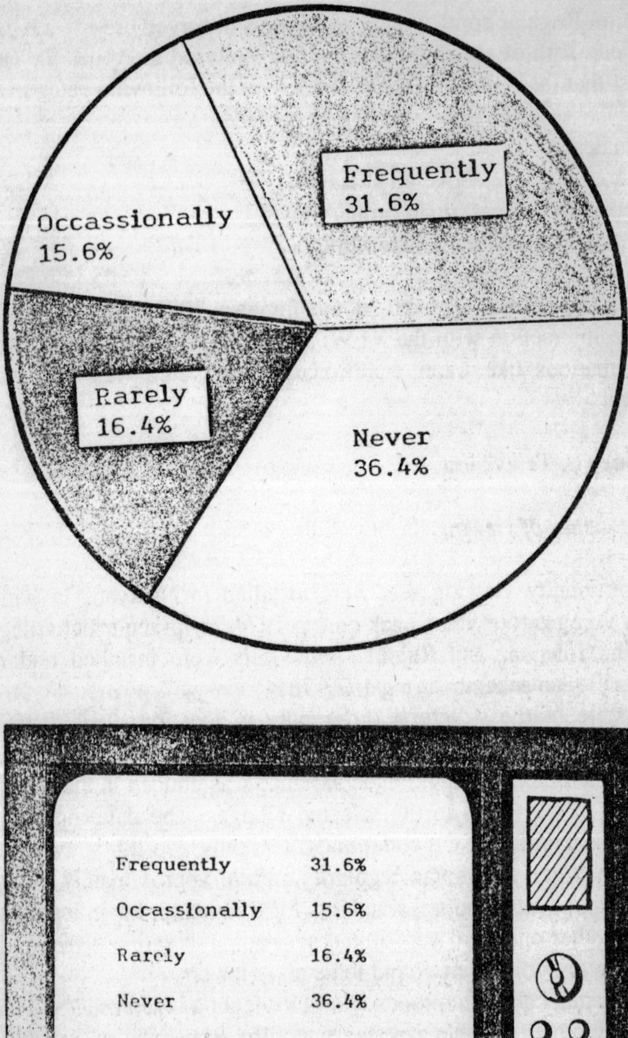


FIG 6.2: Frequency of TV Viewing

TABLE 6.14: Frequency of TV Viewing

| Frequency of TV viewing | Narayan Gayhan | Narodi | Amondi | Taleg-har | Rajpur | All villages | |
|---|---|---|---|---|---|---|---|
| | % | % | % | % | % | N | % |
| Frequently (at lest once a week) | 42.0 | 31.0 | 27.3 | 30.0 | 24.0 | 79 | 31.6 |
| Occasionally (2-3 times a month) | 14.0 | 8.0 | 27.3 | 25.0 | 16.0 | 39 | 15.6 |
| Rarely (once a month or so) | 10.0 | 21.0 | 14.5 | 20.0 | 12.0 | 41 | 16.4 |
| Never | 34.0 | 40.0 | 30.9 | 25.0 | 48.0 | 91 | 36.4 |
| Total | 50 | 100 | 55 | 20 | 25 | 250 | 100.0 |

TABLE 6.15: Regularity of TV viewing during SITE

| As reported by ISRO | Per cent | As reported by Planning Commission | Per cent |
|---|---|---|---|
| Rare viewers (not even once a month) | 37.8 | Do not watch TV | 40.8 |
| Occasional viewers (1-3 times a month) | 41.9 | Less than once a week | 15.6 |
| | | Once or twice a week | 25.8 |
| Frequent viewers (4 times or more a month) | 20.3 | Three or four times a week | 9.1 |
| | | More frequently | 8.7 |

Source: Agarwal, Binod.C, SITE Social Evaluation: Results and Research Experiences, Paper read at the Evaluation and Planning Workshop for Satellite Communication Research, Honolulu, Hawaii, July 15-28, 1979.

## Frequency of TV Viewing by Different Socio-economic Characteristics

With a view to finding the variation in the pattern of exposure and non-exposure to TV, the data on frequency of viewing were analysed by different socio-economic variables. The responses presented in Appendix Table 8 are summarized below:

*(a) By Sex:* The extent of non-exposure among females was observed to be two times higher than that among the males. While as many as one-half of the females never get exposed to TV for one reason or the other, only one-fourth of the males reported non-viewing. Due to constraints like family responsibilities and

social inhibitions not more than one-fifth of the females were observed to get frequent exposure. On the other hand, among the males nearly two-fifths could watch TV frequently.

*(b) By education:* It is generally assumed that television can cut across the literacy barrier and reach the illiterates effectively because of the visual stimuli. But the data support the theory that TV viewing is equally dependent on education as has been found in the case of print and broadcasting media. Among the illiterates the usage of the medium was restricted to 40 per cent and the remaining 60 per cent remained unexposed due to some reason or the other. In contrast six out of seven respondents with college education were found to be frequent TV watchers. The $\chi^2$-test reveals that TV viewing is highly dependent on literacy.[2]

*(c) By occupation*: Comparatively more frequent viewing was noticed among white-collar workers, dependents and those pursing trade and traditional occupations than labourers and cultivators. The least exposed were the labourers among them only one-fifth reported frequent viewing and nearly two-fifths constituted non-viewers.

*(d) Social status*: Tribals and non-harijans were found to receive less exposure than Harijans as a group. Among the tribals as many as 40 per cent never watched TV and frequent viewing was restricted to 22 per cent. Among the Harijans, on the other hand, nearly 45 per cent were noticed to watch TV frequently and among non-Harijans it was limited to 35 per cent. One reason for relatively more exposure to TV among Harijans as compared to tribals could be the location of tribal hamlets far removed from the main habitations (in the non-tribal villages) where the TV sets were located.

*(e) Economic status*: One of the noteworthy findings of this analysis was the lack of any variation in the frequency of viewing according to the levels of living. The $x^2$-test indicated that TV viewing is independent of the economic status of the viewers.[3]

*(f) Distance from TV*: One of the important determinants of the frequency of TV viewing was found to be the distance from the place of residence to the place where the community TV is located. If the TV set is within a half a kilometer from residence, more frequent TV viewing was observed. Any distance beyond one kilometer was found to be certainly an inhibiting factor. In the sample there were 108 persons residing within a kilometer distance

and of them as many as one-half reported frequent viewing, with non-viewing confined to 20 per cent. But, among persons whose houses were located beyond one kilometre, frequent viewing was limited to 16-17 per cent and non-viewing was as high as 50 per cent.

## Reasons for Occasional or Non-viewing of TV

Persons watching TV less than once a week and those who never get exposed to TV were asked to indicate the main reason for not making use of the medium frequently when it was available in the village. The response presented in Table 6.16 suggests that the most important limiting factor is the distance.

TABLE 6.16: Reasons for occasional/non-viewing of TV

| Reason | | Per cent N = 171 |
|---|---|---|
| Distance | .. | 46.8 |
| No time | .. | 24.6 |
| No interest | .. | 12.9 |
| Old age, eye sight, etc. | .. | 9.9 |
| Social constraints (widowhood, etc.) | .. | 3.5 |

One out of every four gave lack of time as the reason for not being able to watch TV more frequently. This was particularly observed to be relevant with house-wives who had no other female member to take care of the children and responsibilities like cooking in the house. Similarly males who had to look after the cattle in the evening often missed the programmes.

Lack of interest in TV was expressed by only 13 per cent and most of them were found to be illiterates past the middle age. Physical disabilities like old age, eye sight etc. prevented another 10 per cent from getting the exposure to TV. One encouraging observation was the negligible proportion of less than four per cent who came out with social constraints like, "husband does not allow". "being a widow does not feel like going out" and it does not look nice sitting with village elders watching" etc. Among the Harijans none except one educated school teacher expressed any reservations for going and watching TV in a public place. Thus, community TV viewing appears to have otherwise got established as an accepted norm in the villages. The reasons for lack of high utilization are something other than the problem of shared viewing.

## Leap-frogging to TV

Studies during SITE by ISRO revealed that about one-fourth of the villagers who had no exposure to any other mass media – print, radio, film could directly make use of TV. These persons were regarded as first-generation media participants and their participation in TV was viewed as "leap-frogging" over other conventional media (Agrawal *et al*: 1977).

In the five selected villages the data were analysed with a view to testing this phenomenon. It was observed that in non-tribal villages, where there is good exposure to communications like roads, buses, media, etc., there are hardly any first-generation media participants. In the tribal villages, however, the percentage of those having exposure to no other mass media except television varied between 8 to 25 per cent.

On the basis of the data presented in Table 6.17 three broad inferences could be drawn:

1. Leap-frogging to TV, cutting across other mass media cannot be assumed in villages which are otherwise exposed to literary and sound broadcasting.
2. In tribal and semi-tribal villages leap-frogging may be expected to a limited extent of 15-20 per cent among males. It would be marginal among females.
3. Most of those who are untouched by print or radio continue to remain untouched by TV medium also.

TABLE 6.17: First-generation media participants

| Village | Percentage of first generation media participants | | |
|---|---|---|---|
| | Males | Females | Total |
| Narayan Gavhan | Nil | Nil | Nil |
| Narodi | 4.5 | 3.1 | 2.0 |
| Amondi | 18.9 | 5.5 | 14.5 |
| Taleghar | 30.0 | 20.0 | 25.0 |
| Rajpur | 14.3 | Nil | 8.0 |
| Total | 8.0 | 4.5 | 6.8 |

## Clustering of Media

As has been stated earlier, one of the important observations was about the increase in TV exposure with the increase in education. Media participation was found to be less among illiterates and increased with the increase in education.

With a view to assessing the association between the exposure to TV and participation in other media, the frequency of TV viewing was analysed according to newspaper regarding and radio listening.

The data presented in Table 6.18 support the general hypotheses of "clustering of media exposure". The more the TV viewing, the more was the paper reading and radio-listening. The lesser the participation in TV, the minimal was the utilisation of print and sound media.

TABLE 6.18: Frequency of TV Viewing According to Exposure to Newspaper and Radio

| Regularity of TV viewing | N | Paper reading | | | | Radio listening | | | |
|---|---|---|---|---|---|---|---|---|---|
| | | Regular | Sometimes | Rarely | Never | Frequently | Occasionally | Seldom | Never |
| Frequently | 79 | 36.7 | 17.7 | 18.9 | 26.6 | 51.9 | 36.7 | 7.6 | 3.8 |
| Occasionally | 39 | 7.7 | 10.3 | 17.9 | 64.1 | 28.2 | 28.2 | 20.5 | 23.1 |
| Rarely | 41 | 7.3 | 17.1 | 12.2 | 63.4 | 39.0 | 22.0 | 24.4 | 14.6 |
| Never | 91 | 5.5 | 9.9 | 4.4 | 80.2 | 26.6 | 13.2 | 20.9 | 37.6 |

Prakash M. Shingi and Bella Mody (1974), who studied the Krishi Darshan experiment in Delhi to find out the persons gaining most from television, similarly noticed that the better educated farmer who was highly exposed to Press, radio and change-agents was the most frequent TV viewer. The exposure to one medium was highly related to exposure to other media. The data presented in Table 6.18 support their observation that utilization of TV would be high among those who are otherwise more exposed to informational channels like radio and newspapers than the media "have-not".

NOTES

1. UNESCO sponsored a Pilot Project on Radio Rural Forums in 1956 and the successful completion of the Project and its encouraging results prompted AIR to

sponsor Radio Rural Forums from other Stations in 1959.

2. The calculated value of $\chi^2$ is 32.95 and the tabulated value at 1 per cent level of significance is 6.65, for one degree of freedom.
3. The calculated value of $\chi^2$ is 1.79 and the tabulated value at 5 per cent level of significance is 9.49, for 4 degrees of freedom.

# 7

# MEETING THE INFORMATION NEEDS

IN THE preceding chapter the analysis was devoted to the assessment of the status of Television, especially in terms of the villagers' exposure to the medium *vis-a-vis* other mass media and personal channels. Continuing this discussion, it is attempted here to analyse the role performance of TV as a communication-aid for rural development. The essential pre-requisite for such an exercise is a broad comprehension of the information needs of the potential audience. For no medium can ever respond unless it identifies the areas in which it can meet the demands.

The basic requirement for survival has been described in a wide variety of terms such as needs, wants, impulses, instincts and drives. In simple terms a need in explained as something lacking or deficient in the individual (Bhatia: 1970). According to Litwin and Stringer, the terms "need" and "want" suggest a lack of something, the attainment of which gives satisfaction (Litwin and Stringer: 1968). David Krech and others explained that "a positive want (e.g. a desire) is an assumed force which impels a person towards the achievement of a goal. A negative want (e.g. anxiety) is a force which repels a person from certain objects or conditions. Common synonyms for positive wants are drives, needs, for negative wants fears, aversions (Krech et al: 1962).

Anthropologists consider culture not merely as a set of stereotyped traditional human reactions, but is terms of its instrumental function in satisfying the needs of man as a highly integrated types of organism. Piddington, basing on Malinowski's need doctrine, classified human needs into three categories: 1. Primary, 2. Derived and 3. Integrative. The primary needs include the biological needs which man shares with animals, like food, rest, defence against bodily injury, protection against climate, sex, reproduction, etc. The Derived needs are socio-genic like the conditioning of the young and socialization process, communication, material satisfaction, social control, leadership etc. The Integrative needs include the expression of collective unity and feeling of confidence, and the aesthetic expression and recreation, etc. (Piddington, 1952).

When a need is felt, the individual is stimulated to respond. Needs generate tension and the individual makes as attempt to remove the tension. This response is described by the psychologists in terms of drive, urge or motive. In the words of Gardner Murphy, motives or drives do not exist for themselves. "The drive or motive is the first step in a cycle of activity or adjustment which leads, if successful, to some reward or goal. The cycle consists of need-tension, followed by effort or striving toward a rewarding goal" (Gardner: 1954). It is imperative that media committed to development goals should provide impetus to generate adequate drive and motivation in the people to develop.

Psychologist A.H. Maslow postulated the theory of specific order of development of needs. He proposed that the needs of man develop in the following sequential order, from "lower" needs to "higher" needs (Maslow: 1954).

1. Physiological needs – hunger, thirst, sex and physical activity
2. Safety needs – security from physical and mental deprivation
3. Belongingness and love needs – affection and identification
4. Esteem needs – prestige, success and self-respect
5. The Need for self-actualization – the desire for self-fulfilment.

Maslow argued that unless the lower need is adequately satisfied the higher need does not emerge in the development of the individual.

According to sociologist Kimball Young, the first-level imperatives (first-order needs) are related to sustenance, sexual demands and protection from physical danger. The second-level motives are those of mastery or power and belongingness. And at the third level are those which grow out of intellectual processes (Young: 1957). Unless the lower order motives are satisfied the higher ones are not effective.

The physiological needs like hunger, thirst and sex are universal and are vital for one's existence. If a person is hungry his goal is to eat. Hence, the individual struggling for survival is conditioned to think only in terms of acquiring some food. Before the fulfilment of this need, it is unlikely that he would feel the urge to seek realization of any other sociogenic need. Holmberg who made a study of the Sirino society, a semi-nomadic Bolivian Indian group, observed that the "man who must grub for food cannot want and seek beauty and intellectual understanding" (Holmberg: 1950). Implied in this argument is that needs related to sustenance of the individual assume top priority in the goal hierarchy. As Gandhiji had rightly remarked that for the millions who have to go without two meals a day, the only acceptable form in which God dare appear is food.

Most of the many needs of the individual are inactive or latent. If the environment is an impoverished one, with very few goal objects available, fewer wants will be triggered off. Wants are aroused with growing aspirations particularly in situations created due to interaction with external sources.

Identification and prioritization of needs was found to be a very complex exercise, because needs are not only multi-dimensional but also vary at different levels and in different contexts. The needs at the village level were found to be of a different order from the needs at the individual, family or community levels. Methodologically, it was considered to be more appropriate to describe the needs in qualitative terms than in quantitative terms. The case study method was, therefore, adopted for presenting a pen picture of the potential TV users and their needs.

## Specific Needs of Individuals

In a broader sense people in the Pune region belong to a distinct culture-area, and share the so-called "western Maharashtra culture". However, Western Maharashtra is only a geographical region, representing a conglomeration of micro-cultural entities, the individual communities. As members of a social group, each community represents a different spectrum of informational needs. Hence, the dominant Maratha peasants and the landless Harijan Mhangs (or neo-Buddhists) who are economically dependent on the former cannot be treated on a par as far as the development needs are concerned. Similar is the case with the tribals. The land-owning progressive Mahadeo Kolis have hardly anything in common with the most underdeveloped nomadic Katkaris, except that both are listed as Scheduled Tribes. Unless their cultural nuances are understood it may be difficult to appreciate the informational needs, specific to each community. Hence, in the following paragraphs the life pattern of each of the major communities is presented with focus on their communication gaps.

(a) *Marathas*: They are the numerically strong peasant community ranking next only to Brahmins in the social hierarchy. As land owners with social status, they are the most assertive and vocal group in the region. Unlike the Brahmins, who are generally the absentee landlords, the Marathas are mostly independent cultivators, keeping the land under their own plough. As farmers they are hard-working and have a zeal to produce more and go up in the economic ladder. Their womenfolk have no inhibitions and there are no social sanctions against working in the fields. As such, except from the rich and aristocratic families, women from the middle and upper middle class families come freely to assist the menfolk in agricultural operations. However, those who have more than marginal holdings depend on farm labourers drawn from castes below in the social order. Frictions with these communities are, therefore, inevitable.

The well-off sections of the Marathas generally remain in joint families to pool up manpower and material resources. Enterprising persons from such families mostly emerge as progressive farmers. With economic power and access to education, these progressive farmers generally assume the role of public opinion leaders in politics and administration. As such, the common aspiration of a typical Maratha farmer is to acquire as much land as possible, work hard, become a resourceful cultivator, provide education to his children, assert as a leader and earn a place of esteem in society.

The interaction of the community with others (whether it is service castes or Harijans) is commanding and domineering. The communication flow is, therefore, one-way with the socially under-privileged groups below reluctantly accepting the authoritative role of the Marathas.

(b) *Malis*: These are the minority peasant community, ranking below the Marathas in social hierarchy. Most of them are small and marginal farmers with only a few rich families. These are the farmers who have come up in competition with the Marathas. Traditionally the Malis are fruit and vegetable cultivators and sellers. Responding to the increasing demand for fruits, vegetables and flowers, many of them have taken to intensive cultivation of these commercial crops and have been quite successful in earning profits, as producers as well as traders. The landless in the community generally migrate to Pune/Bombay cities as fruit and vegetable vendors. Only a small proportion remain in the villages as agricultural labourers.

Malis and Marathas have no traditional rivalry. But they generally live in separate hamlets. If with an improved economic position the Malis claim an equivalent social status with the Marathas, the latter get obviously irritated and treat them badly. Being in a minority, the Malis, therefore, avoid any confrontation with the Marathas. At the same time they join hands with them to resist any move by the Harijans to assert their rights and privileges.

(c) *Service castes*: Grouped under this category are communities like *Sutar* (carpenter/blacksmith), *Nhavi* (barber), *Dhobi* (washerman) and *Kumbhar* (potter). Numerically they are a minority with not more than two or three families from each caste in the village. They are mostly landless but as skilled artisans they earn fairly well. As they are normally initiated into their respective trades at a very early age, most of them are either illiterates or school drop-outs.

Despite their economic independence, they remain under the thumb of the dominating castes – the Marathas or the Malis – as functional groups. Due to little education and social backwardness, they do not have much initiative to go up in the economic ladder. In general it may be said that the aspiration of the service castes is to acquire some land, lease it out if they cannot manage independently, pursue the traditional occupation and lead a care-free life. It there is no demand for the traditional occupation in the village, they invariably migrate to the nearby urban areas to earn a living. Unlike the Marathas and Malis, these communities have a tendency to invest liberally on material goods. They have frequent interaction with people and their exposure to urban influence is also comparatively more, as they move out quite frequently in pursuit of their trade.

(d) *Harijans*: Included in this category are Mangs, Chambhars and Mahars (Neo-Buddhists), who are at the bottom of the social hierarchy. As outcastes (untouchables) they live in separate hamlets away from the main habitation.

Mangs have the traditional occupation of making and selling ropes used for domestic and agricultural purposes. These ropes are made of the fibre of a plant grown in the forest areas. The raw material is not available easily and the technology is very primitive and time-consuming. As such, many of them switch over to agricultural labour, with only one or two in the family pursuing the traditional occupation. Mangs are also traditional drum beaters and musicians, but many of them have given up the art due to lack of demand.

Chambhars are traditionally cobblers. Due to poor workmanship and traditional technology, there is not much demand for their services. Hence, most of them enter the labour force as agricultural and non-agricultural wage earners.

Neo-Buddhists are converts from Mahar communities. Yet they are equally subject to the social disabilities as the non-converts. Due to the advantage of enlightened leadership and some education, they have been able to organize themselves better than other Scheduled Caste communities. As they are more vocal they usually take the lead in asserting the privileges of "weaker sections".

*Adivasis*: There are three tribal communities, all of whom are referred to by the generic name – Adivasis, the aboriginals. Although they are at varying levels of socio-economic development, they are all treated alike for extending special benefits under the Government-sponsored welfare schemes.

(a) *Mahadeo-Kolis*: They are the numerically strong tribal community inhabiting the higher altitudes (above 3,000 ft.) of the Sahyadri mountain range. Most of them possess lands and cultivate minor millets and rice on hill slopes and valleys. But their methods of cultivation are very primitive and consequently the yield levels are poor. Hardly anyone among them uses fertilizers and pesticides. One of their main sources of income is collection of minor forest produce, including Hirada – a fruit having medicinal value and good market.

Mahadeo Kolis have assimilated the socio-economic life pattern of the non-tribal peasant communities and worship Hindu Gods. Their presiding deity is Bhimashankar, whose temple is the most revered pilgrim centre for the local non-tribals. Mahadeo Kolis do not show any signs of primitiveness except illiteracy and ignorance. As an acculturated tribe, they enjoy better social status than the other two communities – Thakkars and Katkaris.

Those who have education find jobs locally as school teachers, forest guards and simultaneously pursue agriculture. There are a few rich families with higher education and these are highly influential and assertive in local polities. Being a single-cropped area most of them, however, remain unemployed for a major part of the year. Agricultural labour and forest work do not keep them busy throughout. There are no small-scale industries to provide them work.

One of the major problems the community faces is acute shortage of drinking water during the summer months due to inadequate perennial sources of water. Thus people collect water from whatever source available and in turn suffer from many water-borne diseases.

(b) *Thakkars*: The community lives normally in the foot-hills and most of them have no cultivated lands. Generally they eke out a living as wood-cutters and agricultural labourers. Some of them resort to the harmful method of shifting cultivation on the hill slopes by cutting the trees to grow millets and groundnuts. Most of them, however, supplement their incomes by rearing cattle and goats. But there is no organized dairy-farming, goat-rearing or poultry-keeping.

As a community, Thakkars are hard-working and sincere. The big land owners from the plains entrust their lands for share cropping to some of them. Thus, with their multifarious activities, they manage to earn a living. However, taking advantage of their simplicity, illiteracy and timid nature, traders, money-lenders, liquor vendors shop-keepers and landlords exploit them by underpayment, high rate of interest on loans and low wages.

(c) *Katkaris*: They are the most backward and the poorest tribal community in Maharashtra. Their original habitation is Konkan but as a wandering tribe they migrate to the tribal areas of Ambegaon, Khed and Junner talukas, crossing the hills on foot, in search of subsistence. They live in temporary grass huts, mostly on river banks, as their principal occupation is fishing. But, they do not use any nets. While the womenfolk hold a piece of cloth dipped in water, the males push a rope tied with stones towards the women, driving the fish into the cloth. As the method is primitive, the catch is very meagre and earnings are small. Occasionally they resort to petty larceny. Most of them are addicted to heavy drinking, particularly the cheap french polish.

As a community, the Katkaris are notorious as "criminals" in the region. The local non-tribals never trust them and do not invite them for agricultural labour. As far as possible they shun any interaction with them. However, taking advantage of the Katkaris' addiction to easy life, they exploit them fully. Particularly, many of the Katkari girls fall a prey to the local non-tribals and resort to prostitution. As such, many in the tribe suffer from sexually transmitted diseases (STD) and other contagious diseases.

Due to abject poverty and nomadic habits, hardly anybody is educated in the community. Their families are highly disorganised and children miss parental care. From the childhood they organize themselves into small groups for petty thieving and end up as delinquents. One of the most urgent needs is to find some gainful occupation for the adult members of the community and slowly wean them away from the nomadic and criminal habits.

Having presented an overall view of the major communities and their cultural background, it is proposed to give a few cases of the individuals, drawn to represent a cross-section of the communities covered above. The objective is to provide an idea of the needs linked to the socio-economic and educational level of the individuals for their ability to respond to the television medium.

**Case 1**
**Yashwant Vithal Bidve**

A 34-year-old Maratha farmer from a joint family. Educated only up to class II, he took up employment as a worker in a small factory in Bombay producing sweets while his family was engaged in agriculture in the village. Later, he persuaded his father to sell off their four acres of dry land and start a factory of their own for making sweets at the nearby Manchar town. The factory so established gave them good returns and the family was able to diversify its business by establishing two grocery shops, one in the village and another at Manchar, which are looked after by his brothers. Availing of a bank loan, they got an electric motor and installed it for dual purposes for running a flour mill as well as lift irrigation. The family has built a house at Manchar and purchased a car for running a taxi service. The income from business is invested in the purchase of land, pumps and other agricultural inputs. They possess about 10 acres of irrigated land and 5-6 acres of dry land. As a rich family, they wield considerable influence in local politics.

**Case 2**
**Indubai Tukaram Kather**

An illiterate Maratha housewife aged 45 years. Her family owns 20 acres of unirrigated land and a large number of cattle. One of her sons is educated and has a white-collar job in Pune city. Her daughter-in-law who is uneducated stays mostly in the village. Indubai is very happy for having fixed the marriage of her youngest daughter also, who is 11 years old and reading in the primary school. She does not know the law prohibiting marriage of girls below 18 years. Her husband knows about it but is not bothered, because the mother is anxious to solemnize the marriage as soon as possible.

**Case 3**
**Bhikaji Shripat Hule**

A 24-year-old Maratha youth from the progressive family owning five acres of irrigated land. His parents sent him to the agricultural college. While he was in the final year (B.Sc.), he discontinued his studies and came back to the village to help his parents in modern methods of farming. He attended a training camp in dairy farming organized by the National Dairy Development Corporation at Anand at his father's suggestion. Afterwards, they tried for a bank loan and got Rs.16,000 for starting a dairy of their own in the village with five Jersey cows. He regularly listens to the radio and reads farm magazines for material on cattle-feed, prevention and cure of their common ailments, etc. He is very much interested in watching TV programmes relating to the use of improved agricultural implements, storage and preservation of the yield for crops like potato, onion, garlic, etc. But, he does not get the opportunity because the TV set in the village remains closed on the days the agricultural programmes are telecast. He had seen a Gobargas plant in one of the houses in the village and got one installed in his house through a voluntary agency.

**Case 4**
**Kumari Venu Maruti Nayak**

A 17-year-old Mali girl from a poor family, having less than one acre of land. Her parents are illiterate and they have a large family to support. She is the eldest in the family and on her teacher's encouragement she continued her studies up to matriculation in the local high school. Afterwards she had to discontinue due to financial difficulties even though she was quite good in her studies as well as sports. She feels that her family can earn some income by rearing goats but no bank is prepared to give any loan to her as she cannot produce any security. She feels unhappy at not being able to help her family in any way financially even though she is educated. They do not want her to work on other farms as a labourer. She has seen many TV programmes like feature films, sports, etc., but none of them could help her learn anything to solve her problems.

**Case 5**
**Maruti Esu Kudam**

A 50-year-old Maratha farmer. As he could not make both ends meet in the village he migrated to Bombay to work as a dock labourer. While he was staying there he contacted VD and after some years came back to the village to eke out a living as a labourer. His wife died issueless due to uterus trouble. Having spent all his earnings and property on the treatment of his own disease and that of his wife, he does not possess anything to fall back upon. He stays with one of his younger brothers who is kind enough to give him shelter during his old age.

**Case 6**
**Janabai Gneneswar Nayak**

A 35-year-old illiterate Mali housewife. Her family grows fruits and vegetables and they are fairly well off. She gave birth to seven children out of whom five died before attaining the age of six years. Having lost her faith in the doctors for not saving her children even after spending a lot of money, she blames her fate and spends most of her time in religious activities. She shuns radio, television, films, etc., and does not also want to mix with people.

**Case 7**
**Basant Bhikari Gaikwad**

A 36-year-old neo-Buddhist educated up to standard IV. After serving in the Indian Army for a number of years, he retired and came back to the village. With the assistance of his relatives he started a poultry farm with 200 birds. He tried for a loan from the local bank but could not get any help. He keeps in touch with those who are in the poultry business to learn about poultry farming and occasionally consults a veterinary doctor.

The relations between the Harijans and Marathas in the village are strained. He is one of the leaders of the Harijans and has proved their strength by voting against the local Sarpanch in the Zilla Parishad elections. The Marathas are, therefore, angry with the Harijans and have even tried to harass them by preventing their womenfolk from taking water from the common tap in the centre of the village. So some of the Harijans damaged the lift pump carrying water to the village Milk Chilling Plant, in which none of them has any interest. He accuses the Maratha leaders of precipitating the issue and adopting pressure tactics.

**Case 8**
**Tukaram Ramji Moremare**

A Mahadeo Koli tribal youth aged 25 years. Son of a traditional leader (village Kotwal) with some landed property, he went to an Asram school and completed his Matriculation, with financial assistance from the Government. Later he joined the Production-cum-Training Centre for the Tribals run by the Government Social Welfare Department, and learnt tailoring. They have given him a sewing machine and he runs a shop of his own in the village now. His other family members are engaged in agriculture.

He regularly reads newspapers and has a radio. He keeps himself abreast of politics and administraticn and takes keen interest in the village Youth Club. He feels that the only way to develop the tribals is to educate them and give them an exposure to the outside world. But, he is very unhappy because the elected village Panchayat members are selfish and greedy. They are least bothered about the welfare of the poor people in the community. He is particularly angry with the Panchayat for keeping the community TV set closed on four days in a week and keeping it open for entertainment film programmes which very few of them understand. He has protested several times, but without any success.

**Case 9**
**Yasodha Pundalik Mohandale**

A 25-year-old Mahadeo Koli tribal woman educated up to Standard V. She is a Gram Panchayat member and her husband works as a postman in the local post office. They are well off with 7-8 acres of land which they have leased out to one of their relatives.

She never reads a newspaper but listens to the radio in the house. Her husband occasionally discusses politics with her. She took the initiative to get the tripple vaccine for all her three children from the Government Primary Health Centre in the village and consults the doctor whenever they are ill. But she also tries local herbs and medicines for minor ailments. She is very unhappy with the inadequate drinking water facilities in the village and blames the leaders for negligence. She feels that women should agitate to get piped water facilities to the village on a priority basis.

**Case 10**
**Sitabai Govind Lohukare**

A 40-year old Mahadeo Koli housewife. Her husband is an alcoholic who does not do any work. They had some land, which they had to dispose of to clear loans. She, therefore, works as a labourer in the Government Forest Nursery to support the family. But, her husband not only takes half of her daily wages for his drinks but also sells off whatever she keeps in the house. On the advice of the local school teacher, she has put two of her sons in the Ashram school in the village.

Her husband suspects her of everything and does not allow her to go out except for work. So, she is not in a position to watch the TV even though it is very near to her house. She is otherwise very much interested to watching the movies on the TV. Even though her married life is quite unhappy, she cannot think in terms of leaving her husband because of her children. She is very hopeful of her son completing Standard X in another two years and taking care of her. Her desire is to see him as a school teacher or Gram Sewak.

**Case 11**
**Kasinath Matarba Kale**

A 20-year old Thakkar youth, educated up to Standard II. He is married and has two children. He lives with his parents in a joint family. His father has taken five acres of dry land from a non-tribal for share-cropping and they grow millets and pulses. They have a few cattle belonging to others for grazing and about 30-35 goats of their own. All of them work on their fields and if they do not have sufficient work at any time they work in others' fields as labourers.

He has heard about 'Hybrid Jowar', but never tried it on his field because his father says that the land is unsuitable. They use only local varieties and apply enough of cowdung and burn it in the field. He feels that the output can be increased much if irrigation facilities are available. They cannot sink wells, because it requires a lot of investment. He has no knowledge how to get a loan from a Land Development Bank.

**Case 12**
**Jijabai Tukaram Kale**

An illiterate woman from the Thakkar tribe, aged 55 years. Her husband died at a very young age due to some illness. But, she did not remarry even though custom permits it. As she had a issue, she preferred to stay with her brother helping their family. They do not have land and cattle. So, they work as labourers and collect firewood from the forest and sell it in the nearby villages. She complained bitterly of the forest guards who always demand money or fowl as bribe for permitting wood-cutting in the forest. She curses them for their unsympathetic attitude.

**Case 13**
**Maruti Mukune**

An illiterate Katkari boy of 15 years. He has guines worms, *naru* disease, which he contracted from one of his cousins who lives with them. Their parents migrated from Konkan area, in search of livelihood. While some of them collect minor forest produce and sell it to the contractors, others are employed as workers with a liquor trader. The trader is a non-tribal and he has an illicit distillery in the forest area. He engages them for the transport and sale of liquor. Mostly the womenfolk are engaged in the business. The income being poor, their parents have not been able to take them to any place for treatment of their diseases. They spend most of the time in the hut. The villagers do not allow them to move about because they are afraid of the spread of the disease.

The cases presented above may be adequate to have a broad idea of the needs of the people. But, they provide only a picture of the socio-economic underdevelopment. Another dimension, related to this cultural impoverishment, is the level of political socialization. The Working Group on Akashwani and Doordarshan, headed by B.G. Verghese observed that "there is little doubt that by opening up new worlds of knowledge and opportunity, broadcasting can be a powerful liberating force. . . . Their power to awaken and *conscientize* is something that no nation can afford to ignore (I&B : 1978).

## Political Socialization

With a view to assessing the level of awareness about the critical issues in focus, at the time of study, three important political personalities were selected. They were: (1) Z.A. Bhutto deposed President of Pakistan, who was hanged for alleged political murders by the military regime; (2) Lok Nayak Jayaprakash Narayan (J.P.) who emerged as the most revered Indian leader after the 1977 general elections. He was critically ill at Bombay Hospital at the time of investigation; and (3) Y.B. Chavan, the most popular political leader of Maharashtra.

The three personalities were elected to represent the international, national and State level political scenes. The respondents were asked to describe, in a few words, each of these leaders, to find out their extent of knowledge (see Table 7.1). It was assumed that the level of awareness would indicate the amount of their concern for political developments and their level of political socialization.

TABLE 7.1: Knowledge of the Current Political Scene

| Awareness | Narayan Gavhan | Narodi | Amondi | Taleghar | Rajpur | All villages | |
|---|---|---|---|---|---|---|---|
| | % | % | % | % | % | N | % |
| 1. Z.A. *Bhutto*: | | | | | | | |
| Aware | 56.0 | 41.0 | 36.4 | 15.0 | 20.0 | 97 | 38.8 |
| Heard name | 2.0 | 6.0 | 3.6 | — | 8.0 | 11 | 4.4 |
| Not aware | 42.0 | 53.0 | 60.0 | 85.0 | 72.0 | 142 | 56.8 |
| 2. *Jayaprakash Narayan*: | | | | | | | |
| Aware | 48.0 | 34.0 | 32.7 | 15.0 | 16.0 | 83 | 33.2 |
| Heard name | 12.0 | 12.0 | 9.1 | — | 4.0 | 24. | 9.6 |
| Not aware | 40.0 | 54.0 | 58.2 | 85.0 | 80.0 | 143 | 57.2 |
| 3. *Y.B. Chavan*: | | | | | | | |
| Aware | 56.0 | 44.0 | 40.0 | 15.0 | 20.0 | 102 | 40.8 |
| Heard name | 18.0 | 12.0 | 21.8 | 40.0 | 16.0 | 48 | 18.0 |
| Not aware | 26.0 | 44.0 | 38.2 | 45.0 | 64.0 | 103 | 41.2 |
| All categories | 50 | 100 | 55 | 20 | 25 | 250 | 100.0 |

It is significant to notice the low awareness of the political personalities, who received the maximum attention in the country during the period of reference. One can, perhaps, conceive to some extent the limited (39 per cent) awareness of the political turmoil and the hanging of Bhutto in Pakistan because it happened in another country. But, complete ignorance of a national leader of the stature of Jayaprakash Narayan among nearly three-fifths of the sample should be an eye-opener for those concerned with bridging the information gaps in rural areas. Y.B. Chavan is the only leader from the region who has risen to the national level. Being a Maratha peasant, it was assumed that he would have at least made an impact as a popular leader. But, it is surprising to note that as many as 40 per cent have no knowledge of him.

Inter-village variations in awareness appear significant. Two reasons that could be attributed to the wide variations are:

(1) Differences in interaction and exposure to outside world, and
(2) Preoccupation with problems of survival particularly in tribal villages and the limited scope for concern for other issues.

The data were further analysed to understand the pattern of awareness according to the socio-economic background of the respondents and presented in Appendix Table 9. It was observed that about 80 per cent of the females were unaware of both J.P. and Bhutto, and only two-thirds had some knowledge of Chavan. While the knowledge was independent of age, illiteracy was found to be the greatest barrier, with 90 per cent of the illiterates not having any knowledge of J.P. and Bhutto and only three-fifths having some knowledge of Chavan.

Another important observation is the association of political knowledge and general awareness of current topics with the habit of newspaper reading. Nearly 85 per cent of those who had no exposure to newspapers had no knowledge of Bhutto or J.P. At the same time almost all those reading newspapers could recount the events easily. But, among those who had only exposure to radio, as many as 50 per cent were found to be unaware of J.P. and Bhutto. Therefore, for political socialization, the critical parameters appear to be literacy and exposure to newspapers rather than exposure to radio and TV.

Having indicated the magnitude of the informational needs both in terms of the socio-economic level of underdevelopment and the low political socialization, it is proposed to continue the discussion with an analysis of the strength of television as a medium that responds to the needs of the audience. The schedule included a number of items on the selection of programmes, their expectations of the medium and their search for different media in solving their problems, etc. The presentation that follows is based on an analysis of this information.

As mentioned in the previous chapter, about 36 per cent of the persons have no exposure to television despite the creation of facilities for community viewing in the villages. While the main reason for their non-utilization was explained as the long distance from their residences of the location of the TV set, two other important limiting

PLATE 7.1: Publicity to Entertainment TV Programmes

PLATE 7.2: Community TV Viewing

factors were lack of time and interest. These responses suggest that either the medium is yet to attract to its fold the audience and establish its genuine interest in responding to their needs, or a better source which is able to satisfy their wants more promptly and with least effort is available to them. To arrive at some broad conclusions, the audience responses to various related issues are discussed in the following paragraphs.

## Programme Preferences on TV

"The thoughts and actions of the individual reflect his wants and goals" is the observation of the social psychologists (Krech *et al*: 1962). We may, therefore, begin the analyses with the programme preferences of the audience. The pattern of selection is assumed to indicate broadly what the audience seek from television.

The data presented in Table 7.2 indicate that as many as three-fifths (62 per cent) of the television viewers in the villages are particularly fond of films. About one-fifth have no selection; they just watch any programme. While 25 per cent indicated preference for agricultural programmes, 21 per cent expressed favour for news items.

TABLE 7.2: Programme Preferences on Television

| Awareness | Narayan Gavhan | Narodi | Amondi | Taleghar | Rajpur | All villages | |
|---|---|---|---|---|---|---|---|
| | % | % | % | % | % | N | % |
| Relevant sample (All TV viewers) (N) | 33 | 60 | 38 | 15 | 13 | 159 | 100.0 |
| 1. Films | 84.8 | 58.3 | 55.3 | 53.3 | 46.2 | 98 | 61.6 |
| 2. Farm and home | 24.2 | 35.0 | 10.5 | 13.3 | 38.5 | 40 | 25.2 |
| 3. News | 36.4 | 15.0 | 18.4 | 6.7 | 30.8 | 33 | 20.8 |
| 4. Plays | — | 6.7 | 18.4 | — | 7.7 | 12 | 7.5 |
| 5. Devotional/light songs | — | 5.0 | 10.5 | 13.3 | 7.7 | 10 | 6.3 |
| 6. Folk items | — | 6.7 | 2.6 | 6.7 | — | 6 | 3.8 |
| 7. Special audience programmes | — | 1.7 | 5.3 | 20.0 | 15.4 | 8 | 5.0 |
| No selection | 9.1 | 23.3 | 31.6 | 20.0 | 15.4 | 34 | 21.4 |

"Wants are conditioned by the experiences. A hungry infant fed with warm milk will develop a want for milk and fed with rice gruel would develop want for rice gruel." This is another cardinal principle in social psychology (Krech *et al*: 1962). It is most likely that the audience programme preferences are conditioned by the type of exposure to the programmes. Most of the persons might be looking for the entertainment film programmes on TV, because they might not be seeing other items and their knowledge is restricted to the telecast of film-based items. To find the answers to this question, the respondents have been asked to indicate their awareness about the telecast of the primary rural audience programme in which the developmental information is delivered.

It may be essential to explain here the broad programme structure of Bombay Doordarshan Kendra at the time of the study.

## Programme Content of Bombay Doordarshan

The weekly transmission time of the TV Centre averages 34 hours. But, as the potential consumers living in Bombay city and suburbs belong to many language groups, it is not possible to ignore their interests. Hence the service is run in four major languages on the following pattern:

| *Language* | *Per cent* |
|---|---|
| English | 22 |
| Hindi | 32 |
| Marathi | 34 |
| Gujarati and others | 12 |

Marathi language programmes constituting approximately 34 per cent of the total output of the Centre, average about 550 minutes per week, excluding the educational programme for schools. The broad content of the output, programmewise is indicated in Table 7.3.

TABLE 7.3: Broad Content of the Marathi Programmes of Bombay TV

| Item | Minutes per week | Per cent to total |
|---|---|---|
| Film and other entertainment programmes | 180 | 32.7 |
| News | 70 | 12.7 |
| Other general audience programmes | 50 | 9.0 |
| Rural-urban social education programmes | 60 | 10.9 |
| Exclusively rural audience programmes | 60 | 10.9 |
| Special programmes for industrial workers | 40 | 7.3 |
| Programmes for women | 30 | 5.5 |
| Programme for youth | 30 | 5.5 |
| Programme for children | 30 | 5.5 |
| Total | 550 | 100.0 |

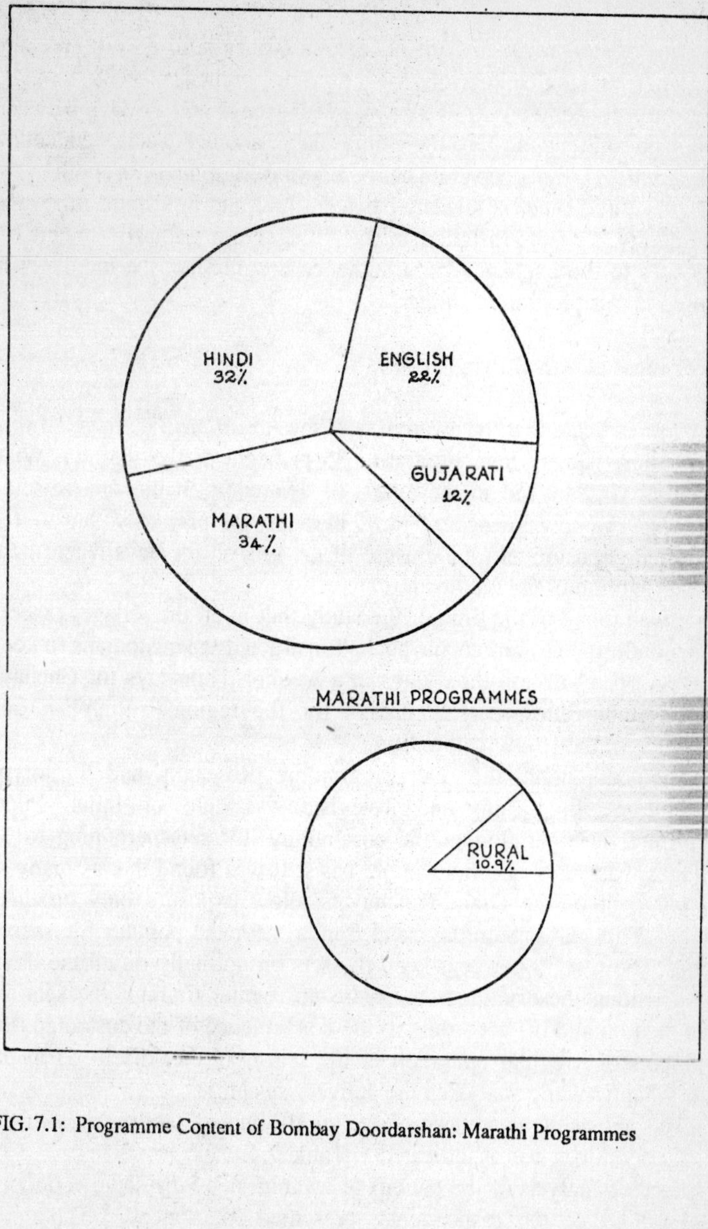


FIG. 7.1: Programme Content of Bombay Doordarshan: Marathi Programmes

The *Amchi Mati – Amchi Manse* (our land – our people) programme meant exclusively for the village audience, of 20 minutes' duration, is scheduled on Mondays, Wednesdays and Fridays between 7.10 and 7.30 p.m. On the same days another social education programme (Dyanadeep/Dainandin Vigyan) designed for both rural and urban audience, is telecast between 7.42 and 8.00 p.m. Since the community TV sets installed in the villages are primarily meant for exposure to the exclusive rural audience programme, the inquiry was limited to this programme alone.

**Awareness of Rural Programmes**

The data indicate that the awareness of the *Amchi Mati – Amchi Manse* programme is very low, limited to 35 per cent of the viewers. Wide variation was noticed in the extent of awareness in the five selected villages. The low awareness may, perhaps, be primarily due to the restricted exposure and the closure of the sets on the days when these rural programmes are on the air.

It was found at the time of the study that in all the villages, except in Amondi, the Gram Panchayats had instructed the custodians to keep the sets open only on three days in a week – Thursdays for Chchaya Geet (Hindi film sons); Saturdays for the regional film/play; and Sundays for the Hindi feature film.

The data with the TV Programme Research and Prototype Production Unit, Film and Television Institute of India, Pune, regarding the operation of the community TV sets pertaining to 35 villages was analysed on a sample basis. It was found that as many as 70 per cent of the Gram Panchayats allow exposure only on three days – Thursdays, Saturdays and Sundays for the popular film-based items. The rest 30 per cent keep the sets on normally on all the days. Even among these villages there are no regular timings, the sets are switched on and off according to the convenience of the custodian (the problems of irregular operation of the sets is further discussed in the next Chapter while analysing the delivery system).

The extent of awareness of the rural-oriented programmes in the selected villages was as indicated in Table 7.4.

Further analysis of the pattern of awareness by the socio-economic background of the respondents, presented in Appendix Table 10, indicates that with the increase in education and frequency of exposure to TV, the awareness increases greatly. The awareness is exceptionally low in the following categories:

TABLE 7.4: Extent of Awareness of the Rural TV Programmes

| Village | Percentage of viewers |
|---|---|
| Narayan Gavhan | 33.0 |
| Narodi | 43.3 |
| Amondi | 26.3 |
| Taleghar | 6.7 |
| Rajpur | 53.8 |
| All villages | 35.2 |

- females
- those who are below 30 years of age
- illiterates
- labourers
- those who watch TV rarely

**Primary Source of Information on Occupation**

The basic informational needs of the individual are mostly dictated by the occupation. With a view to identifying the institutions and channels that they interest most, the respondents were asked to indicate the source from where they normally receive information or seek advice on matters relating to their occupation. Most surprisingly it was found that as many as one-third do not depend on any channel. These persons do not feel the need as they pursue the traditional pattern, learnt from the elders during the process of socialization.

Among the rest two-thirds, "fellow villagers" and "relatives" were found to be the main channels of interaction. Only a small proportion of 8-11 per cent indicated the institutional channels like VLW, Block officials, radio, etc. Conspicuously none mentioned TV as a source of information on matters relating to occupation as could be seen from Table 7.5.

With a view to knowing "who interacts with whom", the data were further analysed. The information presented in Appendix Table 11 shows that majority of the labourers and those who depend on trade and traditional services do not expect to receive any information from any channel about their occupation. Those who need some information approach only relatives and friends. Among the cultivators also most of the interaction is confined to fellow farmers.

PLATE 7.3: Exchange of Information through Personal Channels

PLATE 7.4: Guidance from Experienced Farmers

TABLE 7.5: Primary Source of Information on Occupation

| Source | Narayan Gavhan | Narodi | Amondi | Taleghar | Rajpur | All villages | |
|---|---|---|---|---|---|---|---|
| | % | % | % | % | % | N | % |
| Consults None | 40.0 | 26.0 | 27.3 | 35.0 | 64.0 | 84 | 33.6 |
| Fellow villagers | 24.0 | 46.0 | 36.3 | 15.0 | 20.0 | 86 | 34.4 |
| VLW | 6.0 | 12.0 | 10.9 | 35.0 | — | 28 | 11.2 |
| Radio | 6.0 | 6.0 | 12.7 | — | 8.0 | 18 | 7.2 |
| Block officials | 6.0 | 5.0 | 7.3 | 15.0 | 8.0 | 17 | 6.8 |
| Village officials | 10.0 | 3.0 | 5.5 | — | — | 11 | 4.4 |
| Panchayat members | 4.0 | 1.0 | — | — | — | 3 | 1.2 |
| Books/papers | 4.0 | 1.0 | — | — | — | 3 | 1.2 |
| Television | — | — | — | — | — | — | — |
| All categories | 50 | 100 | 55 | 29 | 25 | 250 | 100.0 |

Contrary to general assumption, seeking information from interpersonal channels increased with the increase in education. This suggests that even among the educated persons the tendency is to rely on personal channels than on institutional channels like radio, VLW, etc. The identification of radio as a source of information on matters relating to occupation was found to be more with traders and farmers than with other categories. Labourers as a group do not seem to expect any information from other sources than friends and relatives.

## Can TV Provide Occupational Information?

Irrespective of the fact whether the respondents look to any source or not, to seek information on their occupation, they were asked to indicate if they consider television as an appropriate medium to provide guidance and information on their respective sources of livelihood. The response was striking.

Data presented in Table 7.6 (Fig. 7.2) indicate that as many as two thirds have no idea if television could provide any information about their occupation. Of the remaining one-third, while majority were positively emphatic, a substantial number doubted if TV could be of any help to them.

Majority of the persons were found to be ignorant of the potentialities of TV in meeting their informational needs pertaining to their occupation mainly due to lack of adequate interaction with the medium. Analyses of the data by frequency of exposure presented in Appendix Table 12 reveals that one-half of the frequent viewers are sure that TV can provide some information about their occupation. Occasional viewers are only sceptical about its potentialities. Analyses by occupation of the respondents reveals that persons engaged in trade and traditional services do not consider TV as an appropriate source to assist them in their occupation. Comparatively there is wider appreciation among farmers and white-collar workers.

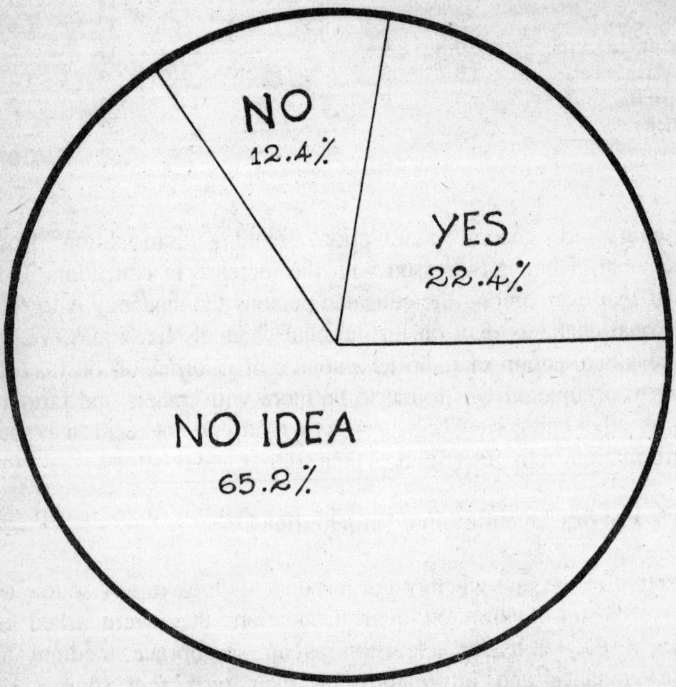


FIG. 7.2: Can TV Provide Information on your Occupation?

**Why Television is Installed in Villages?**

Television is no substitute for inter-personal channels in delivering messages concerning one's occupation and life. It may, therefore, be a far cry to expect TV to achieve the status of an "important channel" for meeting the "urgent informational needs" of the villagers as they are woven round their occupation. But, at the same time it cannot be denied that, by and large, TV is considered to be a "facility" which the people would definitely like to have. Then the question is, what role do they expect it to play? To ascertain the villager's role expectation of TV, all the respondents were asked, why TV has been installed in the village? What is its purpose? The replies were very encouraging.

TABLE 7.6: Can TV provide information on occupation?

| Reply | Narayan Gavhan | Narodi | Amondi | Taleghar | Rajpur | All villages | |
|---|---|---|---|---|---|---|---|
| | % | % | % | % | % | N | % |
| Yes | 24.0 | 25.0 | 20.0 | 15.0 | 20.0 | 56 | 22.4 |
| No | 14.0 | 13.0 | 18.2 | 5.0 | — | 31 | 12.4 |
| No idea | 62.0 | 62.0 | 61.8 | 80.0 | 80.0 | 163 | 65.2 |
| Total | 50 | 100 | 55 | 20 | 25 | 250 | 100.0 |

While 42 per cent in the sample were clear that the facility had been created for the dissemination of general information and knowledge to the villagers, another 17 per cent were of the view that its primary objective was village development. Twenty per cent shared the view that television was purely meant for entertainment as there were no other facilities for relaxation. (See Table 7.7 and Fig. 7.3).

Two broad generalizations that could emerge from the data presented in Table 7.7 are:

1. By and large the villagers have a favourable image of television as a medium for the delivery of useful information. This could be properly exploited to create faith in its capacity to respond to the informational needs of all occupational groups.
2. Potential audience with no idea of what television could offer to them; apparently, have no interaction either direct or indirect with the medium. One of the immediate goals of television should be to reach them with some relevant messages.

In Appendix Table 13 the information was further analysed according to the socio-economic background of the respondents. The Information reveals that the following categories are more convinced of the developmental goals of TV:

TABLE 7.7: Why Television is Installed in the Village?

| | Role expectation | Nara-yan Gavhan | Narodi | Amon-di | Tale-ghar | Rajpur | All villages | |
|---|---|---|---|---|---|---|---|---|
| | | % | % | % | % | % | N | % |
| 1. | For general awareness | 34.0 | 37.0 | 56.4 | 40.0 | 52.0 | 106 | 42.4 |
| 2. | For development | 30.0 | 21.0 | 5.4 | 5.0 | 12.0 | 43 | 17.2 |
| 3. | For entertainment as no other facilities are available | 26.0 | 25.0 | 10.9 | 35.0 | — | 51 | 20.4 |
| 4. | For public viewing | 6.0 | 4.0 | 9.1 | 5.0 | 12.0 | 16 | 6.4 |
| 5. | No idea | 4.0 | 13.0 | 18.2 | 15.0 | 24.0 | 34 | 13.6 |
| | All categories | 50 | 100 | 55 | 80 | 25 | 250 | 100.0 |

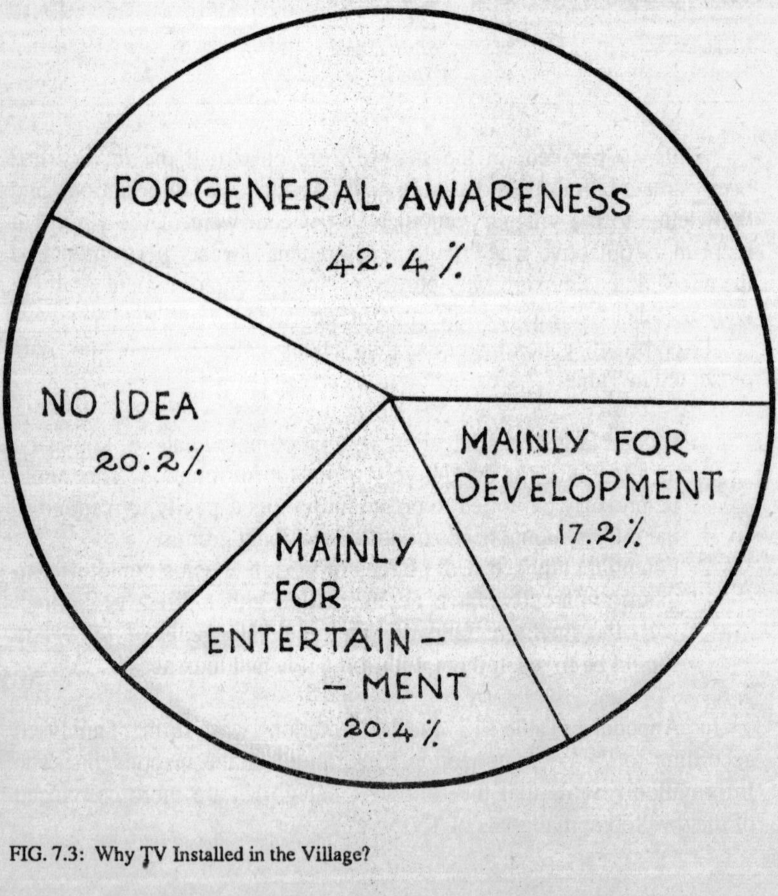


FIG. 7.3: Why TV Installed in the Village?

- males
- those who are below 30 years of age
- those who have at least high school education
- white-collar workers, students and those depending on trade and traditional services
- those who watch TV more regularly.

The categories which think of television basically as an entertainment medium are:

- females
- those who are in the age-group of 45-60 years
- illiterates
- labourers
- those who rarely or never watch TV.

**Preferred Channel for Delivery of Development Messages**

Television is only one of the channels for village development. There are a number of other channels which are available to deliver the messages to the villagers. For identifying the villager's own image of the most effective channel for rural development, the respondents were asked to indicate their preference for any one of the six channels listed in the questionnaire. Sufficient care was taken to avoid the researcher's, bias during the interviews. The six channels included were:

(1) VLW and other Extension personnel;
(2) Fellow villagers;
(3) Panchayat members;
(4) Radio;
(5) Television; and
(6) Newspapers.

Data presented in Table 7.8 indicate that radio is considered to be the most appropriate medium for diffusion of developmental information. The next preferred channel is "fellow villagers". While VLW ranks third in placement, Gram Panchayat members come fourth in the order of choice. TV and newspapers are given the least preference with fifth and sixth positions respectively. Normally television is assumed to have an edge over radio, due to the visual stimuli, particularly with illiterate audiences. Contrary to the belief, the preference for radio suggests that due to its wider accessibility, more transmission hours, facility of exposure within four walls, and wider fare, it has been able to sell more ideas and establish its bona fides as a development medium. TV is yet to establish its strength, vitality and effectiveness as a medium of developmental communication, to win popular support (see Fig. 7.4).

TABLE 7.8: Preferred Channel for Delivery of Development Messages

| Channel | Narayan Gavhan | Narodi | Amondi | Taleghar | Rajpur | All villages | |
|---|---|---|---|---|---|---|---|
| | % | % | % | % | % | N | % |
| 1. Radio | 30.0 | 41.0 | 18.2 | 10.0 | 24.0 | 74 | 29.6 |
| 2. Fellow Villagers | 14.0 | 27.0 | 30.9 | 20.0 | 36.0 | 64 | 25.6 |
| 3. VLW & other Extn. staff | 10.0 | 15.0 | 20.0 | 50.0 | 4.0 | 42 | 16.8 |
| 4. Panchayat members | 36.0 | 4.0 | 9.1 | 5.0 | 20.0 | 33 | 13.2 |
| 5. Television | 4.0 | 2.0 | 7.3 | — | — | 8 | 3.2 |
| 6. Newspapers | 2.0 | 2.0 | 1.8 | — | — | 4 | 1.6 |
| 7. No idea | 4.0 | 9.0 | 12.7 | 15.0 | 16.0 | 25 | 10.0 |
| All Categories | 50 | 100 | 55 | 20 | 25 | 250 | 100.0 |

One of the noteworthy observations was the inter-village differences in preference for various channels. This can, perhaps, be explained mainly in terms of the interaction and past experience of the villagers with the channel. In Narayan Gavhan "Panchayat Members" emerged as the most appropriate and desired channel, as the Sarpanch in that village could establish himself as a person of integrity and work. He is easily accessible to the people and his interactions with ordinary people are cordial. That could be the reason why, as an institution, he could create an impact. Similar was the case in Taleghar. The VLW was found to be a popular figure even though he does not always stay in the village. In Narodi, the community radio set of the Gram Panchayat was found to most effectively used. Even the progressive farmers do not wish to miss exchange of views regarding market rates, availability of pesticides, etc., at the Panchayat listening to the radio. As an institution radio was seen to command a very respectable place for diffusion of information on agricultural development. In the tribal villages of Amondi and Rajpur, there being no such advantages, the "fellow farmers' were the ultimate choice of the majority.

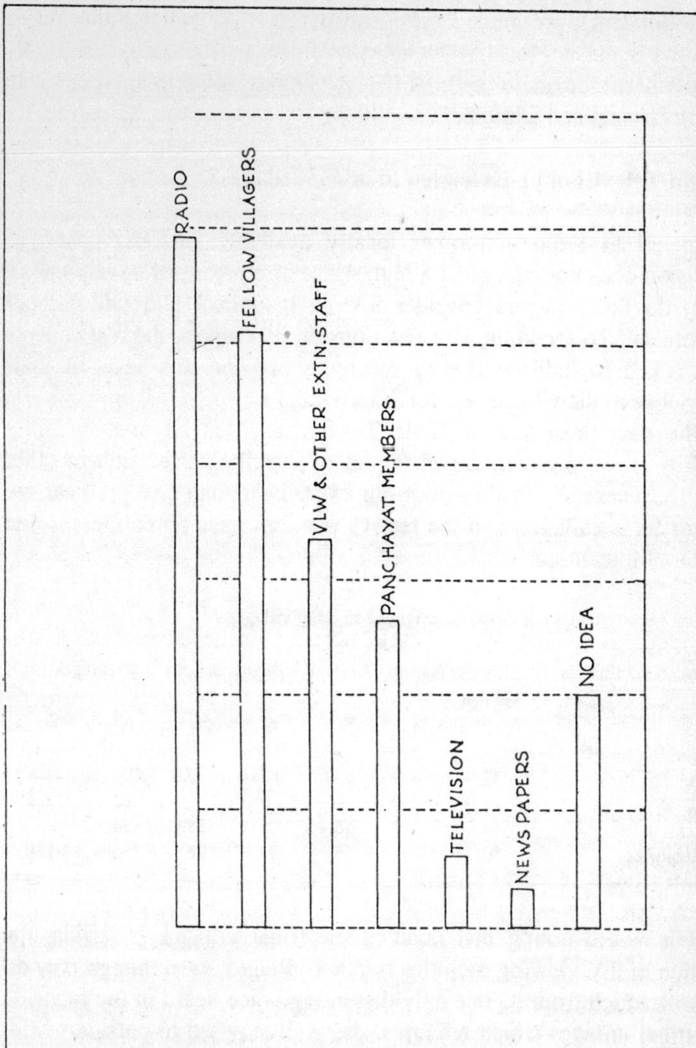


FIG. 7.4: Preferred Channel for Delivery of Developmental Messages

Further analyses of the data by the socio-economic background of the respondents, presented in Appendix Table 14, indicate that while illiterates consider "local villagers" as the best source, those with some education prefer radio and VLW. A similar attitude is noticeable among farmers and white-collar workers.

### Should Television be Extended to other Villages?

Compared to radio and other locally available personal channels, television does not command a high status as a means of development. Then, do the villagers consider TV as redundant and unnecessary investment? To ascertain their reactions on this aspect, the respondents were asked to indicate if they recommended, on this basis of their experience in the village, TV for other villages.

The data presented in Table 7.9 indicate that an overwhelming majority of 80 per cent are in favour of installing television in other villages, where the facility does not exist. Less than five per cent are against its installation and the rest 15 per cent have no comments due to lack of interaction.

TABLE 7.9: Should television be extended to other villages ?

| Whether recommends | Narayan Gavhan | Narodi | Amondi | Taleghar | Rajpur | All villages | |
|---|---|---|---|---|---|---|---|
| | % | % | % | % | % | N | % |
| Yes | 72.0 | 83.0 | 83.6 | 85.0 | 72.0 | 200 | 80.0 |
| No | 14.0 | 5.0 | -- | -- | -- | 12 | 4.8 |
| No opinion | 14.0 | 12.0 | 16.4 | 15.0 | 28.0 | 38 | 15.2 |
| All categories | 50 | 100 | 55 | 20 | 25 | 250 | 100.0 |

It is worth noting that none in the tribal villages is against the creation of TV viewing facilities in other villages, even though they do not seek much from it. The only dissenting voice heard in the roadside non-tribal villages which are otherwise well exposed to outside world. The majority opinion is that TV has more nuisance value than utilitarian value. This group is particularly critical of the adverse influence of the weekly commercial films on TV, on the minds of teenagers and school-going children. However, the majority consider TV as a very useful medium, particularly in enlarging the general consciousness and generating awareness particularly among the younger generation.

No wide variation was observed in the response according to the socio-economic background of the individuals,except that the frequent viewers were more favourably inclined to support the medium and its extension to other villages.

## Utility of TV to self

On what grounds television is recommended to other villages ? How are the villagers convinced of its utility ? If it is not useful to self or family, why is it not considered unnecessary ? On the one hand there is overwhelming support for the extension of the facility to other villages, on the other hand there is extreme underutilization, particularly among the illiterate people. How to explain this paradox ? With a view to reading the minds of those who supported extension of TV, they were specifically asked in what way television had been useful to them individually or their families. The response is presented in Table 7.10.

TABLE 7.10: Specific Utility of TV

| Utility to self or family | Narayan Gavhan | Narodi | Amondi | Taleghar | Rajpur | All villages | |
|---|---|---|---|---|---|---|---|
| | % | % | % | % | % | N | % |
| Relevant sample (N) | 36 | 83 | 46 | 17 | 18 | 200 | 100.0 |
| 1. Mainly information/ knowledge | 55.6 | 32.5 | 45.7 | 41.2 | 38.9 | 82 | 41.0 |
| 2. Mostly entertainment | 25.0 | 15.7 | 17.4 | 23.5 | 16.7 | 37 | 18.5 |
| 3. Self not used for others' benefit | 19.4 | 51.8 | 36.9 | 35.3 | 44.4 | 83 | 40.0 |

The data presented in Table 7.10 support the earlier observation that TV is more identified as a source of information and knowledge than mere entertainment. Only one-fifth of the audience make use of the medium as a pastime. All others, including those who have no direct interaction, support the medium for its informative role.

The argument of the villagers sounded simple and plain. "TV is a facility like any other institution – like post office, bank etc. It is for the common good of the people, not specifically for any group or individuals. People who need the services of a post office go there, others may not go there. That does not mean that a post office is unnecessary in the village. As long as an institution or a facility is harmless to those who do not need its services why should it be opposed". This being the general line of approach, the outlook towards TV appears to be very positive. There is a negligible proportion with negative approach.

One of the most convincing arguments of the people was that by and large most of them have grown without any exposure to the external world, because of lack of communications and facilities like radio and TV. The present generation have an edge over them because of the creation of these facilities. They are gaining more knowledge and becoming conscious of what is happening outside due to increased interaction. They come freely, talk freely and exchange their views more frequently. The contribution of TV in this respect is highly appreciated. The consensus is that the medium may not have any instantaneous benefit. But, in the long run, its impact on children is considered to be very useful. With this positive outlook, it may be concluded that the medium should be able to carve out a more respectable place among the channels of development and respond to their immediate informational needs.

One of the significant findings of the analyses of the data by the background of the individuals, presented in Appendix Table 15, is that even though females do not participate much and flock around TV, they have more appreciation of the informational content. As observed earlier, persons in the middle ages, those who are educated upto the primary level, those who are engaged in farming and white-collar jobs and dependants have a favourable disposition to seek information and knowledge than pure entertainment from TV.

**Preferred Facility for Village Development**

People might justify TV on grounds of its informative and developmental uses. But, in the existing conditions, how indispensable it is in the order of priorities? Given alternative channels which one they prefer most as a channel of development communication? Each village has its distinct problems and it may be necessary to think is terms of different facilities for different villages to solve the specific needs. With a view to finding the general reaction of the villagers, six facilities were listed and everyone was asked to identify one that is considered as the most effective and suitable medium for village improvement. The six facilities listed were: (1) Agricultural expert;

(2) A social worker; (3) An adult education centre; (4) Posts and telegraphs office; (5) Police station; and (6) A television set.

As most of the people were dependent on agriculture, it was not surprising to find their first opinion in favour of an agricultural expert. In this context majority made it clear that they need a person who can practically guide them in the fields, who has more scientific knowledge, who can translate knowledge into action than a person who is inclined to keep busy in moving about and doing "record work". What they have in mind appears to be a skilled technician, instead of a white-collar worker who renders advice and not practical guidance.

The next desired facility was a sincere social worker, a person who can appreciate the needs of the villagers, who can act as a link between them and the administration, who can help them in getting their work done and guide their children in proper training and earning a livelihood. This desire suggests that the institution of Panchayat members could not meet these needs.

Other facilities like the adult education centre, posts and telegraphs office and police station mustered only a negligible support of three to eight per cent in the sample. Television failed to get any support as the most desirable facility. Obviously, the villagers look eagerly for something which is related to their living that can deliver the benefits by itself. Perhaps, it is beyond their comprehension to appreciate the long-term results of TV in solving their social and economic problems. Their thinking is conditioned by the fact that TV cannot create and distribute favours. Under the circumstances, it may be a wishful thinking to project TV as one of the "most desired facilities in villages".

TABLE 7.11: The most desired facility for village development

| Desired facility | Narayan Gavhan % | Narodi % | Amondi % | Taleghar % | Rajpur % | All villages N | All villages % |
|---|---|---|---|---|---|---|---|
| 1. Agricultural Expert | 36.0 | 42.0 | 40.0 | 60.0 | 60.0 | 109 | 43.6 |
| 2. Social worker | 44.0 | 34.0 | 36.4 | 20.0 | 16.0 | 84 | 33.6 |
| 3. Adult education centre | 4.0 | 11.0 | 5.5 | 5.0 | 4.0 | 18 | 7.2 |
| 4. Posts & telegraphs office | 4.0 | 3.0 | 3.6 | 5.0 | — | 8 | 3.2 |
| 5. Police station | 4.0 | 2.0 | — | — | 8.0 | 6 | 2.4 |
| 6. Television | — | 1.0 | — | — | — | 1 | 0.4 |
| 7. No idea | 8.0 | 7.0 | 14.5 | 10.0 | 12.0 | 24 | 9.6 |
| All categories | 50 | 100 | 55 | 20 | 25 | 250 | 100.0 |

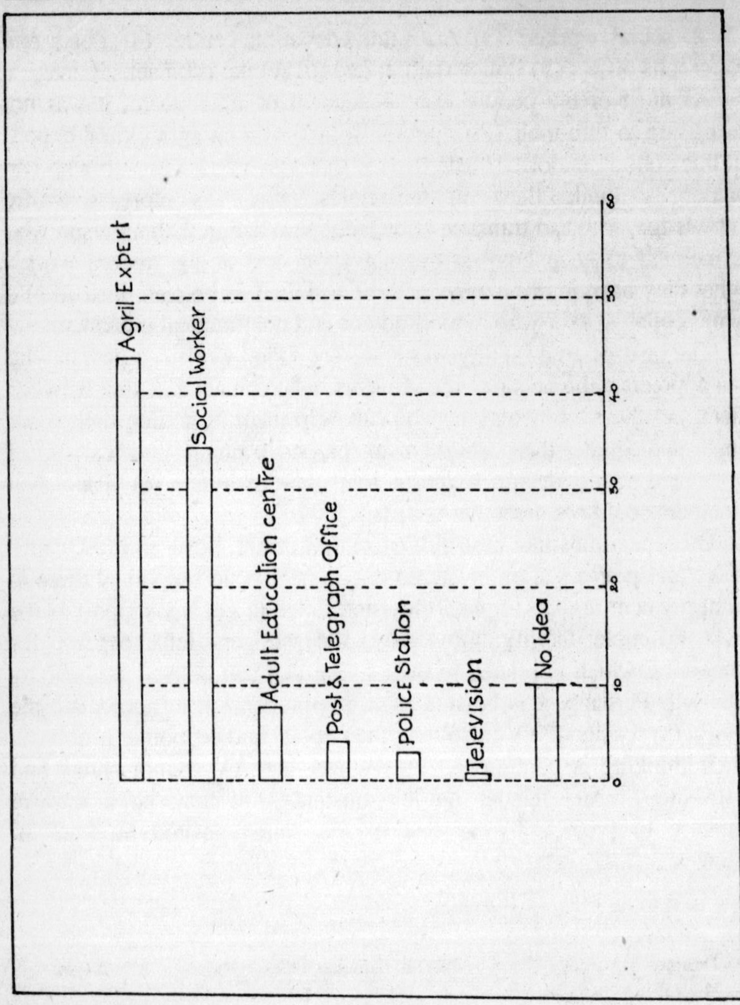


FIG. 7.5: Most Desired Facility for Village Development

With a view to finding "who desires to have what", the data were further analysed according to the background of the individuals. The data presented in Appendix Table 15 reveal the following trend:

1. *Agricultural expert*
   Both small and marginal farmers, independent of sex and age. Preference increased with increase in education.

2. *Social worker*

   All labourers and those living on traditional services, other dependants, white-collar workers. Independent of sex, but preference increased with the increase in age and decrease in education. The desire was more pronounced among the poor with incomes less than Rs.300 per month.

3. *Adult education centre*

   The need was expressed by only a section of the educated persons. This indicates that by and large education of adult illiterates (adult education is mostly understood in terms of literacy alone) is not considered essential for rural development.

4. *Posts & Telegraphs Office*

   Only a section of the persons depending on traditional services and trade opted for such a facility. Agriculturists and labourers mostly considered this as a non-essential facility.

5. *Police station*

   None except two educated Harijans of a non-tribal village desired to have this facility.

6. *Television*

   "Television does not give food" being the general attitude, it could not figure as the most desired facility in any village. The lone supporter was a Sarpanch who brought TV to one of the villages.

Summing up it may be stated that television does not have a place in the priority list of the "most desired facilities" for village development. But, its role as an informational channel, particularly for widening the horizons of the children and creating consciousness of external world among the illiterates is highly appreciated. If it is able to respond more vigorously to the informational needs pertaining to the livelihood of the villagers, it may be able to achieve a respectable status as a channel for village development.

# 8

# THE PARAMETERS OF RESPONSE

FOLLOWING THE popular Lasswell's paradigm of communication process "who says what, in which channel, to whom, with what effect", the determinants of response to television communication may be shown at the source, message, medium and audience levels.

At the *source* level, the political framework under which the broadcasting systems operate, and the role assigned to the medium are the primary determinants of the nature of output. In view of our faith in democratic ideals and the commitment of the medium to the social objectives, it is assumed that there are no constraints at the source level for the application of television for rural development. This assumption, however, ignores other weaknesses such as lack of perception of rural problems among the programme generators, because of their urban background, and the injection of their own values in their productions, as has been observed by some authors (Srinivas: 1976, Deepak Roy: 1979). It is assumed that such constraints could be effectively tackled by evolving suitable recruitment and training systems. It must not be difficult to induct the right type of personnel with rural orientation to man the production positions and provide a development slant to the programmes.

If the controlling variables at the source level are taken care of, two major issues that remain to be effectively managed at message and medium levels are:

1. Content input and presentation of messages, and
2. Effective delivery system to reach the audience.

The socio-cultural attributes of the audience that determine the pattern of exposure, their perception and comprehension of the messages and the physical and financial capabilities of the audience which have a direct bearing on the translation of the knowledge into action assume no significance so long as the content of the programmes is of no concern to the audience, and the medium is out of their reach. In view of this the content and the delivery systems are considered to be the most critical parameters of response.

In the following paragraphs an attempt is made to analyse these two aspects in detail. The basic objective is to find out how best the response to the TV programmes in villages could be increased.

## Content Analysis of the Programmes

With a view to finding the complexion and composition of the programmes presented in the rural service of Bombay Doordarshan *(Amchi Mati Amchi Manse)*, the telecasts during two quarters, October-December 1978, and April-May 1979, totalling a period of six months, were analysed. The source was the producer's log book which is more precise and authentic than the quarterly programme schedules or the weekly Press releases. The producer's log book indicates the duration of each individual item and also the last-minute changes, if any, in the transmission. The composition of the programmes is presented in Table 8.1.

TABLE 8.1: Content analysis of the Rural Service of Bombay TV

| Subject | Oct-Dec 1978 | | April-June 1979 | |
|---|---|---|---|---|
| | Mts. | Percentage | Mts. | Percentage |
| 1. Instructional/ informational programmes on agriculture | 300 | 38.5 | 450 | 57.7 |
| 2. Programmes on animal husbandry | 40 | 5.1 | 60 | 7.8 |
| 3. Employment schemes | 40 | 5.1 | — | — |
| 4. Documentaries on Agricultural Institutions | 70 | 9.0 | 20 | 2.6 |
| 5. Interviews with progressive farmers | 40 | 5.1 | 40 | 5.1 |
| 6. Documentaries on villages | 50 | 6.4 | — | — |
| 7. Cooperation and marketing | 40 | 5.1 | 30 | 3.8 |
| 8. Social education | 100 | 12.8 | 140 | 17.9 |
| 9. Health care | 60 | 7.8 | 40 | 5.1 |
| 10. Other cultural items | 40 | 5.1 | — | — |
| Total | 780 | 100.0 | 780 | 100.0 |

As mentioned earlier, the rural programmes are telecast on three days in a week — Mondays, Wednesday and Fridays — from 7.10 to 7.30 p.m. (20 minutes), preceding the Marathi news programme. It is noticed that normally on Mondays and Wednesdays the hard-core agricultural programmes of general information and instructional nature are scheduled. On alternative Fridays, the experimental programmes prepared by the Television Programme Research and Prototype Production Unit of the Film and Television Institute of India (FTII), Pune, are scheduled. The FTII programmes cover mostly social education themes.

The broad content of the rural programmes is discussed below under four major areas: (1) Agriculture; (2) Social education; (3) Health care; and (4) Cultural items.

1. *Agricultural Programmes*

Table 8.1 reveals that majority of the programmes, accounting for 40-60 per cent of the service, relate to general instruction or information on agriculture. They cover topics like improved agricultural practices, use of modern methods of intensive cultivation, water management, cultivation of commercial crops, proper use of agricultural inputs, selection of seed varieties, storage techniques, etc. For illustration, the items included in the telecast scheduled for April-June 1979, are given in Appendix 16.

One of the important observations is the accent on irrigation and commercial crops. Of the 450 minutes of hard-core and informational programmes telecast during April-June 1979, about two-thirds (300 mt) was utilised for crops which can be grown with irrigation facilities. Such items sound obviously irrelevant to farmers who have only unirrigated land and grow mostly dry crops for survival.

It may be mentioned here that the coverage of Bombay Doordarshan extends to the Konkan region, receiving heavy rainfall, areas with low rainfall but assured irrigation facilities, as well as scarcity areas as in Pune-Ahmednagar districts. As such, it may be difficult to serve both Pune and Bombay regions with the same fare simultaneously. It may also be difficult to apportion the available telecast time to satisfy the audience in both the regions. It must, however, be possible to work out the telecast schedule on the basis of acreage under different crops.

Television may be able to attract the eyes of the ordinary farmers in the Pune region if there is adequate coverage of dry crops like local *jowar, bajri*, millets and pulses specific to the area. Programmes on cotton, sugarcane, fruits and spices are of little relevance to the farmers in the drought-prone areas.

2. *Social Education*

The TV Programme Research and Prototype Production Unit of FTII contributes one programme on fortnightly basis. This is scheduled on alternative Fridays in the rural chunk. The FTII productions are of experimental nature mainly intended for obtaining feedback and testing various methods of presentation techniques and treatment. They cover themes mostly of general relevance to rural areas, but the productions mostly confine to situations specific to the Pune region. However, for wider acceptability these programmes are produced in popular entertainment formats like play, tamasha, waga-natya and other folk formats. The subjects chosen for coverage in this chunk include: superstitions, alcoholism, adult education, untouchability, social evils like nagging of daughters-in-law, dowry, and successful development schemes sponsored by private and government agencies.

Bombay Doordarshan does not have any other social education programme in the rural service other than the FTII contributions (the Dyandeep programmes covering similar themes are directed for both urban and rural audiences). In terms of telecast time the social education programmes in the rural service constitute only 15 per cent. In view of their relevance, the coverage appears to be very inadequate.

3. *Health and Hygiene*

Programmes on health care and hygiene are few and far between in the rural service. There seems to be no fixed frequency and earmarked time for these programmes. In the whole quarter of April-June, 1979, there were only two programmes: one relating to physical education in schools and the other on physically handicapped children. Actuality coverages providing information on the existing facilities and their usage, common diseases in rural areas, practices related to their cure and prevention, and specific messages on simple household remedies are conspicuously missing.

4. *Cultural Items*

The data suggest that there is very little coverage of cultural items relating to the socio-economic life pattern in the villages. While there were no items during April-June 1979, only two items appeared in October-December 1978, accounting for five per cent of the service. Cultural items are considered to be the best means to provide local bias and attract the audience attention. Too much stress on education/instruction and negligence of the cultural life may alienate the viewers as there is very little scope for their identification with the service.

### The Missing Links

Examined in reference to the specific needs of the potential audience in the study area, the data presented in Table 8.1 indicated that the output in rural service is inadequate in respect of the following areas:

1. Simple techniques of increasing the yield levels of common food crops like *jowar*, *bajri*, millets and pulses popular in the area.
2. Scarcity conditions and rural migration.
3. Employment avenues and information on supplementary occupations which can be easily taken up without relying on external help.
4. Animal husbandry programmes particularly goat/sheep rearing, improvement of the local varieties by cross-breeding with Jersey and other popular varieties for dairy farming.
5. Guidance of village artisans and development of household industries with locally available agricultural and forest products like potato, garlic, onion and hirada, etc.
6. Health care and hygiene, with specific reference to water-borne diseases caused by stagnant water, which the people are forced to use due to acute shortage of drinking water wells.
7. Cultural items depicting the social and religious life, to inject local bias in the programmes.

### Feedback on Selected Programmes

Having presented a broad outline of the pattern and composition of the rural service, it is proposed to discuss the actual programme input and presentation of a few selected programmes along with the feedback received from the viewers. Its main objective is to indicate the general pattern of response rather than evaluation of specific formats.

The analysis is based on exercises conducted in three selected villages, by arranging playbacks of programmes. The ideal procedure should have been to obtain the response to the rural programmes as they were telecast. But, unfortunately, during the period of field-work when the researcher was staying in the villages, simultaneous feedback could not be obtained due to two reasons: (a) in two villages the community TV sets were out of order and (b) in the remaining three villages the sets remained either closed or reception was poor on the days when the rural programmes were telecast. It was, therefore, decided to arrange subsequently a playback of a few selected programmes in three villages, viz. Rajapur, Amondi and Narayan Gavhan to study the audience response to specific aspects like content, relevance, clarity and sustenance.

Due to operational constraints it was not possible to carry any agricultural items generated by the Bombay TV centre (as they are recorded only on film). The experimental playbacks were confined to video programmes available with the Film and TV Institute. The programmes selected for obtaining the feedback were different in the three villages. Hence, the results are presented separately giving an outline of the content of the programmes.

**I.Venue: Rajapur**

Content of the programmes:

1. *Bhopali:* A devotional song, sung by one of the devotees to wake up the God while the villagers are assembling for the morning prayers at the temple. Duration: 3 mt.
2. *Bahuroopi:* The traditional entertainer with an invitation for a marriage ceremony and an appeal to all young married girls to limit their families. Duration: 4 mt.
3. *Gondhal:* The folk singers with a message on the increasing craze for anything imported when the traditional village artisan is able to produce the best varieties in the country. Duration: 8 mt.
4. *Bharud:* The popular folk format of the region with a message on family welfare and planning. An aggrieved wife pleads with the village elders to allow her to leave her husband who troubles her year after year with a child unmindful of her health and condition of the family. Duration: 10 mt.
5. *Modern songs:* A compilation of light songs in the film style with

orchestra sung by a popular artiste. Duration: 8 mt.

Audience composition: About 20 men: 20 women: 40 children.

It was a busy agricultural season. But people assembled as soon as the word spread through the children that some programmes are being shown on the television. After the playback brief individual interviews were conducted with 10 males and 10 females to ascertain their views. No structured questionnaire was used. Their responses are summarised below:

1. *Folk Formats Attract the Young and Old Alike*

The items that attracted most of the viewers were the *Bharud* (item 4) and the *Bahuroopi* (item 2) containing the messages on family planning. With witty dialogues, sarcastic remarks and a sprinkle of suggestive actions and double-meaning words (which invariably go with the local folk formats), the items were successful in generating interest and holding audience attention. The language was not only simple but plain. There was no difficulty in understanding the content and the message. Some of the youngsters were observed passing remarks and pulling the legs of an elderly person watching the programme with rapt attention that he should learn a lesson and show sympathy for his wife by not troubling her every year with a child. Perhaps, such identification was possible because of the typical rural style of presentation and the actions and dialogues that are very common to folk presentation in the region.

2. *Irrelevant Themes Escape Attention*

Gondhal is a folk format. But, the content of the programme was irrelevant to the audience who are at the subsistence level of economy. The craze for imported material is a phenomenon associated with middle and upper middle class urban families and rural elite. In the village many of the viewers failed to understand what the Gondhal maharaj was narrating. None could explain the meaning of words like "imported", "label", "market", etc., used in the verse, except an educated youth who was in the army for some time. The audience indicated restlessness and became inattentive after some time and started talking among themselves. Particularly, the womenfolk showed no interest in the programme.

3. *Not Very Much Carried Away by the Glamorous Music*

The melodious music, the elaborate orchestra and the glamorous looks of the artiste who presented the light songs in Hindi were able to attract the audience particularly boys and girls who thought that it was part of a feature film. But after some time the elders left the place giving an excuse that they have got work. Interviews with the viewers revealed that they did not understand the content but enjoyed the music and the visuals, because it was like a "picture".

The consensus was that of all the items the Bharud and the Bahuroopi were the best and most attractive and suitable for the rural audience. Besides lively entertainment, both of them could convey a message which is useful and relevant to the people. Asked if they were given an opportunity to choose between a few film songs, a Bharud play and a programme on jowar cultivation what would be the order of preference, the choice was in favour of jowar cultivation as it happens to be their staple food. It was surprising to get the same reply from both cultivators and agricultural labourers, from men as well as women. Bharud was preferred to film songs because it forms part of their life.

**II. Venue: Narayan Gavhan**

Content of the programme: Studio Production. Duration: 20 mt.

It is a social play in the series on the National Adult Education Programme. The objective is to create awareness on the rights and privileges of villagers as citizens of the country. The play portrays how a revenue official *(Talati)* troubles an illiterate poor farmer making him to run up and down when he approaches for a copy of the land record to get some loan. When the farmer refuses to pay the bribe demanded by the *Talati*, he gets annoyed and rebukes the farmer. On the advice of a friend the farmer tries to lodge a complaint with the police, but he gets a rebuff when he could not write the complaint. The frustrated farmer approaches his friend once again and seeks his help. Taking this opportunity, the friend suggests the farmer and his wife take the advantage of the National Adult Education Programme and learn how to face problems of this nature in life.

Audience composition: About 125 males: 80 females: 75 children.

The feedback was based on individual interviews with 10 adult males and 10 adult females. Due to limited space in the Gram Panchayat building where the playback was arranged the play was shown in two batches. Despite the inconvenience it was watched with rapt attention without any disturbance.

The expressions and behaviour of the innocent looking illiterate farmer, the sarcastic remarks of the Talati, his arrogance and indifferent behaviour generated good interest. Frictions between Talati and small farmers being a common phenomenon, the subject was considered to be not only realistic but very useful. The viewers did not face any difficulty in understanding the dialogues and the message in the satire.

The audience appreciated the value of such programmes in educating the village functionaries as well as the ordinary farmers. However, majority commented that the suggestion to lodge a complaint with the police if the Talati is unhelpful does not sound sensible as it would lead to further problems and make the things worse. It was pointed out that if the Talati is unhelpful, the only way is to approach the village elders like the Sarpanch to bring pressure on him or to report the matter to the Tahsildar who controls the Talati. Except for this critical comment, the programme was well received. It was generally agreed that programmes of this nature would be able to create awareness among the functionaries on how to deal with the public.

**III. Venue: Amondi**

Content of the programme: Field-based programme: Duration 20 mt.

The programme is a documentary on Thakkar community, recorded on $^1/_2$" video. It depicts the life of the inhabitants of a small tribal hamlet in Ambegaon taluka. The focus is on the economic life and the hard-working nature of the Thakkars. The programme explains the areas where improvements are possible like cattle-breeding, goat-rearing, etc., which can be profitably developed for their economic welfare.

Audience composition: 50 men, 30 women, 75 children

The viewers could identify the location where the programme was produced because it is situated very near the village. Some of the menfolk could even identify the familiar faces. The Thakkar tribals who came in large numbers from the nearby hamlet to watch the programme were particularly happy to see their own men and women on the TV screen. Many of them hopefully remarked that one day the television people may even visit their houses to know their miseries. An old man commented that the programme is the best to convey to the higher officers in Pune and Bombay about their problems because they would never be able to come to their village because of the poor communication facilities.

The tribals were convinced with the suggestion that adoption of milk cattle for dairy farming and goat rearing would go a long way in improving their economic standard but remarked that no bank would give them loans because they do not have lands. It was pointed out by some of the educated youth that the programme fails to depict the miseries of the tribals like the problem of drinking water, poor communication facilities, restrictions on firewood collection from the forest, harassment by forest guards, etc. It was suggested that instead of saying a word or two in the commentary about such major problems the villagers should have been asked to speak about their problems.

Women were attracted by the dance sequence and the *Nagapanchmi* song but were critical of the programme for not showing much of their social life. They also expressed that after seeing the programme one may get the impression of everything being fine with the Thakkars. It does not show how they struggle to earn a living.

The non-tribals watched the programme with interest. But, they were not able to offer any critical comments. The tribals watched the programme with some sense of involvement. Hence, the concern for a true reflection of their lives.

### Some Basic Inferences

On the basis of the limited feedback exercises and discussions with the villagers in respect of the content and presentation aspects, the following inferences are attempted:

1. The subject matter should be of immediate practical relevance.

The more it is related to the economic life and subsistence, the more is the interest evinced in the programme.

2. Instead of a generalised approach, specific in-depth analyses of the problem and concrete suggestions are needed.
3. Folk formats are easily accepted because they form part of village life and enjoy the patronage of the young and old alike.
4. Satires on common man's problem are appreciated if they are able to suggest practical solutions. The viewers are not satisfied with mere invocation of sympathy for their problems. What they expect is the way to achieve the ideal presented in the programme.

**Delivery System**

Messages do not travel themselves to hit the audience. They need to be carried and reached at the destination to stimulate response. The system establishing links between the source and the receiver, for effecting the flow of communication is as crucial as the machinery at the pre-production and production stages. The infrastructure for the production and the message content, its relevance, purpose and treatment have no meaning unless there is a system to create interaction of the audience with the medium.

In rural TV communication there is no direct exposure of the audience to the telecasts. The reception of the programmes is dependent on the number of agencies which operate to interlink the Doordarshan transmitters with the audience. Thus, the whole infrastructure for carrying the TV signals from the transmitter to the audience for facilitating their exposure and promoting their interaction constitutes the delivery system. In the ultimate appraisal since the reach and response to the telecasts count significantly, the variables operating within the delivery system warrant a more critical study than the production variables. If the delivery system is not properly planned and organised, the communication cycle gets broken in between and the messages cannot reach the destination. For any effort in strengthening the production inputs must precede an effective delivery system where the communication drain during the process of diffusion is minimised.

Wilbur Schramm (1954) has compared the dissemination of development information to an irrigation system and observed that the need is to ensure an equal flow at the end of the channel taking care to prevent the seepage an route. Shingi and Mody (1974) who studied the Farm Programmes of Delhi TV observed "the organisation and management of the TV reception situation has received much less attention than it deserves. This may have been partly due to lack of information on how important it really is".

The Audience Research Unit of Srinagar TV which conducted a study on the response to community viewing in Kashmir Valley observed that the TV sets installed by the Government to facilitate exposure, remain locked up for most of the time (Ramesh Chandra: 1979). Studies in Lucknow area and SITE continuity clusters of Orissa, Bihar, Madhya Pradesh and Andhra Pradesh similarly point out the exposure of the rural audiences to the TV programmes as far from satisfactory because of some loose ends in the delivery system. In view of its paramount importance it is proposed to critically examine here the delivery system adopted in Maharashtra for taking TV to villages and identify the areas where there is communication loss.

## System for Rural Broadcasting in India

Before outlining the existing delivery system for rural TV in Maharashtra, it may be necessary to mention, in brief, the general frame-work evolved for rural broadcasting in the country.

Broadcasting being a federal subject, the responsibility for originating and transmitting the radio and television programmes rests wholly with the Union Government. All India Radio and Doordarshan thus have the obligation to create infrastructure for the broadcast of radio and TV programmes. But, they do not have the responsibility to provide reception facilities. The beneficiaries are expected to make their own arrangements.

During the late 1930s when AIR launched regular broadcasts for the rural audience, the Provincial Governments were approached for sponsoring Community Listening Schemes for facilitating exposure and utilisation of the broadcasts in villages, as the people could not afford individual sets. The North-west Frontier Province and subsequently the local authorities of Madras and Delhi have created Rural Broadcasting cells for the installation of community radio receiver sets, maintenance and promotion of organised listening under the guidance of a nominee in their respective service areas. This system was followed by other States when the broadcasting facilities were extended.

During 1954 the Central Government decided to promote community listening to radio with the objective of reaching the masses with the Plan messages and accelerating the process of development. The Community Listening Scheme thus formed part of the overall Extension machinery. Under the strategy, the Central Government decided to subsidise 50 per cent of the cost of the community listening sets. The Central participation gave a fillip to the State Rural Broadcasting Departments in extending the facility on a large scale.

With the encouraging response to the Radio Rural Forum Project experimented in Poona, in 1956, the Central Government decided to promote Radio Rural Forums for organised utilisation of rural broadcasts. Under a scheme initiated in 1959, the State Rural Broadcasting Departments were financed by the Central Government to provide listening facilities and organise listening through the appointment of custodians and ensuring the utilisation of the broadcasts.

With the transistor boon in the early sixties the number of radio receiver sets in villages slowly increased and domestic listening picked up. Consequently, the response to community listening decreased. Popular response to Radio Rural Forums (RRF) withered off. Finding no need, the Central Government discontinued the scheme of financing the Community Listening Scheme. Unable to shoulder the burden, the State Governments subsequently disbanded the huge machinery created for the maintenance of the receiver sets in villages and stopped the aid to the RRFs. However, with a skeleton staff most of the State Governments still continue to promote the Community Listening Scheme, by distributing subsidised receiver sets and undertaking their maintenance on a contributory basis.

## Community Television

When television was introduced in 1959 at Delhi, the system evolved for Rural Radio Listening was adopted for promoting community viewing of the experimental TV programmes. Initially community centres and teleclubs were organised for group viewing under the aegis of the Delhi Municipal Corporation as the service was limited to urban areas. Later when the rural service, Krishi Darshan, was introduced in 1967 the local administrations of Delhi and Haryana and U.P. States were entrusted with the installation of community TV sets and organisation of "farm teleclubs" by nominating custodians. Initially, set maintenance in Delhi was taken up by AIR engineers, but subsequently, in 1970, the responsibility was transferred to the Delhi Administration. When the TV network was extended to Maharashtra, Kashmir, Uttar Pradesh and other areas it was envisaged that the community viewing aspect would be fully taken care of by the respective State Governments.

**Rural Broadcasting in Maharashtra**

The Government of Maharashtra created the Rural Broadcasting Department, as early as in 1944, for the installation and maintenance of community radio sets in villages covered by AIR, Bombay. Later the services were extended to the Nagpur and Pune regions when these stations were added in 1948 and 1953 respectively. Two divisional offices were created by the Department for organising Radio Rural Forums and promoting the Community Listening Scheme.

In 1972, when the Television Centre was commissioned at Bombay, the Rural Broadcasting Department took up the responsibility for sponsoring the community viewing in urban, slum and rural areas and created a TV Division at Bombay. With the commissioning of the Pune Relay Centre one more divisional Office was set up at Pune for extending the Scheme to the rural areas covered by the Pune TV transmitter.

**Community Viewing Scheme**

In the management of the Community Viewing Scheme in Maharashtra a number of agencies are involved and it is not the only show of the Rural Broadcasting Department. The operational system is schematically represented in Appendix 17. The general framework of its working is outlined below.

The General Administration Department (GAD) of the Government of Maharashtra is the apex body controlling all the communications institutions under the Directorate General of Information and Public Relations. The Directorate of Rural Broadcasting functions as one of the constituents within the Directorate General of Information and Public Relations, as a technical department, administering the hardware aspects such as procurement, installation and maintenance of the community TV sets.

The District Planning and Development Councils (in which the district officials connected with development and elected representatives of the Zilla Parishad and State Legislature are represented) are in the overall charge of planning of developmental schemes in the district. These Councils allocate funds for the purchase of community TV sets as per budgeted outlay for the district, within the overall ceiling set by the Government. These funds are released to the Directorate of Rural Broadcasting through the Departments of Planning and Finance. The divisional offices of the Rural Broadcasting Department identify the villages for the installation of community TV sets according to the availability of funds.

It may be mentioned here that the community TV sets are primarily meant for installation in villages. But, some of them are provided to the institutions like Panchayat Samitis, Zilla Parishads, Municipalities in urban areas, and Industrial Welfare Centres and slums in cities.

### *Selection of Villages*

No specific criteria in terms of economic or social backwardness or communication exposure have been evolved for the location of the sets. Political pressures and local administrative influences play a significant part in the selection of places. However, the broad guidelines adopted in this connection are:

1. The villages should be within the primarily service area of the transmitter;
2. Should be electrified;
3. Should have a population of at least 1,000; and
4. Should be easily accessible in all seasons to facilitate maintenance.

### *Sets Subsidized by the Government*

The 58 cm (23") Black and White EC TV solid state set with modular construction is selected by the Government for installation under the scheme. A sum of Rs. 750 is collected from the Gram Panchayats or other subscribers as their contribution towards the cost of the set and installation charges. The rest is subsidized by the Government. In additions an amount of Rs. 200 is collected annually from the subscribers as their contribution towards the maintenance cost and the Government provides a matching grant of Rs. 200 per set annually for this purpose. Other accessories like line voltage corrector, antenna booster and the recurring charges of electricity consumption are to be borne by the subscribers.

*Custodians*

It is the responsibility of the institutional owners to nominate a custodian to operate the set, control the viewers and facilitate exposure to the telecasts. The Gram Panchayats generally nominate the Village Level Worker or, in his absence a person residing near the place of location so that he can operate the set on time. There is no system of payment to the custodian. He is expected to provide voluntary service.

*Sets from Central Pool*

The Central Government also participates in the promotion of the scheme. Each year some sets are distributed free of cost from the Central pool, through Doordarshan, to the States sponsoring the community viewing scheme. In Maharashtra these are installed in villages with a population of over 1,200 on the usual contributory basis. Under the scheme about 250 sets were received by the Rural Broadcasting Department from Doordarshan.

*Sets for Tribal Areas*

Under the Tribal sub-plan a small number of sets are earmarked for installation in tribal villages and their cost is fully subsidized by the Government. The subscribers have to meet only the recurring electricity charges.

*Coverage*

There are as many as 35,780 inhabited villages in the State. But, the total number of villages within the transmission area of Bombay and Pune transmitters is estimated to be about 3,900. Making a beginning with 25 sets in Bombay during 1972-73, the Department of Rural Broadcasting has installed about 820 sets for community viewing, by the end of 1978-79. Out of them nearly 750 are located in rural areas. Thus, in terms of coverage it works out to creation of exposure facilities in 20 per cent of the villages within the transmission area.

The growth of community sets over the years in the State is indicated in Table 8.2.

TABLE 8.2: Growth of community TV sets in Maharashtra

| Year | Bombay region | Pune region | Total |
|---|---|---|---|
| 1972-73 | 25 | — | 25 |
| 1973-74 | 93 | 82 | 175 |
| 1974-75 | 116 | 129 | 245 |
| 1975-76 | 214 | 243 | 457 |
| 1976-77 | 302 | 352 | 654 |
| 1977-78 | 333 | 379 | 712 |
| 1978-79 | 376 | 445 | 821 |
| 1979-80 | 386 | 526 | 912 |

Source: Department of Rural Broadcasting, Pune.

## *Outlay and Infrastructure*

The annual Plan outlay for 1979-80 on the scheme is about Rs. 511,000. The budgeted outlay for 1978-83 is Rs. 1.5 million. This excludes the non-Plan expenditure on staff and other establishment costs.

The Department of Rural Broadcasting has set up two divisional offices at Bombay and Pune for the execution of the scheme. The sanctioned staff strength at the divisional level is indicated below:

1. Divisional Engineer (1)
2. Deputy Engineer (1)
3. Technical Asstt. (1)
4. Supervisors (2)
5. TV Mechanics (2)
6. Mechanical Assts. (2)
7. Drivers (2)
8. Helpers (2)

Discussions with the officials reveal that the limitation in the expansion of the viewing facilities in villages is not on account of lack of staff or financial resources. The problems mainly relate to:

(a) small size of the villages;
(b) lack of electricity;
(c) scattered location and poor communication facilities; and
(d) shadow zones due to the hilly terrain.

With a view to estimating the gap between the potential and actual availability of facilities, the data were analysed for the Pune region and presented in Table 8.3.

TABLE 8.3: Community viewing facilities in the Pune region

| | Pune district | Satara district | Ahmed-nagar district | Total |
|---|---|---|---|---|
| Approx. number of villages in the transmission area | 1,200 | 450 | 250 | 1,900 |
| Number of villages having a population of 1,000 and electrified | 437 | 245 | 92 | 774 |
| Number of villages provided with TV as on 31-3-79 | 250 | 100 | 45 | 395 |

Table 8.3 indicates the effective coverage of villages with community TV sets as low primarily because of the poor infrastructure in villages. A typical village with population varying between 500 and 1,000, having no electricity, isolated and cut off from the main road which actually needs the communication exposure may remain untouched by TV for many more years to come. The average size of the village with TV facility in the Pune region works out to 3,525 while the average size of a village in the region is only 970.

*Loss in Communication*

The creation of facilities for group viewing is the basic for the exposure of the villagers to the medium. But, it is wrong to presume that once the community viewing sets are installed the exposure is automatic. There are a number of factors influencing the audience build-up and utilization of the programmes. These can be broadly classified under two heads: (a) physical constraints, and (b) human constraints.

The *physical constraints* include: (a) location of the set, (b) seasonal fluctuations, (c) physical arrangements for viewing, and (d) electricity failures.

Studies during SITE revealed the place of location of the set as an important factor for the utilization of the telecasts. If the set is placed in a centrally located public building where persons from all communities normally go without any inhibition, and if it is easily accessible in all seasons without any difficulty by the young and old alike, it attracts good crowds. But, if it is located in a *Harijan basti* (a ward where the scheduled caste people live), or in an isolated corner with no street lights, or at a place infested with snakes and scorpions, it restricts viewing (Agrawal: 1978, Rao and Ramachandra: 1976). As explained in Chapter 6, a large percentage of the persons particularly elders avoid television if it is located more than a kilometre away from their residences.

The community TV sets are mostly placed in the Panchayat office or the school building. People watch the programmes through an open window. Due to the absence of covered accommodation the exposure is severely restricted during the monsoon and winter seasons. Similarly, during the busy agricultural seasons like transplantation, harvesting, etc., the exposure is extremely low as people are busy with work till late in the evening. They hardly find time to watch TV.

### *Electricity Failures*

Electricity failures and voltage fluctuations are unpredictable in villages, particularly in the areas where electric motors and pump sets are in use for irrigation purposes. During the field work it was noticed that about 11 per cent of the potential exposure time was lost on account of current failures or disturbed power supply. Studies during SITE indicated that about 15 per cent of the total viewing time was lost on account of this constraint (Agrawal: 1978).

### *The Human Constraints*

The major seepage in communication is due to human constraints. The exposure of the villagers to the telecasts is dependent on the mercy of three agencies: (1) the Rural Broadcasting Department which lays the permanent way and takes the TV to villages and maintains the track; (2) the Gram Panchayat which owns and houses the set; and (3) the Custodian who holds the key. We may call these three as the crucial "gate-keepers" for they operate the invisible gates and check the flow of communication.

"Gate-keeping" in communication was first observed by psychologist Kurt Lewin. He pointed out that the longer the informational channel, the larger are the points along the channel at which someone will have the right to say whether the message shall be received and released or not. He added that the power to operate these "gates" and the rules and personalities that govern their operation become crucial in the flow of information (Lewin: 1947).

*Gate-keepers in Rural TV*

The conventional model of electronic communication system developed by Shannon and Weaver does not hold good in the case of rural TV communication process because the former envisages only five elements in the system as indicated below:

*Shannon-Weaver model of communication system*

Source ⟶ Message ⟶ Signal ⟶ Receiver ⟶ Destination

The model assumes that once the message is put on transmission, it is available for reception at the end of the audience. In rural TV the reception and interaction are dependent on the behaviour of three additional element mentioned earlier; the agency providing the set, the agency holding and housing the set, and the agency operating the set. In the flow of communication each agency is capable of acting as a lever, breaking the relay of messages and blocking the interaction of the audience with the medium. Hence, they are labelled the "gate-keepers".

Schematically the rural TV communication system may be represented with the additional filters as under:

Transmitter R.B.⟶ Gram⟶Community⟶ Custodian⟶ Audience
deptt. Panchayat TV set

Since the exposure of the villagers to the telecasts is dependent on the unpredictable behaviour of three agencies operating on their own parameters, they are considered loose ends. In Appendix 18 the different variables in rural TV communication, and how the flow of communication gets thinner as it reaches the destination is diagramatically represented.

In the following paragraphs it is proposed to discuss briefly how the additional elements contribute individually and severally towards seepage and loss in communication in the process of diffusion, before it actually reaches the audience.

## Rural Broadcasting

### *Set Maintenance*

The Rural Broadcasting Department (RBD), which is the service agency for the maintenance of the sets, functions on the presumption that as long as there is no written complaint from the Gram Panchayat, i.e., the *Sarpanch* or the *Gram Sewak*, the sets are functioning all right. Neither the Department nor the originating stations (i.e. Doordarshan) have evolved any machinery for monitoring the operation of the sets and watching their utilization. The people expect the Gram Panchayats to take prompt action regarding set maintenance, as the RBD Department does not take cognizance of their complaints. But it was observed that the Gram Panchayats are indifferent and slow in reporting set breakdowns to the RBD. As a measure of economy, the RBD also waits for a number of complaints to come from a cluster of villages, so that it can plan and attend to the maintenance work at a time instead of making frequent trips.

The cumulative effect of this system of operation makes a set with technical faults to remain inoperative for any period ranging between 15-60 days at a stretch. The department of Rural Broadcasting, however, maintains that it does not take more than 30 days in any case from the date of receipt of the complaint. But, much time is lost before the complaint is actually registered.

During the field work it was observed that two out of the five sets (Narodi and Narayan Gavhan) were out of order and two (Rajpur and Amondi) were defective with poor picture quality. The Gram Panchayat at Narodi gave the impression that it had lodged a complaint about two months earlier but nothing was done. The set at Narayan Gavhan was similarly lying idle for over 20 days due to some technical fault. The custodian informed that the matter was promptly reported to the RBD, but none attended to the set. However, inquiries in the R.B. office revealed the non-receipt of any complaint from the place.

During April-May, 1979, the researcher remained in the selected villages for observation and interviews. Of the 27 days, when efforts were made to monitor the sets and observe the audience response, on as many as 17 days the sets could not be switched on due to breakdowns. This works out to a serious wastage of about three-fifths of the potential exposure time. But, this may seem to be incidental and not a case for generalization. At the same time, the argument of the

RBD that hardly 10 per cent of the set-days are lost due to technical faults appears to be untenable. The RBD does not take into account the number of days lost before the complaint has been received in their office.

Field discussions revealed that a big communication gap exists between the Gram Panchayats and the R.B. Department. There is not co-ordination and interaction either at the District level or at the Block level. Since no records are maintained by the the Gram Panchayats indicating the utilization of the sets, break-downs and power failures, it is not possible to identify and apportion the loss in communication between the agencies. However, a minimal wastage of 7-8 days in a month on account of set disorders may be estimated under the existing circumstances. By and large this has been corroborated by the villagers during informal discussions.

### *Gram Panchayats*

The community TV set is the property of the Gram Panchayat and the responsibility to arrange for its safe custody and operation for public viewing rests on it. As Panchayat Secretaries, the *Gram Sewaks* are officially nominated as the TV Custodians. In practice the responsibility is delegated to the Panchayat Peon *(Sipai)* for three reasons: (1) The *Gram Sewaks* are mostly non-residents, they do not stay regularly in the village, (2) Even if they stay in the village they are quite busy always running up and down from the village to the Block office, getting agricultural inputs, distributing them to the farmers, etc.; and (3) They feel below their status to switch on and off the set and keep a watch over the crowds as an "attendant".

The Panchayat peons are thus *de facto* custodians at most of the places even though the *de jure* custodians are the *Gram Sewaks.* Since there is no system of payment to the custodians, the general attitude at this level is "no pay: no work". The Gram Panchayats also feel that morally they have no right to demand work from the Panchayat peons to come daily after office hours and keep the set open during the transmission, remain there throughout and lock the set when everybody leaves, without any payment.

In view of these considerations the Gram Panchayats as a compromise formula evolved some norms of working of the community TV sets. These are self-evolved ethics and by and large respected as a customary law by most of the Gram Panchayats in the region. Under the system, the Custodians are obliged to keep the sets open on three days in week for specific programmes.

The days are decided on the basis of the schedule of the programmes which draw the "maximum crowds". The pattern of set operation evolved on this principle is indicated below:

- Thursdays for Chayageet (Hindi film songs) from 9.10 to 9.50 p.m.;
- Saturdays for Marathi feature film/long plays from 5.30 to 8.30 p.m.;
- Sundays for Hindi feature film from 5.30 to 9.00 p.m.

The normal practice is to keep the TV set closed on other days, except otherwise instructed by the *Sarpanch.* Special requests are occasionally entertained if the demand is considerable for programmes like sports (cricket matches, etc.), plays and other entertainment items. Sometimes requests for agricultural programmes for specific items of interest from progressive farmers are also honoured. As and when such requests are received (after seeing the local announcements on TV or seeing programme announcements in daily papers) the *Sipai* is requested to open the set and it is left to his convenience and discretion.

The Gram Panchayats justify this policy on the following grounds:

1. They cannot entrust the work to the *Sipai* if it is for all the days. They need some arrangements to be made for paid custodians.
2. Under no circumstances they can skip the popular entertainment items because the demand is maximum for them. Other programmes attract only a limited audience and it is possible to avoid them.
3. Electric consumption would be comparatively very high if the set is kept open daily. To keep the power bills to the minimum, they need to restrict the use of TV.
4. The present arrangement is by and large acceptable to the majority. They have no complaints and there is no need to alter the system.

The practice of the Gram Panchayats to keep the set open only on three days in a week, for popular entertainment items, has no official sanction. On the contrary there are instructions to keep open the sets on all the days for public viewing. But neither the Panchayat Samitis, nor the Zilla Parishad, nor the Rural Broadcasting Department has ever evolved any system to curb the habit of switching on the sets for entertainment items and keeping them closed on other days. No one has ever insisted on the keeping of records showing the utilisation of sets. As the whole system of operation is left to the Gram Panchayats, they have adopted a system which is operationally convenient to them, unmindful of the premises under which they have been provided with the community TV sets. In fact, four out of the five Gram Panchayats where the field-work was conducted gave the impression that since they have been asked to take care of the TV sets and make their own arrangements for their operation, they are free to fix the timings of operation according to their convenience and local demand.

The Gram Panchayats are, thus, apparently the main "gate-keepers" blocking the exposure of the people to almost all the development items. The seepage on account of their decision to keep the sets open only for entertainment items works out to be alarming when compared to other constraints like set breakdowns or power failures. It is essential to remove this snag first to ensure free flow of communication.

### *Custodians*

The custodian is the most crucial link in the channel of communication in the case of rural TV. Since he keeps the key, he acts as the final link between the audience and the medium. He grants the exposure and brings the audience face to face with TV. His involvement and commitment to the medium are essential for the promotion of the viewing habit. Studies during SITE revealed that an inactive and apathetic Custodian acts as a negative factor and discourages viewing (Agrawal: 1978). A Custodian taking pains in organising viewing and evincing personal interest in the programmes is an asset, as he stimulates audience participation (Rao & Ramachandra: 1976).

Chawla who made a study of the community viewing situation in Kashmir valley observed that the Custodians should be able to understand the characteristics of the medium and become a link between the community and the broadcasting scheme (Chawla: 1978).

What stakes the Custodians have in the working of the community TV sets in Maharashtra? Are they in a position to understand the characteristics of the medium and stimulate interaction? To facilitate a discussion on these issues, a brief background of the TV Custodians in the five selected villages is given below:

1. *Narayan Gavhan: Sipai* (the Panchayat peon), a 50-year-old literate from a Scheduled Caste community, is entrusted with the responsibility of looking after the library, community radio as well as the community TV set. He also works as postman on part-time basis. Since he stays in the Panchayat building itself, he does not find it an extra burden to operate the TV set. But, as the Gram Panchayat has instructed him to keep the set open only on three days, he sticks to the schedule.

2. *Narodi:* A 20-year-old Maratha youth educated up to Standard VIII, comes from a family of poor farmers. He works as a salesman in the Consumer Cooperative Society located on the premises of the Panchayat office. As he is free during the evenings and mornings, he accepted the additional job of looking after the Panchayat reading room and community radio for a payment of Rs. 20 per month. He also operates the community TV on three days in a week but he does not get any additional payment for it.

He could recollect the title of the rural programmes, but could not give the timings of their telecast. According to him only occasionally the agricultural programmes are tuned in, on request by progressive farmers.

3. *Amondi:* As the Gram Panchayat does not have a building, the community TV set was placed in the school building and one of the teachers was officially nominated as the Custodian. Since he remains busy, as a personal arrangement he handed over the key to one of the unemployed youths staying next to the school. This boy is a college drop-out, aged about 21 years. He is planning to set up a poultry farm under the self-employment scheme.

As he is free, he finds a good pastime to watch the TV for a few hours in the day. He switches on the set almost daily for the Marathi and Hindi programmes. But, he could not give the timings of the rural programmes and admitted that his interest is confined to film-based items, news, sports and plays.

4. *Taleghar:* A 25-year-old tribal boy from a farmer's family. His brother owns a provision store and a flour mill in front of the temple where the community TV set is located. He accepted the responsibility to operate the set on three days because his shop is located near the temple and he is comparatively free during the evenings. According to

him, there is no lock and key for the window where the set is placed and therefore everybody fiddles with it. Thus, there is no specific person with the responsibility to take care of the set or to operate it at regular timings. The Gram Panchayat hardly takes any interest in the matter.

At the time of field-work the antenna of the set was found broken resulting in very unsatisfactory picture quality. But the Rural Broadcasting Department was not informed of this situation.

5. *Rajapur:* The TV set was originally kept with the *Sarpanch* as the Gram Panchayat does not have a building. He was making use of it daily for his domestic viewing and allowing others only on three days for the film-based programmes. A section of the villagers objected to his using the set for family viewing and brought pressure on other Panchayat members to get the set removed to the village temple which is accessible to everybody. Since then the Sarpanch is indifferent to the TV. He does not take any interest in it.

The set is placed in a wooden case, without any lock and key. Since there is no Custodian, it is handled by everybody. However, the villagers decided in a common meeting to restrict the use of TV to three days to curtail the electricity charges as the bill for the village temple is shared by all the families in the hamlet. The upkeeping of the set was very unsatisfactory at the time of field-work.

It is clear from the background of the Custodians that the sponsors do not expect them to do anything more than mere operation of the set. A Custodian is not visualised as more than an attendant. There is no expectation of their performance as a "catalytic agent" either to promote audience build-up or stimulate interaction.

There is no selectivity in the appointment of the Custodians and no effort is made to induct persons who can appreciate the potentialities of the medium and strengthen the institution. As long as they lack the basic perspective, it is wrong to assume that the Custodian would contribute in any way towards effective utilisation of the medium for development purposes.

One of the reasons attributed for the absence of commitment and devotion to the medium at the level of the Custodians is lack of remuneration for their services. Payment for work does not always ensure positive contribution towards effective working of the system. In Kashmir valley the Custodians are paid a sum of Rs. 50 per month. According to field studies no less than 60 per cent of the Custodians entrust the work to someone else in the family or neighbourhood and shirk the responsibility. In 25 per cent of the cases, the sets remain idle when the Custodians are absent (Rameshchandra: 1978). Similarly, during SITE the Custodians were paid Rs. 15 per month. Even then they were irregular in set operation and entrusted more often than not the work to somebody in the family (Rao and Ramachandra: 1976). All the ills for the low utilisation of the sets cannot, therefore, be attributed to lack of payment to the Custodians.

What seems to be lacking is the comprehension of the human and material investments on the medium and its potentialities primarily at the Gram Panchayat level. As long as they remain unconcerned and indifferent, it may not be possible to achieve the Custodians involvement. Once the Gram Panchayats' commitment to the medium is ensured, it should not be difficult to minimise the wastage in communication at their level as well as the Custodians level.

# 9

# TELEVISION FOR CULTURE CHANGE

TELEVISION ENTERED our country with a promise to provide formal and non-formal education. Currently, it sustains with the assurance of accelerating the process of socio-economic change. Its future is linked with its performance as a supporting medium for promoting development. In the earlier chapters, the goals of the medium, current status, role performance and constraints of operation have been discussed. It is proposed to examine in this chapter its potentialities and limitations as an institution of change in rural areas, and suggest ways and means for better utilisation.

Before initiating the discussion on whether television is in a position to function as a change agent to stimulate development or not, an elucidation of the concepts like culture change, social change, acculturation, industrialisation, modernisation may be useful, because all of them are used, rather loosely, to explain the response to television communication.

## Culture Change

Societies are never static. Modification in social institutions, ideas, values, technology and other products of human interaction, through time, is a universal phenomenon. Culture by Tylor's definition includes "beliefs, art, morals, law, custom and any other capabilities and habits acquired by man as a member of the society". All additions, adjustments, modifications, deprivations in these elements of culture can, therefore, be subsumed under the rubric of culture change. Its scope is wide, meaning any change in learnt behaviour, beliefs and their products. It explains the changes in technology, social organisation and structure, political and economic institutions, human value orientation as well as religion.

### Social Change

Social change implies changes in actual human behaviour. Moore has defined the process as "the significant alteration of social structures (that is, of patterns of social action and interaction) including consequences and manifestations of such structures embodied in norms (rules of conduct), values and cultural products and symbols" (Moore: 1968).

The perspective of social change is considered to be narrower than that of culture change because social change is only a part of culture change. However, since cultures are integrated wholes, changes in the social system affect the larger cultural system and *vice versa*. Social change cannot be singled out and explained as an isolated process. Despite these inter-linkages, the term culture change is preferred to explain the totality of change in societies, as it implies changes in the parts as well as the whole system.

### Acculturation

The process of culture change takes place under two conditions: (1) Internal inventions and readjustments in traditional institutions and (2) External influences, while in interaction with other cultures. The term acculturation (or transculturation) is used to describe the process that occurs when two or more previously separated cultures come into contact with each other, to a degree sufficient to produce changes in either or both. Redfield, Herskovits and Linton as a Committee of the American Anthropologists defined the concept thus: "Acculturation comprehends those phenomena which result when groups of individuals having different cultures come into continuous first-hand contact with subsequent changes in the original culture patterns of either or both the groups" (Kroeber: 1948).

Acculturation denotes a two-way traffic between interacting cultures and explains the changes in various facets of culture due to this interaction. Initially the term was used to describe the changes in the traditional "subordinate societies" under the impact of "superordinate" societies during the colonial days. According to Linton, in the process of acculturation, the changes instigated are almost invariably not spontaneous and automatic but purposively directed or controlled at least in part by the superior society". However, the logical definition offered later by is: "The effect on culture of contact with other cultures. In this would be included the effect on societies that carried the culture" (Kroeber: 1948).

By common acceptance, the concept now denotes all the results of inter-cultural interaction. It is particularly adopted to explain the transformation of societies in conditions of gradual planned change, with no coercion involved.

**Industrialisation**

Industrialisation is a process initially generated by the Industrial Revolution in England and later spread to other countries. The values associated with the process are essentially economic in nature, such as creation and absorption of innovations in technology, higher forces of energy and larger production units. Basically the process suggests a flow of technological innovations from an industrialised society to an unindustrialised society. Slotkin defined industrialisation as a "trait complex with its dominant features as extensive division of labour, formal industrial organisation, use of complex machinery and interdependence between the industrial organisation and wider society" (Slotkin: 1950). In general, industrialisation denotes transfer of technology, application of scientific knowledge, development of production skills and complex material culture.

**Modernisation**

Historically, modernisation is the process of change towards those types of social, economic and political systems that developed in Western Europe and North America from the 18th-19th century and then spread to other European countries, and in the 19th and 20th centuries to the South American, Asian and African countries (Eisenstadt: 1966).

Modernisation is conceived as a process of transformation of traditional societies with awareness plus technology. The basic characteristics of modern society are considered to be liberty, stability and continuity on the one hand and nationality and technical efficiency on the other. According to Inkels and Smith, a modern man is "an informed participant citizen, he has a marked sense of personal efficiency, he is highly independent and autonomous in his relations to traditional sources of influence, especially when he is making basic decisions about how to conduct his personal affairs, he is ready for new ideas and experiences, that is, he is relatively flexible" (Inkeles & Smith: 1974).

The general image of modernity is, however, acceptance of material culture and behaviour which is currently in fashion. Inayatullah has pointed out that "modernity carries an implicit connotation of being like the one which is currently acceptable or fashionable" (Inayatullah: 1967). Thus, it does not seem to include lasting changes in the socio-cultural system of a traditional society open to cross-fertilisation of ideas.

In view of the limited perspective of the modernisation and industrialisation concepts, it is preferred to adopt the generic term of culture change, to interpret the transformation process that is envisaged by exposure to the television medium in villages.

Development is more than mere expansion or sophistication of technology. The role of television does not end with the introduction of technology. Similarly, our philosophy of development is not acceptance in toto of all that is "modern" or associated with Western culture. The objective is to preserve and promote the traditional cultural patterns, that are in harmony with the development goals. Television has an obligation to sustain the traditional art forms and values, like the security of the individual, the well-knit family system, sacrifice of self for group interests, absence of commercial approach, etc. The national leaders have particularly decried the tendency of aping the West in television programmes.

## Changing the Cultures

Anthropological studies have established the change in cultures as a continuous but slow process. They also indicate that culture change does not mean change of equal magnitude in all components of cultures. Herskovits (1950) summarised the basic principles of culture change as under:

1. Borrowing in recognised procedures of society, a new concept, a reorientation of point of view can only come when people agree on the desirability of change.
2. Borrowing, even in most intimate contacts, is selective. The principle of selectivity is basic to the process of any culture

change.

3. Resistance to change or cultural conservatism is universal.
4. Every society has certain focal aspects of culture. Their interests centre on this particular area and institutions relating to it. Where cultures are free in contact, the focal aspect will be the one where new elements are most hospitably received.
5. Hard-core elements like religion and social structure, which form the bedrock of a society are change-resistant, and are least influenced by external forces of change.

Normally the course of change is culture-contact situations is noticed in the following order:

— material culture and technology
— economic life
— social organisation
— other institutions of social structure
— religion and magic
— language

**Changing the Individuals**

Klapper (1960), basing his conclusions on a review of about 270 studies on effects of communication, offered some generalisations. The important among them are summarised below:

1. Mass communication ordinarily does not serve as a necessary and sufficient cause of audience effects, but rather functions among and through a nexus of mediating factors or influences.
2. These mediating factors are such that they typically render mass communication a contributory agent, but not the sole cause in a process of reinforcing the existing conditions.
3. Persuasive communication functions as an agent of reinforcement than as an agent of change.
4. Mass communication is, however, highly effective in creating attitudes on newly arisen or newly evolved issues. It is particularly effective in the case of children who have no knowledge of or attitudes to the subject.
5. Mass media can communicate facts without changing relevant opinions. This indicates their ability in certain types of instruction.

Schramm similarly cautioned us that "the usefulness of mass media does not lie in frontal attacks on strongly held attitudes or long-valued customs. These strongly held positions are in the domain of personal influence and group norms. If changes are to be made on strongly defended customs and beliefs, interpersonal communication is required, because group change is involved. In such major decisions, therefore, the mass media can only indirectly help. They can feed information to the channels of interpersonal influence" (Schramm: 1964).

**Review of the Potentialities of TV in Rural Development**

With the theoretical background given in the preceding paragraphs the potentialities of television in rural development and culture change are critically reviewed in the following paragraphs.

As explained in Chapter 1, the basic goal of development is to satisfy the essential needs – material as well as non-material — of the people, starting with the most underprivileged groups. In the context of our country, the meaning of development is explained as: *sarva jana hitaya, sarva jana sukhaya* (for the good and happiness of all) instead of *"bahu jana hitaya, bahu jana sukhaya"* (for the good and happiness of the majority).

Any strategy of development involves changes in the institutions and functioning of the whole society. The process cannot be compartmentalised and taken up piecemeal. It calls for an integrated approach. Secondly, since the process must be carried out by and with the people, and not for them, it implies socialisation of the people at the grassroot level with the elements of development. This is to equip them to decide for themselves what is essential and desirable for them. It also implies making simultaneously available to them what they want so as to avoid frustration.

Economic development with social justice, establishment of an egalitarian society, freedom from all forms of exploitation, and democratic participation are the fundamental values governing our philosophy of development. These emanate from the goals enshrined in the Constitution. All the functional institutions for planned change and development are created with the responsibility, to contribute directly or indirectly towards the attainment of these goals.

Television is a national institution committed to public service. As a medium of communication, it is assigned with the objective of accelerating the process of socio-economic change in the country. The avowed policy of the Government is to make the television service positively rural-based, so that development of the masses in rural areas could be initiated at a faster pace. The role expectations from the medium, as detailed in Chapter 3, may be summarised as under:

1. To provide an effective communication link between the Government and the people, and to reach the unreached sections through the organisation of community TV.
2. To orient the service to the benefit of the common man instead of the urban elite for their entertainment.
3. To diffuse essentially development-oriented information with particular attention to meet the needs of the underprivileged in rural areas and urban slums.
4. To assist in political socialisation by providing information on current problems and educate the people to participate in the affairs of the nation.
5. To promote interaction, and change the way of life of the people, particularly in social attitudes, and infuse rational thinking.

In the context of these expectations, it is proposed to analyse the performance and potentialities of television, with reference to the field data presented in the earlier chapters.

### 1. *To Provide an Effective Communication Link with the Masses*

In Chapter 4, where the status of television has been analysed *vis-a-vis* other communication media, the data reveal that the exposure of the rural population to television is extremely small. Despite the availability of the facility of community TV, about 36 per cent of the villagers remain completely unexposed to television. Of the remaining 64 per cent, while one-half watch TV once a week or so, the rest watch only very infrequently. The non-participation among females is to the extent of 53 per cent, while it is about 23 per cent among the males.

Illiteracy has been found to be an important barrier to television exposure and this is contrary to the general presumption that TV can effectively communicate with the illiterate audience. The data discouragingly indicate clustering of the media, with those who are exposed to other channels like print, radio, etc., maintaining greater interaction with TV, and those who have no exposure to radio, print and other channels remaining untouched by TV. Maximum utilisation of TV has been noticed among those who have free leisure time like dependents, white-collar workers, traders, artisans, etc., than among farmers and landless labourers.

The present study does not reflect much scope for reaching the unreached masses through the organisation of community TV as it exists in the Pune region. The community TV facilities exist only in better-off villages (except in the case of tribal villages covered under the Tribal sub-plan), which otherwise enjoy the essential infrastructure, and have better exposure in terms of media reach, interaction with urban areas, contact with extension agents, etc. In the study area, the average population of the village with community TV viewing facility has been found to be around 3,500 as against the average size of 970 of an ordinary village. The data also do not support the contention of sizable "leapfrogging" to television, cutting across other conventional media like radio and print. The exposure of the people to radio being fairly widespread, the proportion of first-generation media participants, having direct exposure to television communication, is meagre particularly in the non-tribal villages.

One of the basic determinants of exposure to TV in the community viewing situation, is the distance from the residence to the place of location of the set. The data indicate that even persons residing at a distance of about a kilometer or so from the community TV, seldom avail of the facility due to problems like walking in the night, lack of street lights, etc. Those, who are residing in the hamlets far away from the main village, continue to remain mostly unexposed to the medium. Under these circumstances, television does not seem to be in a position to establish an effective communication link between the masses scattered in the interior villages and the Government. At present it is able to provide benefit primarily to those who are already served by other media. The interior villages mostly depend upon traditional channels like the weekly market, kin groups, friends, local leaders, and to a fairly large extent the radio. Among the mass media, the potentialities of radio are appreciably higher than either newspapers, or TV or films. Both in terms of proliferation and exposure, radio commands a better position than other media.

### 2. *Orientation of the Service to the Benefit of the Common Man*

The potential audience of the Bombay Doordarshan Kendra is essentially concentrated in Bombay city and suburban areas. But the relay centre at Pune covers primarily rural areas. Taken as a whole, the proportion of the rural population in the service area of the two transmitters works out to 36 per cent of the total 12.5 million population. But the number of the community television sets located in the villages hardly exceeds 750 out of the total 1,99,000 domestic sets in the region, which are mostly concentrated in Bombay, its suburbs and Pune city. Under these circumstances, it is unreasonable to expect the service to have a rural bias.

The analysis of the output of the Centre in Chapter 7 indicates that to meet the demands of the cosmopolitan audiences in the service area, the programmes are generated in four languages, viz. English, Hindi, Marathi and Gujarati. The non-Marathi programmes take nearly two-thirds of the total telecast time and these are wholly urban-oriented.

In the Marathi language service, the exclusive rural programmes constitute approximately 11 per cent with 60 minutes' duration per week. In terms of the total output of the Centre, however, this works out to hardly three per cent. The general Marathi language service is primarily oriented towards the elite both in entertainment and informational content. Hardly one-third of the programmes excluding the news and feature films are aimed at the common man.

### 3. *Diffusion of Purposeful Programmes for Rural Audiences*

As indicated earlier, the total duration of the rural service is only 60 minutes per week. The content analysis of these programmes given in Chapter 8 indicates that nearly two-thirds of the time is utilised for hard-core instructional programmes on agriculture and animal husbandry. A further analysis of these instructional items reveals that they are mostly oriented towards the progressive farmers, who have the resources like education, pump sets, modern agricultural implements and money. The small farmers mostly cultivating traditional varieties on rain-fed land are not able to derive any significant benefit. In addition, a substantial proportion of the programmes relates to crops specific to the Konkan area, having no relevance to the Pune region.

The general image of the hard-core instructional programme on agriculture and animal husbandry, in terms of their relevancy and utility to the average farmer, is low, particularly among village functionaries and the Extension officials. No efforts are made to organise viewing of these programmes for promoting interaction. Even the consensus among the farmers is that the programmes are superfluous for all farmers: small, medium and progressive. The contention is that the small farmers, particularly the illiterates, are not in a position to comprehend the content and make use of the information. The medium and progressive farmers depend mostly on the Extension officials, the radio and books, because they need specific and detailed information. The information provided on TV is not new to them and sounds redundant.

The coverage of other non-agricultural programmes like social education, health care, occupational avenues for artisans, supplementing incomes by adopting small-scale and cottage industries is so little that the viewers have not been able to feel their impact.

The needs of the small farmers and village artisans and the landless agricultural labourers are not only simple but essentially centre round their survival. Most of the information they exchange relates to their occupation and food. TV is not able to establish its bona fides as a channel to meet their basic informational needs. As such, they continue to depend on the traditional channels like family members, kin-groups, local leaders, etc.

The mass audience consisting of the agricultural labourers, small and marginal farmers and housewives do not get what they need from the instructional programmes. As a natural consequence, they tend to show keen interest in entertainment programmes, particularly the feature films and plays. This is due to the negative effect, and it cannot be interpreted as a positive preference for entertainment items over the instructional items. The feedback on selected purposeful programmes with a rural bias indicates that the desire to see meaningful programmes concerning rural life is much higher than the interest to watch pure entertainment programmes. This observation has been supported by earlier studies by SAC during SITE. Thus, when the feed is not according to the need, the needs are reconditioned to the feed. Unless the pattern of output is altered to meet the essential requirements of the audience in rural areas, it may be difficult to discourage them from the growing addiction to film-based entertainment programmes.

Despite the limited output of programmes covering rural life, the image of television as a medium of "knowledge" and "utility" is encouragingly high. The data presented in Chapter 7 indicate that the presence of TV is regarded as an asset rather than a source of nuisance. Its benefit to children in enlarging their horizons, creating awareness of the happenings in other parts of the country is highly appreciated and acknowledged. There is a positive feeling that exposure to television equips the children to think in terms of a better life. Secondly, their attitude to community viewing and watching the programmes together with all communities is considered to be a great asset for removing tensions in the long run. There is a demand for the extension of TV on these considerations and from no quarters is there a suggestion for its removal.

### 4. *Political Socialisation*

The potentialities of television in creating political awareness and generating interest on current issues seems to be limited. In this context, newspapers have been observed to pay the major role and the contribution of the radio is also meagre. The data presented in Chapter 7 indicate that those who have frequent exposure to daily newspapers are in a better position to explain the topical issues at the regional, national and international levels. Political awareness is found to be basically associated with literacy. The exposure of the illiterates to radio or TV does not seem to contribute towards assimilation of any political knowledge. The main problem is lack of comprehension to digest such information. Their selection is, therefore, limited to entertainment items.

Another important observation is that those who are mostly worried about their survival (like small and marginal farmers and agricultural labourers) are not psychologically oriented to receive any news that does not concern their immediate family. The question of their direct or indirect exposure to TV to gain political news or news on current issues of the nation is a remote possibility. Under the circumstances, TV does not seem to be in a position to contribute in any significant way towards political socialisation of the illiterate masses. However, it helps the educated and politically conscious persons to verify their information from newspapers and other sources.

### 5. *To Promote Interaction and Change Attitudes*

Television for the rural audience and the institution of community TV are inseparable; one goes with the other. When television expansion plans were mooted with the commitment that the medium would be utilised for rural development, it was assumed that the respective State

Governments would take the responsibility of promoting Community TV in villages. But neither Doordarshan nor the State Governments have made efforts to evolve organised systems for group viewing and follow up discussions. There is no in-built mechanism for regular feedback on the monitoring of the sets and the response to the programmes.

The data presented in Chapter 8 indicate that the system existing in Maharashtra for community TV viewing in villages is weak and non-functional. In most of the villages, the people do not get exposure to the developmental programmes as the television sets remain open only for the film-based programmes.

The basic reason for the unsatisfactory utilisation of the service is the psychology of "mind thy business" among the agencies involved in the project. Doordarshan, the State Rural Broadcasting Department and the Gram Panchayats function in their respective grooves, in isolation, without any mutual interaction. Doordarshan, as an agency responsible for the production and transmission of the programmes, functions with the feeling that the responsibility to organise the community TV viewing rests with the State Government, and as a third party it has nothing to say in organisational matters. The State Rural Broadcasting Department, which is entrusted with the installation and maintenance of the sets, feels that the responsibility of organising community TV sets rests wholly with the Zilla Parishads, Panchayat Samitis and Gram Panchayats. As a technical service department, RBD does not see any role for it in the managerial aspects of the scheme. The Gram Panchayats, on the other hand, feel that it cannot be held responsible for the organisational matters as there is no provision for the appointment of a regular Custodian at the village level.

Thus the system operates without the provision for the institution of a regular Custodian to take care of the essential elements such as switching on and off the set, promoting viewing, initiating follow-up discussions, providing feed-back on programmes to the TV centre, maintenance of records, and reporting of faults to the Rural Broadcasting Department. These aspects were not seriously considered assuming that TV would automatically attract audiences, provide a stimulus for discussion, and the Village Level Workers would take care of the sets as Panchayat Secretaries. These premises have been proved wrong but no corrective action has been taken.

The Gram Panchayat are the main "gate-keepers" blocking the exposure of the people to the programmes. Their argument for keeping the sets open only for the "popular" film-based programme is that there is no arrangement in the system for payment to the Custodian, and that nobody wants to do the job on a voluntary basis on all the days. The second argument is that the attendance for the rural programmes is thin, and so it does not warrant taking the trouble of switching on and off the set for a few persons who may not even understand the programmes.

The Panchayat Samitis and Zilla Parishads which control the Gram Panchayats have not been able to take any corrective measures except issuing some routine circulars reminding the Gram Panchayat of their obligation to provide facilities for community viewing of TV. The taluka level Panchayat Extension Officers are expected to supervise the utilisation of the sets. But in practice they hardly exercise any control. The Gram Panchayats do not keep any records of the monitoring of the sets and set breakdowns. Neither the Panchayat Samitis nor the Rural Broadcasting Department has evolved any system for their maintenance.

There is no organised feedback on the monitoring of the sets or on the programme content. Doordarshan has an Audience Research Unit at the Bombay TV Centre. But so far no studies have been conducted and results released. Thus, all the departments are functioning unaware of the situation at the receivers' end.

Another serious lacuna in the system is the communication gap between the Rural Broadcasting Department and the Gram Panchayats regarding the maintenance of the sets. The observations indicate that the information about the set breakdowns is not promptly communicated to the Rural Broadcasting Department by the Gram Panchayats. The RBD does not take cognizance of the complaints from the viewers. Secondly, it does not take into consideration the amount of loss in communication before a formal complaint is received by it. Thirdly, it may take its own time, anywhere between 8 and 30 days, for repairs due to problems of transport, spares, staff, etc. The cumulative effect of all these constraints is a loss of about 20-25 per cent of the potential exposure time.

The delivery system being unorganised and ineffectively controlled, the interaction of the villagers with the medium is extremely poor, specifically as regards the developmental programmes. As such, they have not been able to locate TV as a potential medium to meet their basic informational needs. Comparatively the position of the radio is better than even that of personal channels like the Village

Level Worker. With its wider fare and better reach, the radio has been able to assert itself as an effective diffusion agent, particularly in the communication of agricultural information.

The role of television is appreciated as a useful source for opening the window to the world and widening the horizons of the youngsters. Its presence is invited for providing an exposure to women and children, who are otherwise confined to a limited world, without any interaction. The expansion of TV is overwhelmingly recommended. But to initiate and promote development in the village, only personal channels which could deliver the goods have been cited, and not TV. This indicates that for guiding change and get the things done, television is not visualized as an appropriate medium. Its potentialities are much appreciated as a diffusion agent than as a change agent. This could be due to two reasons: (1) the people have not had the opportunity to taste fully the feed of television; and (2) whatever has been the feed, it was too ineffective to provoke any significant changes.

**Outlook for Future**

To conclude, the present status of rural television in India, with the positive and negative aspects, may be shown as under:

| *Positive aspects* | *Negative aspects* |
|---|---|
| 1. The attitude of the villagers to television is positive | 1. Meagre programme input, and bias towards the better off sections |
| 2. Its image as a source of awareness and "widow to the world" particularly for grooming the women and children is high | 2. Weak and ineffective delivery system and considerable seepage in communication during diffusion. |
| 3. The response to community TV is uninhibited | 3. Absence of feedback |

Television is a potential diffusion agent, rather than a change agent. It cannot substitute the personal channels and rank as the most suitable communication medium for bringing about development. As such, there are no two opinions on its utility as an informational channel.

Technology is fast growing and the exploitation of television for social ends will immensely increase in the near future. Under the circumstances, it may be naive to think in terms of restricting its growth and proliferation. The major constraints in exploiting the potentialities of television for utilization by villagers are mostly operational. With a meaningful programme input, effective delivery system and organised interaction with the medium, it should be possible to diffuse developmental information and supplement the extension effort. The interaction of the people with personal extension channels being not significant at moment any contribution by TV in this direction needs to be appreciated and encouraged.

**Suggestions for Improvement of the Service**

Three aspects that need immediate attention for improving the rural TV service are: (1) Reorganization of the delivery system, (2) Correction in the imbalances in the programme content, and (3) Evolving a regular feedback system. With modifications in these three elements, it should be possible to ensure a regular flow of communication and minimize wastage.

(1) *The Delivery System*

(a) *Selection of villages*: The norms for the identification of villages for the location of community TV sets have to be revised. At present, the facility is mostly created in bigger villages which are otherwise well exposed to media. Instead villages which are relatively small and underdeveloped in terms of communication facilities, media reach, educational facilities, dependence on traditional agriculture, etc., need to be given priority. The basic problem in this approach would be availability of power supply. Among the villages which have the power supply, first preference may be given to small and interior villages. The utilization of community TV in such villages is usually much better than in big villages with urban influence.

(b) *Coordination at the zonal level*: At present there is no system for the coordination of the working of the community TV scheme and periodical review of its working, either at the zonal or the District level. It is suggested that a suitable body may be created at the Zonal level (one each for the Pune and Bombay regions) with representatives from the State Rural Broadcasting Department, Doordarshan, Zilla Parishads, and State Electricity Board. Periodical interaction between the concerned executing agencies may help in streamlining the operation to ensure effective utilization of the sets.

(c) *Panel of Custodians at the village level*: At the present there is no system for organized exposure to the telecasts at the village level. Appointment of a paid custodian may not ensure regular tuning of the sets and keeping effective liaison with Doordarshan and the State Rural Broadcasting Department. The concept of community ownership of common facilities in the villages, traditionally existent in the villages, may be exploited for better utilization of the TV set. Instead of identifying the Gram Panchayat as the institutional owner, if the TV set is entrusted to a panel of Custodians nominated by the village elders, the notion that TV belongs to the "Government" may be rectified.

The panel of Custodians may share among themselves the responsibilities like opening and closing the set, maintenance of records and keeping a link with the Rural Broadcasting Department. They may also encourage direct interaction of the viewers with the TV centre, instead of going through the Custodian.

Continuation of the community TV in the village may be linked to its utilization. If the local inhabitants do not show adequate interest, there should be a provision for the withdrawal of the set with the approval of the zonal-level coordination committee.

(2) *Programme Input*

(a) *Daily rural service*: In the context of the present realities it may not be logical to suggest earmarking of the 30-40 per cent of the transmission time to rural service, or running an alternative channel for their exclusive benefit. However, it should be reasonable to propose a service of at least 60 minutes' duration on all the days for hard-core and cultural items relating to rural life.

(b) *Diversification of programme input*: At present there is more stress on agricultural hard-core information and very little time is devoted for programmes on other aspects of rural life. There +is need for increasing the programmes on health care, household industries, employment benefits, vocational guidance, social education and cultural activities. Secondly, the programmes should be mainly related to the immediate needs and pressing problems of the common people than to harping on long-term benefits.

(c) *Need for "how-to-apply type" of information*: The various rural development agencies, radio and other channels have created awareness among the people about the existence of improved innovations. Taking advantage television may concentrate on "how-to-apply" type of information. Otherwise, there is very little scope for change. Information redundancy has to be avoided for better results.

(d) *Training of personnel*: One of the most important needs of the improvement in programme quality is training in development communication. Most of the television production staff are drawn from urban areas with very little exposure to rural life. As such, their image of rural problems, and perception of needs is dependent on imagination and books. It is necessary to give them an extensive orientation training on the socio-economic structure and institutions at the village level.

The present input of rural orientation during the in-service training at the Film and Television Institute of India is insufficient. The system of training is heavily oriented to studio production, with marginal practical input on programmes relating to village development. The trainees are excepted to produce about five programmes during the training as part of their exercises. But, there is no obligation that at least one of them should be village-oriented. As such, the tendency is to originate entertainment oriented programmes directed to an urban audience. This trend needs to be corrected by drawing the practical and theoretical inputs in training according to the accepted objectives of the medium.

(3) *Feedback on Programmes*

The television centres are poorly equipped for ascertaining audience response to programmes. There is heavy dependence on the viewer's mail. The studies by the Audience Research Unit are limited to mostly urban problems and there is practically no formative research. As such, the programme producers mostly grope in the dark, with no scope for making any changes in the programme input according to the audience needs or tastes.

Under the existing circumstances, it may not be possible to evolve any strong machinery for feedback from the village level. As an alternative it may be necessary to strengthen the Audience Research Units for undertaking periodical assessment studies and qualitative reporting on the programmes.

# APPENDICES

*APPENDIX 1*

## Pattern of Exposure to Newspapers

| Category | N | Regular % | Sometimes % | Rarely % | Never % |
|---|---|---|---|---|---|
| *Sex:* | | | | | |
| Male | 162 | 22.8 | 15.4 | 13.6 | 48.2 |
| Female | 88 | 3.4 | 10.2 | 10.2 | 76.2 |
| *Age:* | | | | | |
| 15-30 yr. | 83 | 19.3 | 14.5 | 21.7 | 44.5 |
| 31-45 yr. | 88 | 18.2 | 12.5 | 7.9 | 61.4 |
| 46-60 yr. | 57 | 12.3 | 10.5 | 7.0 | 70.2 |
| Above 60 yr. | 22 | 4.5 | 22.8 | 9.1 | 63.6 |
| *Education:* | | | | | |
| Illiterate | 103 | — | — | — | 100.0 |
| Standard I-VII | 109 | 17.5 | 23.8 | 22.0 | 36.7 |
| Standard VIII-X | 31 | 48.4 | 22.6 | 22.6 | 6.4 |
| College | 7 | 85.7 | 14.3 | — | — |
| *Occupation:* | | | | | |
| Agriculture etc. | 154 | 16.2 | 13.6 | 11.1 | 59.1 |
| Labour | 42 | — | 2.4 | 11.9 | 85.7 |
| Trade & traditional services | 26 | 15.4 | 15.4 | 15.4 | 53.8 |
| White-collar & others | 28 | 39.3 | 28.6 | 17.9 | 14.2 |
| All categories | 250 | 16.0 | 13.6 | 12.4 | 58.0 |

*APPENDIX 2*

## Frequency of Radio Listening

| Category | N | Frequently % | Occasionally % | Rarely % | Never % |
|---|---|---|---|---|---|
| *Sex:* | | | | | |
| Male | 162 | 40.1 | 29.7 | 16.0 | 14.2 |
| Female | 88 | 32.9 | 14.8 | 19.3 | 33.0 |
| *Age:* | | | | | |
| 15-30 yr. | 83 | 40.9 | 22.9 | 15.7 | 20.5 |
| 31-45 yr. | 88 | 32.9 | 25.0 | 23.9 | 18.2 |
| 46-60 yr. | 57 | 38.6 | 26.3 | 10.5 | 24.6 |
| Above 60 yr. | 22 | 40.9 | 22.7 | 13.7 | 22.7 |
| *Education:* | | | | | |
| Illiterate | 103 | 17.5 | 23.3 | 26.2 | 33.0 |
| Standard I-VII | 109 | 45.8 | 25.7 | 13.8 | 14.7 |
| Standard VIII-X | 31 | 67.7 | 22.6 | 3.2 | 6.5 |
| College | 7 | 71.4 | 28.6 | — | — |
| *Occupation:* | | | | | |
| Agriculture etc. | 154 | 39.0 | 23.4 | 20.1 | 17.5 |
| Labour | 42 | 11.9 | 33.3 | 21.5 | 33.3 |
| Trade & traditional services | 26 | 38.4 | 30.8 | 7.7 | 23.1 |
| White-collar & others | 28 | 67.9 | 10.7 | 3.6 | 17.8 |
| All categories | 250 | 37.6 | 24.4 | 17.2 | 20.8 |

*APPENDIX 3*

## Awareness of Radio Rural Programmes

| Category | Narayan gavhan % | Narodi % | Amondi % | Taleghar % | Rajpur % | All villages % |
|---|---|---|---|---|---|---|
| *Sex:* | | | | | | |
| Male | 90.9 | 85.3 | 70.3 | 60.0 | 85.7 | 81.5 |
| Female | 76.5 | 62.5 | 33.3 | 60.0 | 63.6 | 59.1 |
| *Age:* | | | | | | |
| 15-30 yr. | 89.5 | 85.7 | 56.3 | 33.3 | 57.1 | 74.7 |
| 31-45 yr. | 93.7 | 88.2 | 50.0 | 75.0 | 83.3 | 78.4 |
| 46-60 yr. | 77.8 | 60.9 | 61.5 | 66.7 | 100.0 | 66.7 |
| Above 60 yr. | 66.7 | 50.0 | 100.0 | 100.0 | 75.0 | 68.2 |
| *Education:* | | | | | | |
| Illiterate | 70.0 | 58.5 | 35.3 | 50.0 | 64.7 | 57.3 |
| Standard I-VII | 95.5 | 92.1 | 64.5 | 63.6 | 100.0 | 82.6 |
| Standard VIII-X | 100.0 | 87.5 | 83.3 | 100.0 | 100.0 | 90.3 |
| College | 100.0 | 100.0 | 100.0 | NR | NR | 100.0 |
| *Occupation:* | | | | | | |
| Agriculture etc. | 80.0 | 80.0 | 67.7 | 53.8 | 80.0 | 75.3 |
| Labour | 100.0 | 66.7 | 35.7 | 50.0 | 66.7 | 61.9 |
| Trade & traditional services | 100.0 | 63.6 | 57.1 | 100.0 | NR | 73.1 |
| White-collar & others | 81.8 | 90.0 | 66.7 | 66.7 | 100.0 | 82.1 |
| All categories | 86.0 | 78.0 | 58.2 | 60.0 | 76.0 | 73.6 |

*APPENDIX 4*

## Frequency of Exposure to Films

| Category | N | Frequently % | Occasionally % | Rarely % | Never % |
|---|---|---|---|---|---|
| *Sex:* | | | | | |
| Male | 162 | 3.7 | 9.9 | 17.9 | 68.5 |
| Female | 88 | 1.1 | 4.6 | 22.7 | 71.6 |
| *Age:* | | | | | |
| 15-30 yr. | 83 | 3.6 | 15.7 | 22.9 | 57.8 |
| 31-45 yr. | 88 | 4.5 | 5.7 | 18.2 | 71.6 |
| 46-60 yr. | 57 | — | 3.5 | 19.3 | 77.2 |
| Above 60 yr. | 22 | — | — | 13.6 | 86.4 |
| *Education:* | | | | | |
| Illiterate | 103 | — | 1.0 | 8.7 | 90.3 |
| Standard I-XII | 109 | 1.8 | 10.1 | 24.8 | 63.3 |
| Standard VIII-X | 31 | 6.5 | 19.3 | 35.5 | 38.7 |
| College | 7 | 42.8 | 28.6 | 28.6 | — |
| *Occupation:* | | | | | |
| Agriculture etc. | 154 | 2.6 | 6.5 | 20.8 | 70.1 |
| Labour | 42 | — | 7.1 | 4.8 | 88.1 |
| Trade & traditional services | 26 | 3.8 | 7.7 | 23.1 | 65.4 |
| White-collar & others | 28 | 7.1 | 17.9 | 32.1 | 42.9 |
| All categories | 250 | 2.8 | 8.0 | 19.6 | 69.6 |

*APPENDIX 5*

## Contacts with Urban Area

| Category | N | Regularly % | Occasionally % | Rarely % | Never % |
|---|---|---|---|---|---|
| *Sex:* | | | | | |
| Male | 162 | 56.8 | 16.0 | 13.0 | 14.2 |
| Female | 88 | 23.9 | 10.2 | 14.8 | 51.1 |
| *Age:* | | | | | |
| 15-30 yr. | 83 | 38.6 | 15.7 | 10.8 | 34.9 |
| 31-45 yr. | 88 | 47.7 | 11.4 | 19.3 | 21.6 |
| 46-60 yr. | 57 | 47.4 | 15.8 | 10.5 | 26.3 |
| Above 60 yr. | 22 | 54.5 | 13.6 | 9.1 | 22.8 |
| *Education:* | | | | | |
| Illiterate | 103 | 31.1 | 12.6 | 16.5 | 39.8 |
| Standard I-VII | 109 | 49.5 | 15.6 | 13.8 | 21.1 |
| Standard VIII-X | 31 | 64.5 | 16.1 | 6.5 | 12.9 |
| College | 7 | 100.0 | — | — | — |
| *Occupation:* | | | | | |
| Agriculture etc. | 154 | 48.0 | 17.5 | 11.7 | 22.8 |
| Labour | 42 | 19.0 | 9.6 | 21.4 | 50.0 |
| Trade & traditional services | 26 | 50.0 | 11.5 | 15.4 | 23.1 |
| White-collar & others | 28 | 64.3 | 3.6 | 10.7 | 21.4 |
| All categories | 250 | 45.2 | 14.0 | 13.6 | 27.2 |

*APPENDIX 6*

## Contacts with Block Headquarters

| Category | N | Frequently % | Occasionally % | Rarely % | Never % |
|---|---|---|---|---|---|
| *Sex:* | | | | | |
| Male | 162 | 67.3 | 13.0 | 7.4 | 12.3 |
| Female | 88 | 44.3 | 17.0 | 9.1 | 29.6 |
| *Age:* | | | | | |
| 15-30 yr. | 83 | 55.4 | 13.2 | 7.2 | 24.2 |
| 31-45 yr. | 88 | 60.3 | 19.3 | 6.8 | 13.6 |
| 46-60 yr. | 57 | 70.2 | 5.3 | 10.5 | 14.0 |
| Above 60 yr. | 22 | 40.9 | 22.7 | 9.1 | 27.3 |
| *Education:* | | | | | |
| Illiterate | 103 | 43.7 | 18.4 | 11.6 | 26.3 |
| Standard I-VII | 109 | 69.7 | 11.9 | 5.5 | 12.9 |
| Standard VII-X | 31 | 74.2 | 9.7 | 6.5 | 9.6 |
| College | 7 | 57.1 | 14.3 | — | 28.6 |
| *Occupation:* | | | | | |
| Agriculture etc. | 154 | 61.6 | 14.3 | 10.4 | 13.7 |
| Labour | 42 | 54.8 | 11.9 | 7.1 | 26.2 |
| Trade & traditional services | 26 | 57.7 | 15.4 | — | 26.9 |
| White-collar & others | 28 | 53.6 | 17.8 | 3.6 | 25.0 |
| All categories | 250 | 59.2 | 14.4 | 8.0 | 18.4 |

*APPENDIX 7*

## Contacts with Village Level Workers

| Category | N | Frequently % | Occasionally % | Rarely % | Never % |
|---|---|---|---|---|---|
| *Sex:* | | | | | |
| Male | 162 | 28.4 | 11.1 | 6.2 | 54.3 |
| Female | 88 | 10.2 | 8.0 | — | 81.8 |
| *Age:* | | | | | |
| 15-30 yr. | 83 | 14.5 | 9.6 | 2.4 | 73.5 |
| 31-45 yr | 88 | 19.3 | 9.1 | 6.8 | 64.8 |
| 46-60 yr. | 57 | 33.3 | 10.5 | 3.5 | 52.7 |
| Above 60 yr. | 22 | 31.8 | 13.6 | — | 54.6 |
| *Education:* | | | | | |
| Illiterate | 103 | 10.7 | 8.7 | 2.9 | 77.7 |
| Standard I-VII | 109 | 30.3 | 10.1 | 5.5 | 54.1 |
| Standard VIII-X | 31 | 29.0 | 12.9 | — | 58.1 |
| College | 7 | 28.6 | 14.2 | 14.2 | 43.0 |
| *Occupation:* | | | | | |
| Agriculture etc. | 154 | 27.9 | 12.9 | 3.9 | 55.3 |
| Labour | 42 | 4.8 | 7.1 | 4.8 | 83.3 |
| Trade & traditional services | 26 | 7.7 | 7.7 | — | 84.6 |
| White-collar & others | 28 | 28.6 | — | 7.1 | 64.3 |
| All categories | 250 | 22.0 | 10.0 | 4.0 | 64.0 |

APPENDIX 8

## Frequency of TV Viewing

| Category | N | Frequently % | Occasionally % | Rarely % | Never % |
|---|---|---|---|---|---|
| *Sex:* | | | | | |
| Male | 162 | 37.0 | 17.9 | 17.9 | 27.2 |
| Female | 88 | 21.6 | 11.4 | 13.6 | 53.4 |
| *Age:* | | | | | |
| 15-30 yr. | 83 | 38.5 | 16.9 | 14.5 | 30.1 |
| 31-45 yr. | 88 | 36.4 | 15.9 | 15.9 | 31.8 |
| 46-60 yr. | 57 | 21.0 | 12.3 | 22.8 | 43.9 |
| Above 60 yr. | 22 | 13.6 | 18.2 | 9.1 | 59.1 |
| *Education:* | | | | | |
| Illiterate | 103 | 10.6 | 17.5 | 14.6 | 57.3 |
| Standard I-VII | 109 | 40.5 | 15.6 | 21.0 | 22.9 |
| Standard VIII-X | 31 | 58.1 | 12.9 | 9.7 | 19.3 |
| College | 7 | 85.7 | — | — | 14.3 |
| *Occupation:* | | | | | |
| Agriculture etc. | 154 | 27.9 | 15.6 | 16.2 | 40.3 |
| Labour | 42 | 21.4 | 28.6 | 11.9 | 38.1 |
| Trade & traditional services | 26 | 42.3 | 3.9 | 26.9 | 26.9 |
| White-collar & others | 28 | 57.2 | 7.1 | 14.3 | 21.4 |
| *Social status:* | | | | | |
| Non-Harijans | 161 | 33.5 | 13.8 | 16.1 | 36.6 |
| Harijans | 25 | 44.0 | 12.0 | 20.0 | 24.0 |
| Adivasis | 64 | 21.9 | 21.9 | 15.6 | 40.6 |
| *Economic status:* | | | | | |
| Poor | 89 | 29.2 | 16.9 | 19.1 | 34.8 |
| Average | 125 | 31.2 | 14.4 | 16.0 | 38.4 |
| Upper Middle | 36 | 38.9 | 16.7 | 11.1 | 33.3 |
| *Distance from TV:* | | | | | |
| Near TV | 108 | 50.0 | 15.7 | 13.9 | 20.4 |
| 1-2 km | 118 | 17.8 | 16.1 | 16.9 | 49.2 |
| More than 2 km | 24 | 16.7 | 12.5 | 25.0 | 45.8 |
| All categories | 250 | 31.6 | 15.6 | 16.4 | 36.4 |

*APPENDIX 9*

## Knowledge of Current Political Scene

| Category | N | Aware of | | |
|---|---|---|---|---|
| | | Bhutto % | JP % | Y.B. Chavan % |
| *Sex:* | | | | |
| Male | 162 | 56.0 | 54.4 | 71.6 |
| Female | 88 | 21.0 | 22.0 | 35.2 |
| *Age:* | | | | |
| 15-30 yr. | 83 | 49.4 | 51.8 | 60.2 |
| 31-45 yr. | 88 | 37.5 | 38.6 | 58.0 |
| 46-60 yr. | 57 | 47.4 | 38.6 | 57.9 |
| Above 60 yr. | 22 | 77.3 | 36.4 | 59.1 |
| *Education:* | | | | |
| Illiterate | 103 | 8.7 | 9.7 | 27.2 |
| Standard I-VII | 109 | 58.7 | 56.9 | 76.1 |
| Standard VIII-X | 31 | 90.3 | 90.3 | 93.5 |
| College | 7 | 100.0 | 100.0 | 100.0 |
| *Paper reading* | | | | |
| Yes | 105 | 85.7 | 81.0 | 93.3 |
| No | 145 | 12.4 | 15.2 | 33.8 |
| *Radio listening* | | | | |
| Yes | 198 | 51.5 | 51.0 | 67.2 |
| No | 52 | 11.5 | 11.5 | 26.9 |
| *TV viewing* | | | | |
| Yes | 159 | 55.3 | 55.3 | 73.0 |
| No | 91 | 22.0 | 20.9 | 34.1 |
| All categories | 250 | 43.2 | 42.8 | 58.8 |

*APPENDIX 10*

## Awareness of Rural TV Programmes

| Category | Narayan gavhan % | Narodi % | Amondi % | Taleghar % | Rajpur % | All villages % |
|---|---|---|---|---|---|---|
| *Sex:* | | | | | | |
| Male | 30.3 | 30.9 | 27.0 | 10.0 | 28.6 | 28.4 |
| Female | 5.9 | 15.6 | — | 10.0 | 27.3 | 11.4 |
| *Age:* | | | | | | |
| 15-30 yr. | 15.8 | 22.9 | 12.5 | — | 14.3 | 16.9 |
| 31-45 yr. | 25.0 | 44.1 | 18.2 | — | 41.7 | 31.8 |
| 46-60 yr. | 22.2 | 8.7 | 23.1 | 22.2 | 33.3 | 17.5 |
| Above 60 yr. | 33.3 | 12.5 | 25.0 | — | — | 18.2 |
| *Education:* | | | | | | |
| Illiterate | — | 9.8 | 5.9 | — | 29.4 | 9.7 |
| Standard I-VII | 36.4 | 14.8 | 25.8 | 18.2 | 28.6 | 30.3 |
| Standard VIII-X | 28.6 | 57.5 | 16.7 | — | — | 29.0 |
| College | 100.0 | 60.0 | — | — | NR | 57.1 |
| *Occupation:* | | | | | | |
| Agriculture etc. | 32.0 | 27.1 | 29.0 | 7.7 | 40.0 | 27.9 |
| Labour | 12.5 | 22.2 | — | — | 11.1 | 9.5 |
| Trade & traditional services | — | 27.3 | 14.3 | — | NR | 15.4 |
| White-collar & others | 18.2 | 20.0 | — | 33.3 | — | 17.9 |
| *TV viewing* | | | | | | |
| Frequently | 38.1 | 64.5 | 40.0 | 33.3 | 66.7 | 50.6 |
| Occasionally | 42.9 | 37.5 | 20.0 | — | 50.0 | 28.2 |
| Rarely | — | 14.3 | 12.5 | — | 33.3 | 12.2 |
| All categories | 22.0 | 26.0 | 18.2 | 10.0 | 28.0 | 22.4 |

*APPENDIX 11*

## Primary Source of Information on Occupation

| Category | N | Consults None | Fellow villagers | Radio | VLW | Other Block staff | Other Sources |
|---|---|---|---|---|---|---|---|
| | % | % | % | % | % | % | % |
| *Sex:* | | | | | | | |
| Male | 162 | 33.3 | 28.4 | 8.0 | 14.2 | 9.3 | 6.8 |
| Female | 88 | 34.1 | 45.4 | 5.7 | 5.7 | 2.3 | 6.8 |
| *Age:* | | | | | | | |
| 15-30 yr. | 83 | 30.1 | 42.2 | 4.8 | 7.2 | 4.8 | 10.9 |
| 31-45 yr. | 88 | 34.1 | 36.5 | 7.9 | 6.8 | 6.8 | 7.9 |
| 46-60 yr. | 57 | 31.6 | 26.3 | 7.0 | 22.3 | 10.5 | 1.8 |
| Above 60 yr. | 22 | 50.0 | 18.2 | 13.6 | 13.6 | 4.6 | — |
| *Education:* | | | | | | | |
| Illiterate | 103 | 55.3 | 30.1 | 1.9 | 9.8 | 1.0 | 1.9 |
| Standard I-VII | 109 | 22.9 | 34.9 | 11.9 | 14.7 | 9.2 | 7.3 |
| Standard VIII-X | 31 | 6.5 | 41.9 | 12.9 | 6.5 | 12.9 | 19.3 |
| College | 7 | — | 57.1 | — | — | 28.6 | 14.3 |
| *Occupation:* | | | | | | | |
| Agriculture etc. | 154 | 26.6 | 39.0 | 8.4 | 14.9 | 7.8 | 3.3 |
| Labour | 42 | 54.8 | 33.3 | — | 4.8 | — | 7.1 |
| Trade & traditional services | 26 | 57.7 | 15.4 | 11.6 | 3.8 | 7.7 | 3.8 |
| White-collar & others | 28 | 17.9 | 28.6 | 7.1 | 7.1 | 10.7 | 28.6 |
| All categories | 250 | 33.6 | 34.4 | 7.2 | 11.2 | 6.8 | 6.8 |

*APPENDIX 12*

## Can TV Provide Information on Your Occupation ?

| Category | N | Yes % | No % | No idea % |
|---|---|---|---|---|
| *Sex:* | | | | |
| Male | 162 | 24.7 | 15.4 | 59.9 |
| Female | 88 | 18.2 | 6.8 | 75.0 |
| *Age:* | | | | |
| 15-30 yr. | 83 | 24.1 | 13.2 | 62.7 |
| 31-45 yr. | 88 | 22.7 | 12.5 | 64.0 |
| 46-60 yr. | 57 | 21.0 | 12.3 | 66.7 |
| Above 60 yr. | 22 | 18.2 | 9.1 | 72.7 |
| *Education:* | | | | |
| Illiterate | 103 | 7.8 | 8.7 | 83.5 |
| Standard I-VII | 109 | 31.2 | 15.6 | 53.2 |
| Standard VIII-X | 31 | 29.1 | 16.1 | 54.8 |
| College | 7 | 71.4 | — | 28.6 |
| *Occupation:* | | | | |
| Agriculture etc. | 154 | 23.4 | 7.1 | 69.5 |
| Labour | 42 | 19.0 | 14.3 | 66.7 |
| Trade & traditional services | 26 | 11.5 | 42.3 | 46.2 |
| White-collar & others | 28 | 32.1 | 10.7 | 57.2 |
| *TV viewing* | | | | |
| Frequently | 79 | 50.6 | 20.3 | 29.1 |
| Occasionally | 39 | 28.2 | 23.1 | 48.7 |
| Rarely | 41 | 12.2 | 14.6 | 73.2 |
| Never | 91 | — | — | 100.0 |
| All categories | 250 | 22.4 | 12.4 | 65.2 |

*APPENDIX 13*

## Why TV is Installed in the Village ?

| Category | N | Mainly for Development % | For General awareness % | Mainly for Entertainment % | For Public use (Not specific) % | No idea (cannot any) % |
|---|---|---|---|---|---|---|
| *Sex:* | | | | | | |
| Male | 162 | 22.8 | 45.1 | 19.8 | 7.4 | 4.9 |
| Female | 88 | 6.8 | 37.5 | 21.6 | 4.5 | 29.6 |
| *Age:* | | | | | | |
| 15-30 yr. | 83 | 18.1 | 45.8 | 21.7 | 2.4 | 12.0 |
| 31-45 yr. | 88 | 20.5 | 40.9 | 15.9 | 7.9 | 14.8 |
| 46-60 yr. | 57 | 15.8 | 36.8 | 26.3 | 7.0 | 14.1 |
| Above 60 yr. | 22 | 4.6 | 50.0 | 18.2 | 13.6 | 13.6 |
| *Education:* | | | | | | |
| Illiterate | 103 | 9.7 | 31.1 | 23.3 | 9.7 | 26.2 |
| Standard I-VII | 109 | 20.2 | 47.7 | 20.2 | 5.5 | 6.4 |
| Standard VIII-X | 31 | 29.0 | 58.1 | 12.9 | — | — |
| College | 7 | 28.6 | 57.1 | 14.3 | — | — |
| *Occupation:* | | | | | | |
| Agriculture etc. | 154 | 14.9 | 41.6 | 22.1 | 7.1 | 14.3 |
| Labour | 42 | 16.7 | 40.5 | 16.7 | 4.7 | 21.4 |
| Trade & traditional services | 26 | 26.9 | 46.1 | 11.6 | 7.7 | 7.7 |
| White-collar & others | 28 | 21.4 | 46.4 | 25.0 | 3.6 | 3.6 |
| *TV viewing* | | | | | | |
| Frequently | 79 | 31.6 | 50.6 | 15.2 | 1.3 | 1.3 |
| Occasionally | 39 | 10.3 | 61.6 | 17.9 | 5.1 | 5.1 |
| Rarely | 41 | 22.0 | 43.9 | 19.5 | 7.3 | 7.3 |
| Never | 91 | 5.5 | 26.4 | 26.4 | 10.9 | 30.8 |
| All categories | 250 | 17.2 | 42.4 | 20.4 | 6.4 | 13.6 |

*APPENDIX 14*

## Preferred Channel for Delivery of Developmental Messages

| Category | N | VLW % | Fellow villages % | Panchyat Members % | Radio % | TV % | Papers % | No idea % |
|---|---|---|---|---|---|---|---|---|
| *Sex:* | | | | | | | | |
| Male | 162 | 19.1 | 21.6 | 12.3 | 33.3 | 3.8 | 1.9 | 8.0 |
| Female | 88 | 12.5 | 33.0 | 14.8 | 22.7 | 2.3 | 1.1 | 13.6 |
| *Age:* | | | | | | | | |
| 15-30 yr. | 83 | 14.5 | 24.1 | 15.7 | 30.1 | 3.6 | 1.2 | 10.8 |
| 31-45 yr. | 88 | 12.5 | 28.4 | 11.4 | 33.0 | 4.5 | 3.4 | 6.8 |
| 46-60 yr. | 57 | 22.8 | 24.6 | 10.5 | 26.3 | 1.8 | — | 14.0 |
| Above 60 yr. | 22 | 27.3 | 22.7 | 18.2 | 22.7 | — | — | 9.1 |
| *Education:* | | | | | | | | |
| Illiterate | 103 | 13.6 | 34.0 | 16.5 | 17.5 | — | — | 18.4 |
| Standard I-VII | 109 | 20.2 | 22.9 | 9.2 | 35.8 | 4.6 | 1.8 | 5.5 |
| Standard VIII-X | 31 | 12.9 | 9.7 | 19.4 | 41.9 | 9.7 | 6.4 | — |
| College | 7 | 28.6 | 14.3 | — | 57.1 | — | — | — |
| *Occupation:* | | | | | | | | |
| Agriculture etc. | 154 | 17.6 | 29.2 | 11.0 | 31.2 | 2.6 | 1.3 | 7.1 |
| Labour | 42 | 11.9 | 31.0 | 19.0 | 14.3 | — | — | 23.8 |
| Trade & traditional services | 26 | 11.5 | 11.5 | 19.3 | 30.8 | 3.8 | 7.7 | 15.4 |
| White-collar & others | 28 | 25.0 | 10.7 | 10.7 | 42.9 | 10.7 | — | — |
| All categories | 250 | 16.8 | 25.6 | 13.2 | 29.6 | 3.2 | 1.6 | 10.0 |

*APPENDIX 15*

## Most Preferred Facility in the Village

| Category | N | Agriculture Expert % | Social worker % | Adult Education Centre % | Posts & Telegraphs office % | Police station % | TV % | No idea % |
|---|---|---|---|---|---|---|---|---|
| *Sex:* | | | | | | | | |
| Male | 162 | 44.4 | 33.9 | 7.4 | 3.7 | 2.0 | 0.6 | 8.0 |
| Female | 88 | 42.0 | 33.0 | 6.8 | 2.3 | 3.4 | — | 12.5 |
| *Age:* | | | | | | | | |
| 15-30 yr. | 83 | 39.8 | 32.5 | 10.8 | 2.4 | 4.8 | — | 9.7 |
| 31-45 yr. | 88 | 47.7 | 31.8 | 6.8 | — | 2.3 | 1.1 | 10.3 |
| 46-60 yr. | 57 | 42.1 | 35.1 | 5.3 | 10.5 | — | — | 7.0 |
| Above 60 yr. | 22 | 45.5 | 40.9 | — | — | — | — | 13.6 |
| *Education:* | | | | | | | | |
| Illiterate | 103 | 36.9 | 33.0 | 7.8 | 2.9 | 1.9 | — | 17.5 |
| Standard I-VII | 109 | 48.6 | 32.1 | 7.3 | 3.8 | 1.8 | 0.9 | 5.5 |
| Standard VIII-X | 31 | 45.2 | 45.2 | — | 3.2 | 6.4 | — | — |
| College | 7 | 57.1 | 14.3 | 28.6 | — | — | — | — |
| *Occupation:* | | | | | | | | |
| Agriculture etc. | 154 | 54.5 | 27.3 | 7.8 | 1.3 | 1.3 | 0.7 | 7.1 |
| Labour | 42 | 28.6 | 38.1 | 7.1 | 2.4 | 2.4 | — | 21.4 |
| Trade & traditional services | 26 | 11.5 | 42.3 | 7.8 | 15.4 | 11.5 | — | 11.5 |
| White-collar & others | 28 | 35.6 | 53.6 | 3.6 | 3.6 | — | — | 3.6 |
| *Economic Status:* | | | | | | | | |
| Upper Middle | 36 | 66.7 | 24.9 | 2.8 | — | 2.8 | — | 2.8 |
| Average | 125 | 51.2 | 31.2 | 8.8 | 4.0 | 1.6 | — | 3.2 |
| Poor | 89 | 23.6 | 40.4 | 6.7 | 3.4 | 3.4 | 1.1 | 21.4 |
| All categories | 250 | 43.6 | 33.6 | 7.2 | 3.2 | 2.4 | 0.4 | 9.6 |

*APPENDIX 16*

## Telecast Schedule of Bombay Doordarshan for April-June, 1979

*April 1979:*

| | |
|---|---|
| 2-4-79 | Lift irrigation in Sangli district |
| 4-4-79 | NSS Camp at Pirangut, Pune district |
| 6-4-79 | Physical education in schools |
| 9-4-79 | Vegetable cultivation: creepers: fruit trees: Dalim and Mangoes, Soil conservation |
| 13-4-79 | *Thingi*–Play on Alcoholism (FTII presentation) |
| 16-4-79 | Care of vegetables |
| 18-4-79 | Cultivation of Ginger |
| 20-4-79 | Mango products |
| 23-4-79 | Interview with the Prize Winner in Sugarcane |
| 25-4-79 | Farm Experiences |
| 29-4-79 | *Sansarachi Taraha* – Play on alcoholism (FTII presentation) |
| 30-4-79 | Cross-breeding of cows |

*May 1979*:

| | |
|---|---|
| 2-5-79 | Hybrid *jowar*: Seed production |
| 4-5-79 | Arrangements for Kharif harvest |
| 7-5-79 | Konkan Agricultural University: Orchard Research |
| 9-5-79 | Use of improved agricultural implements |
| 11-5-79 | *Sansaracha Iskot* – Play *(Tamasha)* on alcoholism (FTII presentation) |
| 14-5-79 | Sugarcane cultivation<br>Multipurpose Service Centre |
| 16-5-79 | Kharif vegetables |
| 18-5-79 | Fruit trees in Konkan: coconut, pineapple. |
| 21-5-79 | Water management in heavy rainfall areas, green manuring sprinkler irrigation. |
| 23-5-79 | Mango cultivation |
| 25-5-79 | *Duniya Adhanichi Nahi* – Play on National Adult Education Programme (FTII presentation) |
| 28-5-79 | Dairy farming |
| 30-5-79 | *Masala* crops in Konkan: black pepper, cardamom |

*June 1979*:

| | |
|---|---|
| 1-6-79 | Fruit trees in Konkan |
| 4-6-79 | Kharif campaign |
| 6-6-79 | Rehabilitation of handicapped children |
| 8-6-79 | *Ya Sathi Sikhla Payije*: Play on National Adult Education Programme (FTII presentation) |
| 11-6-79 | Bombay District Central Coop. Bank |
| 13-6-79 | Hybrid *jowar* |
| 15-6-79 | Kharif pulses |
| 18-6-79 | Kharif oilseeds |
| 20-6-79 | Dry-land horticulture |
| 22-6-79 | *Navi Sakal* – Play on National Adult Education Programme (FTII presentation) |
| 25-6-79 | Selection of milch animals |
| 27-6-79 | Experience of a cultivator: Cotton-crop grower |
| 29-6-79 | Paddy seed beds. |

APPENDIX 17

## Community TV in Maharashtra

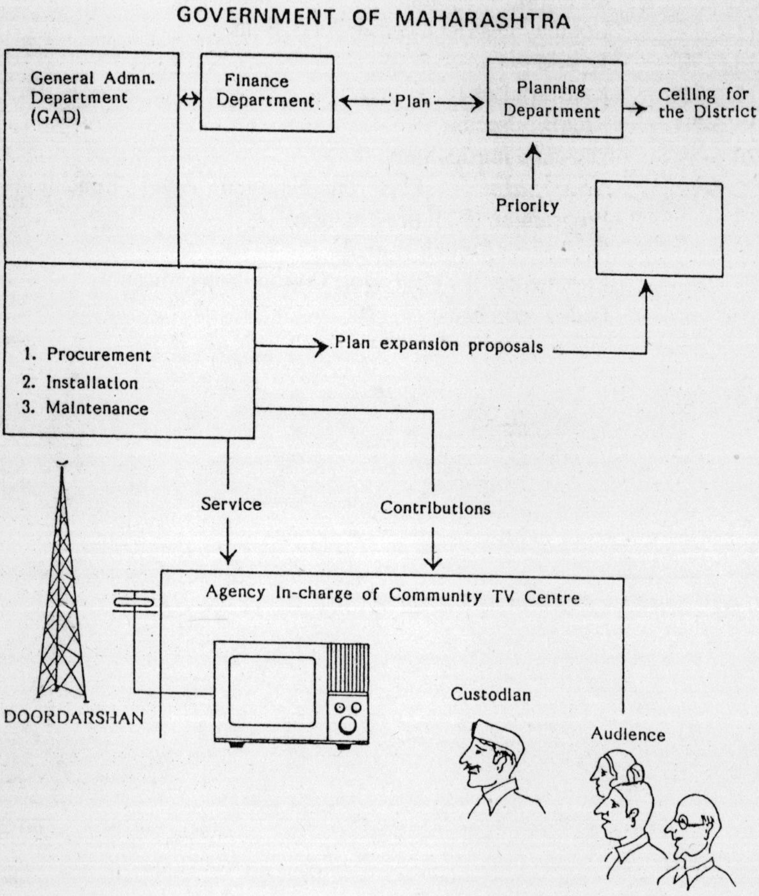

*APPENDIX 18*

## Variables of Rural TV Communication

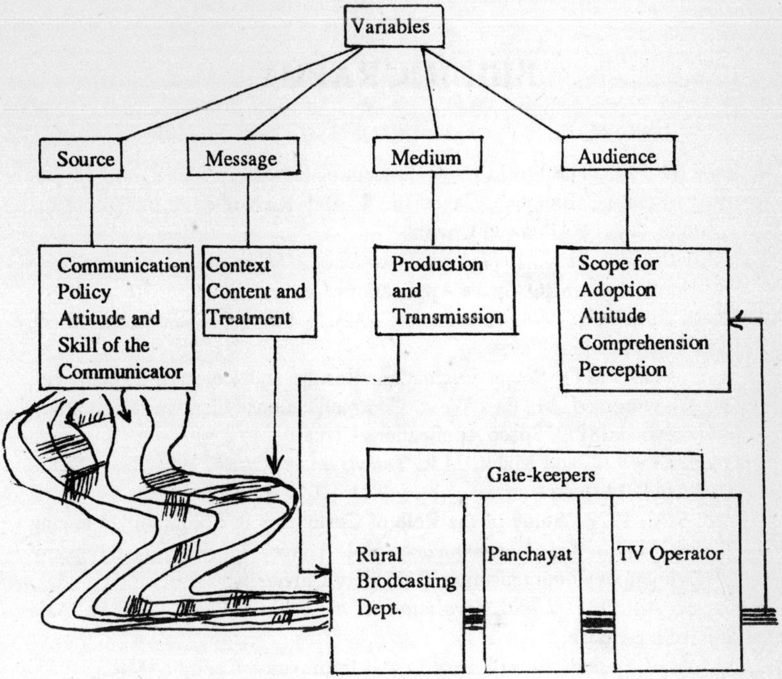

# BIBLIOGRAPHY


Adler, J.H., 1972. The World Bank Concept of Development, *in Development and Planning*, Bhagvati, Jagadish N. and Richards, S. Eckaus, Eds., London, George Allen and Unwin.

Agrawal, Binod C. *et al.*, 1977. *Social Impact of SITE on Adults*, Volume I and II, Ahmedabad, ISRO, Space Applications Centre.

Agrawal, Binod C., 1978. *Television Comes to Village*, Ahmedabad, ISRO, Space Applications Centre.

——— 1979. 'SITE Social Evaluation: Results and Research Experience', Paper presented at East-West Communications Institute (Honolulu), Ahmedabad, ISRO, Space Applications Centre.

Agrawal, Binod C. and Malik, M.R. *Television in Kheda*, 1986, New Delhi, Concept Publishiers.

Ahmed, S.A., 1977. 'Study of the Role of Custodians in Community Viewing during SITE', *The Communicare*, Vol. 1, No. 1, 1976-77, Bangalore Department of Communication, Bangalore University.

Aiyappan, A., 1965. *Social Revolution in a Kerala Village*, Bombay, Asia Publishing House.

Asian Mass Communication Research and Information Centre (AMIC), 1965. *Study Seminar on Development Communication*, Guy-de-Fontgalland, ed., Singapore, AMIC.

Awasthy, G.C., 1965. *Broadcasting in India*, New Delhi, Allied Publications.

Bailey, F.G., 1960. 'An Oriya Hill Village', *in Indian Villages*, Srinivas, M.N., ed., Bombay, Asian Publishing House.

——— 1963. *Politics and Social Change in Orissa*, Berkeley, California, University of California Press.

Beteille, Andre, 1965. *Caste, Class and Power: Changing Patterns of Stratification in Tanjore Village*, Berkeley, California, University of California Press.

Berlo, David K., 1960. *The Process of Communication*, Inc. New York, Holt, Rinohart and Winston.

Berelson, Bernard and Steiner, 1964. *Human Behaviour: An Inventory of Scientific Findings*, New York, Harcourt, Brace and World.

Bernett, H.G., 1953. *Innovation: The basis of Cultural Change*, New York, McGraw-Hill.

Bhagvati, Jagadish N. and Richards, S. Eckaus, 1972. *Development and Planning*, eds., London, George Allen and Unwin.

Bhatia, B.S., 1979. 'SITE: What it did not do', *Vidura*, Vol. 16, No. 3, June, 1979. New Delhi, Press Institute of India.

Bhatia, B.S. and Chauhan, Ajay, 1978. *SITE Utilization*, Ahmedabad, ISRO, Space Applications Centre.

Bhatia, Hansraj, 1970. *Elements of Social Psychology*, Bombay, Somaiya Publications.

Bhatt, V.V., 1978. *Some Aspects of Development Strategy and Policies*, Bombay, Vora.

Brookfield, H., 1975. *Interdependent Development*, London, Methuen.

Commonwealth Broadcasting Association (CBA), 1976. 'Broadcasting and National Development', *Proceedings of the 11th Conference at Singapore*, London, CBA.

Chatterjee, P.C., 1979. Two Voices: Essays in Communication and Philosophy, New Delhi, Hem Publishers.

Chatterjee, R.K., 1973. *Mass Communication*, New Delhi, National Book Trust.

Chawla, N.L., 1978. 'Prospects for TV', *Times of India*, Bombay, dated July 8, 1978.

Coyle, David Cushman, 1963. *National development and how it works*, New York, the New American Library of World Literature.

Danda, A.K. and Danda, Dipali, 1971. *Development and Change in Basudha*, Hyderabad, National Institute of Community Development.

Dandekar, V.N. and Rath, Nilakanth, 1971. *Poverty in India*, Poona, Indian School of Political Economy.

Damle, Y.B., 1955. *Communication of Modern Ideas and Knowledge in Indian Villages*, Poona, Deccan College.

DeFluer, Melvin. L., 1970. *Theories of Mass Communication*, Inc. New York, David Mckay.

Desai, M.V., 1977. *Communication Policies in India*, Paris, UNESCO.

Dharap, B.V., 1979. *Indian Films 1977 & 78*, Pune, Motion Picture Enterprises.

Dhavan, B.D., 1974. *Economics of Television in India*, New Delhi, S. Chand.

Doob, Lionard W., 1961. *Communication in Africa: A Search for Boundaries*, New Haven, Yale University Press.

Dua, M.R., 1979. *Programming Potential of Indian Television*, New Delhi, Communication Publications.

Dube, S.C., 1958. *India's Changing Villages*, London, Routledge and Kegan Paul.

———— 1974. *Contemporary India and its Modernization*, Delhi, Vikas Publishing House.

——— 1978. 'Anthropology and Challenges to Development: A view from Third World', Inaugural address, Xth International Congress of Anthropological and Ethnological Sciences, New Delhi, ICAES.

Dubashi, P.R., 1979. 'Communication and Integrated Rural Development', Paper presented in the Seminar on Rural Development and Communication Policies at Hyderabad, New Delhi, Indian Institute of Mass Communication.

Dumazedier, J., 1956. *Television and Rural Adult Education*, Paris, UNESCO.

Eapen, K.E., 1979. 'The Limited Relevance of SITE', paper presented in the Seminar on Rural Development and Communication Policies at Hyderabad, New Delhi, Indian Institute of Mass Communication.

Eisensdadt, S.N., 1966. *Modernization, Protest and Change*, New Jersey, Eagle Wood, Cliffs.

——— 1973. *Tradition, Change and Modernity*, New York, John Wiley and Sons.

Epstein, T.S., 1962. *Economic Development and Social Change in South India*, Manchester, Manchester University.

Firth, Raymond, 1957. *We, the Tikopia*, London, George Allen and Unwin.

Fonseca, A.J., 1971. *Challenge of Poverty in India*, ed., Delhi, Vikas Publications.

Foster, G.M., 1962. *Traditional Cultures and Impact of Technological Change*, New York, Harper and Row.

Fuller, C.J., 1976. *Changing Cultures: The Nayars of Today*, Cambridge, Cambridge University Press.

Gaikward, V.R. *et al.*, 1973. *Rural Social Structure and Communication in an Indian Village*, Ahmedabad, Indian Institute of Management, Centre for Management in Agriculture.

Gardner, Murphy, 1954. 'Social Motivation', *In Hand Book of Social Psychology*, Lindzey Garner, ed., Boston, Addison-Wislay.

Golding, Peter, 1974. *The Mass Media Aspects of Modern Sociology*, London, Longman.

Groombridge, Brian, 1972. *Television and the People — A Programme for Democratic Participation*, Middlesex, Harmondsworth, Penguin Books.

Higgins, Benjamin, 1970. *Economic Development and Culture Change*, Chicago, University of Chicago.

Hovland, Carl, J., 1954. 'The Effects of the Mass Media of Communication', *in* Gardner, Lindzey, ed., *Handbook of Social Psychology*, Boston, Addison-Wesley.

Ministry of Information and Broadcasting (I&B), Government of India, 1959. *Annual Report for 1958-59*, New Delhi, Ministry of I&B, Government of India.

—— 1962. *Annual Report for 1962-63*, New Delhi, Ministry of I&B, Government of India.

_____ 1964. *Report of the Study Team for Five Year Plan Publicity*, New Delhi, Ministry of I&B, Government of India.

_____ 1965. *Annual Report for 1964-65*, New Delhi, Ministry of I&B, Government of India.

_____ 1966. *Radio and Television, Report of the Committee on Broadcasting and Information Media*, New Delhi, Ministry of I&B, Government of India.

_____ 1978 *Akash Bharati*, Volumes I and II, Report of the Working Group on Autonomy for Akashvani and Doordarshan, New Delhi, Ministry of I&B, Government of India.

Indian Institute of Mass Communication (IIMC). 1979. *Rural Development and Communication Policies*, Proceedings of the Seminar at Hyderabad (February 21-24, 1979), New Delhi, Indian Institute of Mass Communication.

International Encyclopaedia of the Social Sciences. 1968. *Articles on Economic Growth and Development*, Volume IV, Inc. New York, Macmillan Company and the Free Press.

Inayatullah. 1967. Towards a Non-Western Model of Development, *in Communication and Change in the Developing Countries*, Lerner Daniel and Schramm, Wilbur, Eds., Honolulu, East-West Centre.

Katz, Elihu and Lazarsfeld, Paul F. 1955. *Personal Influence*, Glencoe, Ill., Free Press.

Kivlin, Joseph, E. *et al*. 1971. *Innovation in rural India*, Ohio, Bouling State University.

Klapper, Joseph T. 1960. *The Effects of Mass Communication, New York, The* Free Press.

Krech, David *et al*. 1962. *Individual in Society*, Inc., New York, McGraw Hill.

Kroeber, A.L. 1948. *Anthropology*, Inc., New York, Harcourt, Brace and World.

Kuppuswamy, B. 1972. *Social Change in India*, Delhi, Vikas Publications.

Lasswell, Harold. 1960. *Mass Communications*, Schramm, Wilbur, ed., Urbana Ill, University of Illinois Press.

Lazarsfeld, Paul F., Bernard, Berelson and Hazel Gaudet. 1948. *The People's Choice*, New York, Columbia University Press.

Lerner, Daniel. 1958. *The Passing of Traditional Society*, Glencoe, Free Press.

Lerner, Daniel and Schramm, Wilbur. 1967. Communication and Change in the Developing Countries, Eds., Honolulu, East-West Communication Centre.

Lewin, Kurt. 1947. "Group Decision and Social Change", *in Readings in Social Psychology* Newcomb, T.M. and Hartley, E.L., eds., New York. Holt.

Lewis, W. Arthur. 1959. *The Theory of Economic Growth*, London, Allen and Unwin.

_____ 1966. *Development Planning*, London, George Allen and Unwin.

Lewis, Oscar. 1958. *Village Life in Northern India*, Urbana, University of Illinois.

Litwin, George H. and Stringer, Robert A. 1968. *Motivation and Organisational Climate*, Boston, Harward University, Graduate School of Business Administration.

Malinowski, Bronislaw. 1922. *Argonauts of Western Pacific*, London, Routledge and Kegan Paul.

Masani, Mehra. 1976. *Broadcasting and the People*, New Delhi, National Book Trust.

Maslow, A.H. 1954. *Motivation and Personality*, New York, Harper.

Mathur, J.C. and Saksena, H.P. 1963. *Social Education through Television*, Paris, UNESCO.

Mathur, J.C. and Neurath, Paul. 1959. An Indian Experiment in Farm Radio Forums, Paris, UNESCO.

Mazumdar, D.N. 1958. *Caste and Communication in an Indian Village*, Bombay, Asia Publishing House.

Mead, Margaret. 1953. *Cultural Patterns and Technological Change*, Paris, UNESCO.

Menon, K.P.A. 1979. *Rural Development — The Tasks Ahead*, Keynote address, Seminar on Rural Development and Communication Policies at Hyderabad, New Delhi, Indian Institute of Mass Communication.

Menon, Narayana. 1976. *The Communication Revolution*, New Delhi, National Book Trust.

Moore, Wilbert. 1968. 'Social Change', Article in *International Encyclopaedia of Social Sciences*, Vol.14, Inc., New York, Macmillan and Free Press.

Myrdal, Gunnar. 1968. *Asian Drama*, New York, Pantheon.

Murray, J. Leaf. 1972. *Information and Behaviour in a Sikh Village — Social Organization Reconsidered*, Delhi, Oxford University Press.

Narayan Andal, 1987. *Impact of TV on Viewers*, Bombay, Sonaiya Publications.

Nash, M. 1968. *Primitive and Peasant Economic Systems*, San Francisco, Chandler.

National Council of Educational Research and Training (NCERT). 1967. *Krishi Darshan; Agricultural Television Project, Continuous Education Report I*, New Delhi, Department of Adult Education, NCERT.

Ogburn, Willium. 1964. *On Culture and Social Change*, Duncan Otis Dudley, ed., Chicago, University of Chicago Press.

Olson, David R. 1974. *Media and Symbols: The Forms of Expression, Communication and Education*, ed., Chicago, Illinois, The National Society for the Study of Education.

Oommen, M.A. 1973. *Development: Perspectives and Problems*, ed., Bangalore, Ecumenical Christian Centre.

Paliwal, R.K. 1987. *Impediments to Rural Communication*, Meerut, Research India.

Piddington, Ralph. 1937. *An Introduction to Social Anthropology*, Volumes I and II, London, Oliver and Boyd.

Planning Commission (Government of India). 1952. *The First Year Plan*, New Delhi, Planning Commission, Government of India.

—— 1956. *Second Five Year Plan*, New Delhi, Planning Commission, Government of India.

—— 1961. *Third Five Year Plan*, New Delhi, Planning Commission, Government of India.

—— 1974. *Draft Five Year Plan*, 1973-78, New Delhi, Planning Commission, Government of India.

—— 1978. *Draft Five Year Plan*, 1978-83, New Delhi, Planning Commission, Government of India.

Ploman, Edward, 1979. *Rural development in the context of overall development*, paper presented in the Seminar on Rural Development and Communication Policies at Hyderabad, New Delhi, Indian Institute of Mass Communication.

Ponsioen, J.A. 1968, *National Development: A Sociological Contribution*, The Hauge, Mouton, N.V. Publishers.

Pool, Ithiel de Sola, 1963, "The role of Communication in the process of Modernization and Technological Change", In *Industrialization and Society*, Hoslite and Wilbert. Moore, Eds., The Hauge, Mouton.

Pye, Lucien. 1963, *Communication and Political Development*, ed., Princeton, New Jersey, Princeton University Press.

Ramesh Chandra, 1979. Community Television Viewing in the Kashmir Valley, *Indian Journal of Communication Arts*, Vol. IV, No.IX, New Delhi.

Rao, BSS, 1977. 'Where are Mass Media?' *Indian Express*, New Delhi, December 1, 1977.

Rao, BSS and Ramachandra, D.P. 1976. *One video-Two audio Transmission in SITE*, New Delhi, Directorate General, Doordarshan.

Rao MSA. 1957. *Social change in Malabar*, Bombay, Popular Book Depot.

—— 1972. *Tradition, Rationally and Change*, Bombay, Popular Prakashan.

Rao, YVL. 1963. Communication and Development: *Study of two Indian Villages*, Minneapolis, University of Minnesota Press.

Reddi, Adivi.A. 1979 *What ails Rural Development ?* paper presented in the Seminar on Rural Development and Communication Policies at Hyderabad, New Delhi, Indian Institute of Mass Communication.

Ricardo, W.A. and Charles, E.D. 1964. *Development and Underdevelopment*, Los Angeles, University of California.

Rogers, Everett, H. 1962. *Diffusion of Innovation*, New York, Free Press of Glencoe.

—— 1976, *Communication and Development*, ed., London, Beverly Hills. Sage Publications.

Rogers, Everett. H and Shoemaker, Floyed. F. 1971. *Communication of Innovations: A Cross-Cultural Approach*, (Second Edition), New York, The Free Press.

Rostow, W.W. 1960. *The Stage of Economic Growth*, Cambride, Cambridge University Press.

Roy, Deepak, 1979. 'Television in India, Much ado about Nothing,' Vidura August, 1979, New Delhi, Press Institute of India.

Roy, Pradipto *et al*. 1969. *The Impact of Communication on Development*, Paris UNESCO.

Sachchidananda, 1968. *The Tribal Village in Bihar*, Delhi, Oriental Publishers and Book Sellers.

——— 1977. *The Harijan Elite*, Faridabad, Thomson Press.

Sampath, N. 1977. *SITE Costs and Management*, UN-UNESCO Panel Meeting on SITE Experience, Ahmedabad, ISRO, Space Applications Centre.

Schekele, Rainer. 1973. 'Economic Development: A Broad Perspective,' in Development Perspectives and Problems, Oommen, M.A, ed., Bangalore, Ecumenical Christian Centre.

Schramm, Wilbur, 1964. *Mass Media and National Development*, Paris, UNESCO.

——— 1973. *Men, Messages and Media*, New York, Harper and Row.

——— 1977. *Big Media, Little Media: Tools and Technologies for Instruction*, London, Beverely Hills, Sage Publications.

Siepman, Charles, A. 1950. *Radio Television and Society*, New York, Oxford University Press.

Sekhar, M.C. 1968 *Social Change in India : First Decade of Planning*, Poona, Deccan College, Post-Graduate Research Institute.

Shanmugam, A.V. *et al*. 1977. *Working Document on SITE*, National Seminar on SITE Evaluation, Bangalore, Department of Communication, Bangalore University.

Sharma, S.C. 1987. Media Communications and Development, New Delhi, Rawat Publications.

Shingi, P.M. and Mody, Bella. 1974. *Farmers' Ignorance and the role of Television*, Ahmedabad, Indian Institute of Management, Centre for Management of Agriculture.

Singer, Milton. 1972. *When a great tradition modernises*, Delhi, Vikas Publishing House.

Singh, Jagadish. 1971. 'A study of the Factor Influencing the viewing behaviour of the farmers towards Agricultural Programmes on Television in Delhi villages.' (Unpublished Ph.D Thesis), New Delhi, Indian Agricultural Research Institute.

Singh, K.N. 1979. *Farm Information Development and Transfer Systems*, paper presented in the Seminar on Rural Development and Communication policies at Hyderabad, New Delhi, Indian Institute of Mass Communication.

Singh, Y.P. 1970. Studies in Agriculture Communication in India. *In Research in Extension for Accelerating Development Process*, Singh, K.N. *et al* (Eds), New Delhi, Indian Society of Extension Education.

Slotkin, J.S. 1950 *Social Anthropology*, New York, Macmillan.

Soedjatmoko. 1969. *South-East Asia Today and Tomorrow*, Honolulu, East-West Centre.

Spicer, H. Edward. 1952. *Human Problems in Technological Change*, ed., New York, Russel Sage Foundation.

Srinivas, M.N. 1976. *A Remembered Village*, Delhi, Oxford University Press.

Srinivas, R. 1979. 'The SITE Programme Producers - A Study,' *The Communicare*, Vol.1, No.1, 1976-77, Bangalore, Department of Communication, Bangalore University.

Steimberg, Charles, S. 1966 *Mass Media and Communication*, ed, New York, Hasting House Publishers.

Umadevi.K. 1977. 'An Evaluation of the Multi-Media Training for Extension Workers and Farmers.' *The Communicare*, Vol.1, No.1, 1976-77, Bangalore, Department of Communication, Bangalore University.

UNESCO. 1960. *Rural television in Japan*, Paris, *UNESCO*.

UNESCO. 1969. *Television Development and Training (India)*, Report by Willings, John and others, Paris, *UNESCO*.

_____ 1975 *World Communication*. Paris, *UNESCO*.

_____ 1978 *Interim Report on Communication Problems in Modern Society*, (MacBride Commission), Paris, New York.

Vidyarthi, L.P. 1970 *Socio-Cultural Implications of Industrialisation in India*, New Delhi, Planning Commission, Research Programme Committee.

Walter, B. Emery. 1969 *National and International Systems of Broadcasting*, East Lansing, Michigan State University Press.

Williums, Roymond. 1962. *Communication*, Middlesex, Penguin Books.

Woods, John. L. 1976 *Report on the International Conference on Integrated Communication for Rural Development*, Honolulu, East-West Communication Institute.

Wright, Charles.E. 1959. *Mass Communication : A Sociological Perspective*, New York, Random House.

Young, Kimball. 1957. *Hand Book of Social Psychology*, London, Routledge and Kegan Paul.

# INDEX


Acculturation, 214
Adivasi Maha Mandal (Tribal
    Development Corporation), 122
*Adivasis*, 108, 156
Adult education, 36, 57, 183
    programmes, 84
Adulteration of food, 63
Africa, television in, 59
Agrawal, Binod C., 18, 55, 86, 88, 92,
    204
Agricultural Broadcasts, awareness of,
    133
Agricultural extension, 66
    programmes, 188
Ahmed, S.A, 88
Aiyappan, A., 18
Ajanta ranges, 106
Akashwani, 163
Ambegaon Panchayat Samiti, 139
Ambegaon taluka, 99, 111
Animal husbandry, 117
Antyodaya, 27
Aristotle, 40
Asia, television in, 59
Audience, 192, 196
    composition, 194
Audio transmission, 82
Autonomy, 49, 53
Auxiliary Nurse Midwife (ANM), 115

Bahuroopi, 193
Bailey, F.G., 18
*Bajri*, 189, 190
Basic inferences, 195
Basic needs model, 27
Bavaji Arjun Chimte, 16
Beehive, 107
Berelson, Bernard, 40
Berlo, David K., 40
Bhagvati, Jagadish N., 20
Bharud, 192, 193
Bhatt, V.V., 21
Bhatia, B.S., 88
Bhatia, Hansraj, 151
Bhutto, Z.A., 163, 165
Block headquarters, 139, 140, 238
Bombay Doordarshan Kendra, 168
    programmes, 93
    telecast schedule of, 248
Brookfield, H., 21
*Burrakatha*, 56

Cash crops, 108
Chanda, Ashok K., 52, 66
Chavan, Y.B., 164
Chawla, N.L., 209
Citizenship programmes, 63
Clusters, 87, 89
Command Area Development Programme
    (CADP), 35
Commercial crops, 16, 108, 154
Communications, 182
    channels of, 42
    development, 39, 44, 50
    facilities, 111
    functions of, 41
    resources, 53
    satellites, 75
    system, 15
Community development programme, 33
    listening facilities, 131
        scheme, 198-99
    television, 198
        viewing scheme, 98, 199
Constraints, 15, 87, 119, 147, 186, 191,
    207, 213
Consumer cooperative store, 122
Cosmopolitan audiences, 221
Coyle, David Cushman, 22
Cricket matches, 208
Culture area, 106, 213
Cultural heritage, 41

items, 189
Current political scene, 241
Custodians, 207, 209, 211, 224, 228
Custom, 163

Daily rural service, 228
Danda, Ajit Kumar, 18
Deepak Roy, 186
Delivery system, 196, 227, 246
Demographic variations, 107
Development of Women and Children in Rural Areas (DWCRA), 36
Dimba irrigation project, 112
Direct Broadcast System (DBS), 176
Doordarshan Kendras, 63, 110
Drinking water, 17, 121
Drought Prone Area Programme (DPAP), 35, 113
Dry crops, 189
Dube, D.C., 26

Eapen, K.E., 87
Economic status, 146
Education, 38, 146
Educational programme, 168
television programmes, 57, 82
Eisensdadt, S.N., 125
Electronic communication system, 205
Employment Guarantee Schemes (EGS), 112-13
Entertainment formats, 189
programmes, 222
Epstein, T.S., 18
Evaluation cell, 81
Expansion proposals, 66
Exploitation, 28, 42, 218, 227
Extension, 28, 42, 218, 27
Extension services, 54
workers training programme, 84

Family planning, 85
Farm teleclubs, 65
Feedback system, 227
Field-based programme, 194
Fifth Five Year Plan, 31, 70
Film-based programmes, 118, 211, 224
First Five Year Plan, 29, 50
Food crops, 108
Foodgrains import, 29
Fourth Five Year Plan, 30, 52, 69

Gordner, Murphy, 152
General election, 1971, 31
Glamorous music, 193
Godavari, 106
Goulit, Demis, 22
Gram Panchayat, 102, 115, 116, 118, 127, 132, 140, 170, 200, 201, 207, 208, 224
Gram Sewak, 116, 120, 140, 206
Gross National Product (GNP), 21
Gujarati Programmes, 81

Harijans, 105, 108, 130, 146, 155, 160, 204
Health care and hygine prcgramme, 189
Higgins, Benjamin, 25
Hindi film programmes, 123, 210
Holland, 61
Hovland, Carl J., 40
Human Constraints, 204
problems, 95

Inayatullah, 216
Indian Institute of Mass Communication (IIMC), 50
Indian Adult Education Association, 63
Indian Space Research Organisation (ISRO), 77, 86
Industrial revolution, 20
Industrial Welfare Centres, 200
Industrialisation, 24, 215
Installation, 201
Instructional programmes, 222
Integrated rural development, 36
Intensive Agriculture Area Programme (IAAP), 34
Irrigation facilities, 17, 112, 115, 162
system, 196
Italy, 57

Jagdish Singh, 65
Janata Party, 71
Japan, rural television in, 68
*Jatra* 56
Jayaprakash Narayan, 163, 164
Joint family, 158
Joshi, P.C., 92

*Karbharis*, 125
Karl Marx, 20
Kashmir valley, 197
*Katkaris*, 157
Keynesion model, 21
Kharif crops, 115, 119-20
Kheda district, 70
Klapper, Joseph, T., 217
Kondiba, 17
*Konkan*, 106
Krech, David, 151, 167
Krishi Darshan, 65, 69, 149
Kroeber, A.L., 215

Lasswell, Harold, 40
Latin America, television in, 59
Lazersfeld, Paul F., 43
Leapfrogging, 148, 220
Lerner, Daniel, 45
Lewin, Kurt, 204
Lewis, Arthur W., 25
Litwin, George, H., 151
*Loksatta*, 110

Mahadeo Kolis, 122, 156
Maharashtra, 98, 199
*Maharashtra Times*, 110
Mahatma Gandhi, 33
Malek, M.R., 92
Malinowski, Bronislaw, 96
Marathi Newspapers, 116
Marathwada, 98
Marginal Farmers and Agricultural Labourers Development Agency (MFALDA), 35
Masani, Mehra, 68
Maslow, A.H., 152
Mass Media, 43, 110
  channels, 47
  clustering of, 149
  participation in, 104
Mathur, J.C., 62
Mead, Margaret, 17
Menon, K.P.A., 35
Minimum Needs Programme, 35, 36
Mody, Bella, 149, 197
Modernisation, 215
Municipalities, 200
Myrdal, Gunnar, 22

*Nachni*, 112, 122
*Nagapanchmi*, 195
Narayan, Andal, 93
National Aeronautics and Space Administration (NASA), 75, 86
National Adult Education Programme, 193
National Broadcast Trust (NBT), 71
National communication policy, 49
National Extension Servive (NES), 50, 54
National integration, 85
National Rural Employment Programme (NREP), 36
Net Domestic Product, 108
New Delhi, industrial fair, 61
New nationalism, 22
Newspapers, 125, 233

Observation technique, 102
Occupation, 146
Occupational information, 173
Oommen, M.A., 23, 26
Operational Constraints, 101
  definitions, 107

Paliwal, R.K., 93
Pakistan, 163
Panchayat Samiti, 200, 224, 225
Parner Taluka, 99, 101, 113
Physical variations, 107
Piddington, Ralph, 96, 152
Pij, 70, 71
Pilot project, 62
Planning Commission, 28, 32, 50, 51, 53, 61, 91, 143
Ploman, Edward, 27
Political socialization, 163, 223
Ponsioen, J.A., 20, 22
Poor communication facilities, 141, 195
Population growth, 37
Poultry farm, 160
Poverty, 37
Programme generation, 81
  references, 167
Primary Health Centres (PHC), 34, 120
Primary school children, telecasts for, 69
Prioritization, 153

Quebral, Nora, 47

Rabi crops, 115
Radio listening, frequency of, 131, 234
Radio rural forum programmes, 133
  awareness of, 231
  scheme of, 51
  project, 198
  treatment, 46
Ramachandra, D.P., 88, 204
Rao, Y.V.L., 18
Reservation, 147
Ricardo, W.A., 24
Rogers, Everett, 59
Rostow, W.W., 25
Rural areas, infrastructures in, 108
Rural audiences, 197, 221, 223
Rural broadcasting, 123, 206
  systems, 197-99
Rural development
  communication aid, 151
  effective channel for, 177
  potentialities of, 218
  problems, 186
  programmes, 133, 170, 188, 191
  strategy for, 33
Rural landless Employment Guarantee Programme (RLEGP), 36
Rural-oriented radio programmes, 51, 103, 170
Rural T.V. communication, 205, 251
  programmes, 74, 171, 227, 242
Rural works programmes, 113

Sachchidananda, 18
Sarpanch, 206
Satellite Instructional Television Experiment (SITE), 18, 68, 75, 143
  clusters, 80
  cost effectiveness, 90
  coverage of, 78
  evaluation of, 85
  Hindi programmes, 88
  instructional programmes, 85-86
  objectives of, 77
Scheduled caste communities, 156
Schickele, Rainer, 24
School education, 66
  television, 64
School going children, 180
Schramm, Wilbur, 45, 46, 47, 196, 218
Science education programmes, 81
Second Five Year Plan, 30, 57, 61
Selected programmes, feedback of, 103, 190
Seventh Five Year Plan, 32, 74
Sexually Transmitted Diseases (STD), 157
Shanmugam, A.V., 89
Share-cropping, 162
Sharma, S.C., 93
Shifting cultivation, 122
Shingi, P.M., 197
Sixth Five Year Plan, 32, 53, 74
Small Farmers Development Agency, 35
Small land holdings, 37
Smith, Adam, 20
Social change, 214
Social education, 189
  programmes, 62
  status, 146
Socialization, 41, 171
Socio-economic characteristics, 145-46
Space Application Centre (SAC), 77
Spicer, H. Edward, 17
Srinivas, M.N., 18, 186
Srivastava, U.K., 92
Stolkin, J.S., 215
Swaminathan, M.S., 65

*Tamasha*, 56
Technological revolution, 15
Telecast pattern, 82
Television software planning, 91
*Thakkars*, 157, 194
Third Five Year Plan, 30
Training of Rural Youth for Self Employment (TRYSEM), 36
Training and visits (T&V) System, 54
TV viewing, frequency of, 145, 240

Umadevi, K., 89
UNESCO, 57, 61, 63, 68
United Nations Organisation (UNO), 21
Urban Area, 237
  expansion in, 72
  problems, 230

Vidarbha, 98
Vidyarthi, L.P., 18

Village development, 182
functionaries, 194
Village Level Workers (VLW), 16, 18, 201, 225, 226, 239

Weekly commercial films, 180
Weekly market, 16
Weekly transmission, 168
White-collar workers, 105, 130, 136, 174, 182, 220
Williams, Raymond, 40
Willings, John, 67
World War II, 21

Young, Kimball, 152
Youth club, 118

Zilla Parishad, 112, 116, 119, 121, 160, 200, 209, 224, 225

[illegible]